The Dressed Society

Theory, Culture & Society

Theory, Culture & Society caters for the resurgence of interest in culture within contemporary social science and the humanities. Building on the heritage of classical social theory, the book series examines ways in which this tradition has been reshaped by a new generation of theorists. It also publishes theoretically informed analyses of everyday life, popular culture and new intellectual movements.

EDITOR: Mike Featherstone, *Nottingham Trent University*

SERIES EDITORIAL BOARD
Roy Boyne, *University of Durham*
Mike Hepworth, *University of Aberdeen*
Scott Lash, *Goldsmiths College, University of London*
Roland Robertson, *University of Aberdeen*
Bryan S. Turner, *National University of Singapore*

THE TCS CENTRE
The Theory, Culture & Society book series, the journals *Theory, Culture & Society* and *Body & Society*, and related conference, seminar and postgraduate programmes operate from the TCS Centre at Nottingham Trent University. For further details of the TCS Centre's activities please contact:

The TCS Centre
School of Arts and Humanities
Nottingham Trent University
Clifton Lane, Nottingham NG11 8NS, UK
email: tcs@ntu.ac.uk
web: http://sagepub.net/tcs/

Recent volumes include:

Informalization: Manners and Emotions Since 1890
Cas Wouters

The Culture of Speed: The Coming of Immediacy
John Tomlinson

Consumer Culture and Postmodernism
Mike Featherstone

Advertising in Modern and Postmodern Times
Pamela Odih

The Dressed Society

Clothing, the Body and Some Meanings of the World

Peter Corrigan

SAGE Publications
Los Angeles • London • New Delhi • Singapore

First published 2008

SAGE Publications Ltd
1 Oliver's Yard
55 City Road
London EC1Y 1SP

SAGE Publications Inc.
2455 Teller Road
Thousand Oaks, California 91320

SAGE Publications India Pvt Ltd
B 1/I 1 Mohan Cooperative Industrial Area
Mathura Road
New Delhi 110 044

SAGE Publications Asia-Pacific Pte Ltd
33 Pekin Street #02–01
Far East Square
Singapore 048763

Library of Congress Control Number: 2007921860

British Library Cataloguing in Publication data

A catalogue record for this book is available from the British Library

ISBN 978–0–7619–5206–0
ISBN 978–0–7619–5207–7 (pbk)

Typeset by Newgen Imaging Systems (P) Ltd., Chennai, India
Printed in India at Replika Press Pvt. Ltd
Printed on paper from sustainable resources

To my parents

To my parents

Contents

Acknowledgements

I would like to thank Brian Torode of Trinity College, Dublin, my former sociological colleagues at Keele University and my present colleagues at the University of New England for encouraging my research endeavours in ways both general and specific. Special thanks to David Gray for making me think about the sense-based sociology mentioned in the introductory chapter, to Frances Gray for suggesting the title of Chapter 7, and to Peter Forrest for pointing out that Chapter 3 was not about time but rather about times. Part of Chapter 5 appeared originally in the journal *Sociology*, and part of Chapter 2 appeared in *Body & Society*.

1

Introduction: Dress in the Sensory World

This is a book about the meaningful adventures of dress in the world. Like any material object, clothing can be looked upon in terms of its brute concrete reality or as an element in some greater conceptual scheme transcending its mere materiality. For the social scientist, the relationship between the concrete and the conceptual is of central interest because it reveals in practice how we may make sense of the world in which we find ourselves – and even of the worlds that we have imagined.

But where shall we begin? With a foundational question that sociology has not, perhaps, asked often enough: how do we apprehend the world? My answer is: through data provided by the senses. Until recently, the senses had rather an unreliable reputation: famously, René Descartes (1984 [1641]: 12, 16) wrote that 'from time to time I have found that the senses deceive, and it is prudent never to trust completely those who have deceived us even once . . . Anything which admits of the slightest doubt I will set aside just as if I had found it to be wholly false'. For him, the 'inter-mingling of the mind with the body' led to 'confused modes of thinking' (1984 [1641]: 57) that would never let us get at the truth of the world. But the person plunged into the busy world of actions and events does not have the contemplative analytical time of the philosopher 'sitting by the fire, wearing a winter dressing-gown' (1984 [1641]: 13), and this is the person that is of interest to the sociologist (who may well be sitting by the laptop, wearing a winter dressing-gown). We must set aside Descartes, and accept that the embodied creatures of the confused modes of thinking who inhabit the streets, the squares, the stadia and the shops are the very subject matter of sociology. These people are pragmatic operators rather than philosophical analysts, but this does not mean that they are not also sophisticated navigators of the world.

Henri Bergson (1929 [1908]: 29, 34) suggests something of the sophis-tication of these navigators when he writes that 'The images [i.e., any sort of sense data, not just visual – PC] which surround us will appear to turn towards our body the side . . . which interests our body . . . [perception is] reduced to the image of that which interests you'. Put more bluntly, we se(ns)e what we need to se(ns)e in a given context. We are not at all *confused*, even if we are *wrong*. Furthermore, the contemplative analytical time of the philosopher is drastically short-circuited through habit and memory: 'The bodily memory, made up of the sum of the sensory-motor systems organized by habit, is then a quasi-instantaneous memory to which the true memory of the past serves as a base' (1929 [1908]: 197). Our sensate bodies help us make decisions quickly and clearly. They do not operate in the transcendent realm of truth, but in the immanent kingdom of the real.

The neurologist Antonio Damasio (1994; 1999) links the senses, emotions, thoughts and actions, and shows that the intermingling of mind and body leads less to the confused modes of thinking of the Cartesian view than to sharpened modes of thinking. He observes that

> The environment makes its mark on the organism in a variety of ways. One is by stimulating neural activity in the eye . . . the ear . . . and the myriad nerve terminals in the skin, taste buds, and nasal mucosa. Nerve terminals send signals to circumscribed entry points in the brain, the so-called sensory cortices of vision, hearing, somatic sensation, taste, and olfaction. (Damasio, 1994: 90–1)

These sensing surfaces give rise to emotions as a primary effect, then to feelings and finally to reasoning (Damasio, 1999: 55). For Damasio, body-based emotions and feelings do not so much get in the way but rather orientate us appropriately to the salient features of the world, allowing us to think and thus act more swiftly than would otherwise be the case. The emotions do not operate in a social vacuum, but are tempered by what Bergson calls 'habit' and Damasio (1994: 200) expresses as the 'cultural prescriptions designed to ensure survival in a particular society'. Emotion and habit conspire to produce the *intuition* that guides our everyday acts: 'emotion ha[s] a role to play in intuition, the sort of rapid cognitive process in which we come to a particular conclusion without being aware of all the immediate logical steps . . . Intuition is simply rapid cognition with the required knowledge partially swept under the carpet, all courtesy of emotion and much past practice' (Damasio, 1994: xii–xiii). So our senses operate in a particular scenario and lead to emotions, and feeling these emotions 'provide[s] an automated detection of the scenario components which are more likely to be relevant' (Damasio, 1994: 175). Our emotions may bias us, but they are trained by habit to bias us in what is, on the average, an appropriate direction (which does not mean that the direction is necessarily appropriate in a given circumstance). As Damasio (1994: xi, xvii) puts it, '[emotion] allows the possibility of making living beings *act* smartly without having to *think* smartly . . . At their best, feelings point us in the proper direction, take us to an appropriate place in a decision-making space, where we may put the instruments of logic to good use.'

The senses, then, are fundamental to how we grasp the world and behave in it. For the sociologist Georg Simmel (1997 [1908]: 110), 'every sense delivers contributions characteristic of its individual nature to the construction of sociated experience.' The focus in this introductory chapter will be on sketching what a sensual sociology might look like in the present context. As an introduction to thinking about clothing, then, I propose that we begin with the classic five senses and endeavour to work out what each can tell us about clothing in the world. Of course, the senses would not normally be of equal importance in terms of the breadth and depth of what they could allow us to understand in the case of any given social phenomenon, and the reader will quite rightly suspect that sight provides the richest data of all for our current concerns. That is not the same as saying that it is the only relevant sense. There are also higher-level logics at work such as Bergson's 'habits' and Damasio's 'cultural prescriptions', and we shall deal with these as well.

Hearing

What would an analysis in terms of the sense of *hearing* tell us? After all, clothing and accessories can and do make sounds: they may swish, rustle, creak, clink, clank and click. Such sounds may announce a presence before it becomes visible and so serve as an advance warning and aid in the preparation of the appropriate social face. Swishings and rustlings of silks and satins slide easily into the erotic imaginary, as sound here depends upon and evokes the sensual existence of the (generally female) body through the physical movement needed to create the sounds. In the words of Miss Littlestar, Dominatrix of Fun (2005), 'What other hidden delights exist beneath the rustle and swish of silk and satin?' A satisfied customer of Caroline B (2005) takes the time out to remark that 'Not least is the charm of the *sound* of pure nylon . . . when my wife crosses her legs'. The creak of leather, the clicks of high heels and the clinking of jewellery may also slip easily into the erotic domain. The auditory dimension of clothing, although relatively limited, nevertheless exists and is capable of orientating human behaviour and imaginings.

Touch

Like hearing, *touch* has a strong erotic dimension. We may experience metonymic shivers of pleasure if we touch the clothing of desired others (whether they are wearing the item at the time or not), and we may find more direct delights in the sensory characteristics of the materials themselves: fur, velvet, silk, suede, leather, linen, lycra, wool, cotton and so forth, all these have different feels and are capable of evoking ranges of meanings, memories and emotions. If the latter are unpleasant, then we may seek to avoid the touch of certain coverings. Touch also has a political dimension: who can touch what, when and under what circumstances.

Taste

Sensory *taste* in the case of dress seems to belong almost entirely to the erotic universe. Edible bras, briefs and panties seem to compose the world of edible clothing, to judge by what is advertised on the Internet (e.g., Caperdi Trading, 2005). Taste here may be a way of metonymically devouring the other in a most intimate way, but the status of the body of the other may not be quite as straightforward as it appears at first bite. If the relationship to the body in its brute reality was the prime aim, then edible underwear should soak up the flavours of a specific body and deliver those tastes through the act of consumption. But the body does not seem to be so directly transmissible, because I could find no advertisements that proposed anything other than pre-flavoured underwear for both men and women: for example, cherry, passion fruit, pina colada, strawberry and chocolate, pink champagne, mai tai (Sex Toys, 2005). If there is no time, desire or opportunity for edible clothing to pick up body flavours, then we have a rather coy metonymy at work: we consume symbolically without having to deal with the taint of the real. The specificities of peculiar bodies can be disregarded, and one can displace the tastes of intimate flesh into 'safer' flavours representing culturally sanctioned pleasures in the gustatory sub-domains of desserts and cocktails. These tastes can imaginatively be mapped on to any bodies or collections of bodies that we like. It is all very clean. But if edible clothing is worn for a while, then what presumably is tasted is the intermingling of specific body and general (pre-existing) non-body flavours. A given body is here marked by something coming from outside the immediate shroud of intimacy, and that makes it a body in a particular collective. The brute reality of the body is not here disregarded as it was earlier, but is rather accepted as part of a conglomeration of matter and concept: the social body. It is all very elemental. Taste in the gustatory sense may not be a large dimension of dress, but it certainly makes certain social practices possible.

Smell

What can the sense of *smell* contribute to an understanding of clothing? Obviously it can function as an indicator of levels of acceptable and unac-ceptable cleanliness for the wearer and others, it can broadcast news about where we have been lately as clothing fibres absorb odours from their surroundings, and it can be made to carry meanings we want it to carry (or hope it will carry) by the calculated use of scents. One could easily imagine a future where the smell of clothing could be manipulated technologically for the creation of certain atmospheres, and there is some evidence that this is already possible (see Eng, 1999). To judge by advertisements for soap powders and the like, though, the currently most desirable clothing smell is 'fresh'. This is presumably another way of saying 'clean', and it is cleanliness that is highly desired and respected in our hygienized societies. Here, the native scent of a particular body is likely to be interpreted as signalling a degree of uncleanliness and concomitant unacceptability. Smelling 'fresh' is a way of making one's bodily presence inoffensive to others, and is perhaps the nearest we can get to smelling of nothing at all except cleanliness. But anything beyond this risks the disruption of the community solidarity of the clean by a specific bodily presence. Perfume draws attention to the body of the wearer, and imposes itself on the company inescapably. It is 'dirty' in the Mary Douglas (1966) sense of 'matter out of place' in those contexts where the peculiarities of individual bodies are not supposed to matter (most workplaces and public spaces, for example). But in circumstances where it may be appropriate for individual bodies to be present to others in their own way, such as meetings between lovers, then individual perfumes or even natural body odours may be more acceptable than the degree zero of the fresh. Although perfume bans such as those in Canada (McLaren, 2000) may have been predicated on notions of multiple chemical sensitivity, our analysis suggests that there is something more fundamentally social at stake: the status of appropriate body in the world.

The power of clothing to retain smell makes it possible for the presence of a wearer and their relevant qualities to be evoked even when that person is no longer at the scene. This could be a specific loved one who may be away or who may even be deceased, but it could also be a person or category of person who has never been met by the one holding the clothing. One example of the latter can be found in the notorious trade in the unwashed underwear of (particularly) schoolgirls in the *burusera* shops of Japan: 'items that have been worn for extended periods without laundering and those that retain certain, er, discharges are said to command a higher price' (Schreiber, 2001). Clearly part of the erotic imaginary, such trade has recently been regulated in Tokyo: 'Secondhand clothes stores are allowed to buy items such as school uniforms and underwear from children, only with their parents' permission' (Anonymous, 2004). Smell is a sense that links us with others in an intimate way not only because given odours are attached to given persons (or categories of person, in the case of anonymous Japanese schoolgirls) but because smell undercuts our more analytical senses: it is 'primitive', forcing itself onto our minds without the degree of careful processing we can give to the meanings of sights or sounds. We cannot easily hold it at a discriminating distance. This characteristic, indeed, is what can make it so invasive. An 'overpowering' smell overpowers these other senses and that is what makes it 'overpowering' in the first place: it fills our consciousness in a way that seems to lie outside our control.

Sight

None of the senses so far encountered provide as many possibilities for fine distinctions and meaning-making as the sense of *sight*, which is primary to an understanding of clothing. Appearances parade before us in often pre-formulated arrays, providing us with (more or less) instantly navigable social worlds. The social order is a dressed order: occupation, class, age group, sexuality, gender, region, religious affiliation, activity, sub-group membership and so forth are all announceable and readable through appearance.

Natural phenomenologists, we generally take the world to be as it appears to announce itself to us. We will be skilled, subtle and swift readers of differences that are significant to who and where we are in the world at the time, and less skilled and somewhat rougher readers of appearances that orientate to categories more remote from our concerns. We operate by trusting our instant readings. As Marshall Sahlins (1976: 203) remarks:

> 'Mere appearance' must be one of the most important forms of symbolic statement in Western civilization. For it is by appearances that civilization turns the basic contradiction of its construction into a miracle of existence; a cohesive society of perfect strangers. But in the event, its cohesion depends on a coherence of a specific kind: on the possibility of apprehending others, their social condition, and thereby their relation to oneself 'on first glance'.

Indeed, Frédéric Monneyron (2001: 20, 39, 47) believes so much in the power of appearances to create reality that he grants changes in fashion the power to bring about changes in society: designer creations change the image of the body and therefore the behaviours that are possible for the body (e.g., the availability of trousers for respectable women makes huge social change in the workplace possible). Sociologists would no doubt mutter something about social change making fashion change possible in response, but there may be a dialectic that has been overlooked: social change may lead to fashion change, but fashion change confirms the social change and brings it into the realm of the thinkable, the practicable and the embodiable for the greater public. It makes social change more real and less challengeable.

This trust in appearances has led to attempts to control and manipulate them, from the sumptuary laws of the medieval period that prescribed specific dress for specific classes to the claims to identity staked by those who wish to be taken as other than they are – or who simply wish to close any gap between who they think they are and who they appear to be. Indeed, the emulation of the appearances associated with higher social classes, and the subsequent changes made by the latter in order to retain a distinguishing difference, was considered by Simmel (1906) to be the very driver of fashion change in clothing. But such imitation does not have to be socially upwards: as Crane (2000: 14) has remarked, 'Since the 1960s, the "bottom-up" model, in which new styles emerge in lower-status groups and are later adopted by higher-status groups . . . has explained an important segment of fashion phenomena.' But this may just be a case of higher classes including 'lower' items as part of a much broader repertoire than those with lesser amounts of the various sorts of capital that it can manage. This is one way in which class distinction can be maintained in democratic societies where everyone has a claim to equality: have not only a number of items common to all classes, but also have ever-widening collections for those higher and higher up the economic and cultural scale. The analyses of Bennett *et al.* (1999) suggest that this process is what structures consumer practices generally in Australia, a country known for the ideological power of notions of egalitarianism and mateship.

Mostly, though, emulation is likely to be horizontal: we want to (or may be required to) look like everyone else in our part of classified social space, as Bourdieu (1984 [1979]) has so convincingly shown in his study of distinction. Goblot (1925) catches the situation well in his phrase 'la barrière et le niveau': the 'barrier' separates us from different social groups (we appear different from them) while the 'plateau' unites us as members of the same group (we look the same as they do). I prefer to render 'niveau' as 'plateau' rather than as the more literal 'level', because I do not wish to imply that a hierarchy is *necessarily* involved in difference. Goblot's concepts are clearly also applicable to social differences other than class, and to sub-barriers and sub-plateaux within larger barriers and plateaux. Although there may be minor modulations of difference within any given plateau (individualizations of various sorts), these are normally unlikely to breach a barrier. That is not to say that barriers are inviolable, of course. When we change age groups, class, countries, religions, or even gender, we try to move to a different plateau with its associated appearances. The change may be playful or it may be serious, which matters not to the general idea. Although writers such as Finkelstein (1991) and Lipovetsky (1987) place personal identity and individualism at the core of their understandings of dress, these concerns are of lesser import than the more general social sides of appearance we have been addressing here.

The visual aspect of clothing, then, is fundamental to knowing where we are in the world, who we are in the world, and what the world seems to be. That very foundational quality also means that it can pose dangers to the order of the present world. The potential confusion brought by change is no doubt one reason why dress in the imaginary perfect world created by utopian writers that we meet in a later chapter is almost always frozen in unambiguous timeless signalling. Political movements can colonize particular aspects of appearance for revolutionary ends, from the red shirts of Garibaldi in the nineteenth century through the brown shirts of the National Socialists in the 1930s to the orange scarves and ties of Ukraine in 2004.

A case study: Islamic dress in French schools

But it is perhaps time to be a little less general, and to look at how the spectacle of clothing is fundamental to social order in the context of a very particular case. This case is variously referred to as the 'affaire du voile' or the 'foulard islamique' and concerns the role of female Islamic dress in French state schools, an affair that began in 1989 and culminated in the law of 15 March 2004 banning conspicuous religious signs in schools. Here we begin to meet some of the higher-level logics with which the senses are articulated.

Is the sight of an Islamic head covering a threat to the foundations of the French Republic? The short answer is yes, it is – at least from the point of view of the French Republic. The reasoning behind this is to be found in the two-volume 2003 Parliamentary Report on the question of the wearing of religious signs at school, which I shall refer to as the Debré Report after its chair and rapporteur.

The key to understanding French political readings of such dress is found in the notion of *laïcité*. This is normally translated as *secularism*, but the Debré Report (2003: 32) makes a distinction between *laïcité* and *sécularisme*. The former derives from a confrontation between the State and a Church with overarching power pretensions, such as is the case in a historically Catholic country like France, while the latter is associated with the simul-taneous liberalization of the State and the Church in Protestant countries. In this view, Church and State are to be kept very clearly distinct in France whereas the boundaries are a little more permeable and confused in many other places. The Church/State separation is enshrined in the law of 9 December 1905, where the role of the State is to be neutral with respect to religions and, by extension, to ensure that public places under its control – such as state schools – are also sites of religious neutrality. *Laïcité* is central to the French Republic's very definition of itself, as can be seen from the *Article Premier* of the Constitution of 4 October 1958: 'La France est une République indivisible, laïque, démocratique et sociale'. So if something that is not *laïque* wishes to claim rights of residence in a space that is defini-tionally *laïque*, then this must logically be prevented from happening. There is no room for compromise here because the matter touches a founding principle. The crucial role of the state school in embedding this principle in apprentice citizens is nicely expressed in an informal term for the state primary school system: *'la laïque'*.

Laïcité is a mode of organization of society inherited, according to Debré (2003: 13), from the Rousseauist notion of the *volonté generale*. For him, this means that specific rules cannot be granted to particular groups because that would lead to the breakdown of society. It is not that French society is not breakable into all sorts of groups, because it most certainly is. But this means that there must be a space where this multiplicity is not a disturbing factor: 'When faced with a pluralist and diversified civil society, a principle of unity is required' (Debré, 2003: 47). It is the principle of *laïcité* that is to provide a guarantee of social cohesion in such circumstances.

The space where multiplicities are turned into a unity is the state school, and this must be a space free of the pressures stemming from the divisions marking broader French society: 'the law of the street should not be the law of the school' is how Debré (2003: 56) summarizes the views of school principals. A religious sign here belongs to the 'law of the street', and, according to the Council of State in its comments on the 1989 situation, conspicuous religious signs in the school can constitute 'an act of pressure, of provocation, of proselytizing or of propaganda' (*Circulaire du 12 décembre 1989*: 4). The Education Minister made similar points in 1994, stating rather more strongly that 'These signs are *in themselves* proselytizing or discrimina-tory elements' (Bayrou, 1994: 9, my emphasis). For Debré (2003: 65), wearing a sign showing particular allegiances is also to affirm in advance what is to be believed and to close oneself off to new knowledge that might throw these beliefs into doubt. So the signs both put illegitimate pressures on others in a space where this should not happen and prevent the knowledge development that is the job of the school. All this is very far from a view that would bring diversity and all its resonances directly and visibly into the school, and it may well appear strange to people from countries whose constitutions are not based on such a notion of *laïcité*.

But constitutional factors are not the only ones mobilized in the parliamentary report. The young women who wear the scarf are seen as acting under pressure from their families or the environment in which they live (Debré, 2003: 8) and their voices are thus written out of consideration. Even the government mediator responsible for dealing with schools and their veil problems, Hanifa Chérifi, insists that the veil is not a sign of being a Muslim but a sign of allegiance to fundamentalist Islam (Debré, 2003: 80).

Outside the polished committee rooms of parliament, the voices are less constrained. For the feminists Vigerie and Zelensky (nd), the veil symbolizes the submission of women to men, and those women who desire it are dismissed on the grounds that the dominated are the most fervent supporters of their own subservience. For members of the women's groups gathered under the name *Égalité*, the veil is again a symbol of the oppression of women and of their negation as independent individuals (Comité National Coordination des groupes de femmes Egalité, 2003), while the website of the *Union des Familles Laïques* condemns the veil because it does away with personal qualities and turns social status into human destiny (Kintzler *et al.*, 2003). Both Vigerie and Zelensky (nd) and the French National Front (Lang, 2003) see the veil as the tip of the iceberg, the former understanding it as part of the attempt by Muslim groups to control young people and the latter warning against the threat of revolutionary Islam to the integrated nature of France. These latter readings are independent of cool and sophisticated arguments about *laïcité*, and most likely represent the more common non-Muslim interpretations of the veil prevalent in Europe and, indeed, North America (Mohsin Moudden, 2003a; Naheed Mustafa, 2003). As we have just seen, they were also at least partly at work in some of the less constitutionally centred sentiments expressed in the Debré Report.

Muslim writers on the 'affaire du voile' are not inclined to play in the *laïcité* discourse, and one dismisses the notion as a complete myth designed to keep Muslims in ghettos (Mohsin Moudden, 2003b). Instead, they work with notions of religious obligation, personal choice and sexual protection. In the latter case, seduction through the gaze is prevented through modest dress but the notion of modesty stands outside history because it has been set down for all time. Temporally sliding Westerners tend to see modesty as a moveable feast, with one era's seductive apparel being the height of modesty (or at least embarrassment) for the next – the reverse direction may hold too. That cannot be the case when the characteristics of modest dress have been spelled out in the Qur'an. Modest dress is relative in fashion-marked societies, but matters are very different when relativity is not permitted to be a factor. It is even more different when timeless dress is also considered to show obedience to God. For many of the writers, showing obedience in this way is seen as a personal choice (Abdallah, nd: 30; Al-Shouli, 2004; Naheed Mustafa, 2003; Sound Vision Staff Writer, 2004), and such choices may be incomprehensible to those accustomed to the notion of personal choice being located within consumerist discourse. On the one hand, 'personal choice' here not only gains legitimacy from its omnipresence as a consumer value in our world but, on the other, also disturbs the latter because of the nature of the choice.

The view of the veil as the sign of the submission of women is located by one writer (Anonymous, 2003) in the tendency of Europeans to interpret religious elements through the prism of their meaning in Christianity. The First Epistle to the Corinthians establishes a dominance of men over women and symbolizes this through head coverings for the latter, but this is not the case in Islam: *both* sexes are required to be modest in dress with the aim of preventing inappropriate relations from developing through the seduction of the eye. For this writer, Europe's Christian collective unconscious underpins a misreading of the veil.

For the French Republic, there can be no 'others' in the public space of the state school; there can only be apprentice citizens. For some of the young Muslim girls concerned, throwing off the protections of modest dress and the sign of obedience to God must seem like a very difficult price to pay for access to the protected space of citizens *en formation*.

Although the visual side of clothing is intrinsically open to instant readings and although we cannot navigate the world without doing this, we cannot either, as analysts, afford to content ourselves with such instant semi-wisdom. Reluctantly or no, we may have to don Descartes' winter dressing-gown and think long and hard by the fire. As we have just seen in the short case study, visual interpretations of clothing are not always easy and evident, and can be caught up in subtle and intricate ways with very large and fundamental social and political questions. Sensual episte-mology can range from instantaneous judgements to sustained analyses, and from the broad canvas to the finest of details. Much of the rest of this book is concerned with sustained analyses of fine details in the context of broader topics, linking micro concerns and macro themes in theoretical and empirical ways.

Chapter 2 considers the place of dress in a discourse that shares with sociology the aim of elaborating systematic accounts of the social world, but that accomplishes this end through narrative fiction rather than the more argument-oriented rhetoric of a specific social science. Utopian texts are born out of criticisms of the social world in which their authors live, and their themes thus serve as clues to the key tensions of the times. Utopian discourse both pre-dates sociology and continues to run in parallel with it, and we look at the tradition from Thomas More's *Utopia* of 1516 to the feminist science fiction of the 1970s. Topics include the ways in which dress signals social status, relations of power and ruling in the cases of the state and gender, body–clothing relations as understood through notions of nudity and comfort, aesthetics, the gendered division of labour, gender differences and sexuality in dress, and the historical shift from the dangers of luxury to the imperative of consumption.

Chapter 3 is devoted to the exploration of a topic that has hitherto been primarily the domain of philosophers and theoretical physicists but which has become the subject of much sociological discussion only since about 1990, namely time. This chapter attempts to describe the socio-temporal structuring of dress, and considers the year, seasonal time, hebdomadary time, diurnal time, the notion of the 'now', body time, age time, political time and the times of dominant cultures and classes. It shows that the dress–time nexus is complex and detailed in its social significance.

Like Chapter 3, Chapter 4 considers a topic to which sociology paid little attention until relatively recently: the body. It first discusses the 'classical' body in relation to early anatomy, nature, aesthetics, health and the dress reformers of the nineteenth century, and then elicits the elements of Marx's understanding of the social and economic nature of the body from an analysis of the 1844 Manuscripts, *The German Ideology* and *Capital*, relating this to the ideas of the Soviet Constructivist clothing designers in the early years of the USSR. It then examines how the body has been constructed through articles and advertisements in a sample of fashion magazines. The material considered in this chapter permits the proposal of a new history of key moments of the aesthetic body from eighteenth-century anatomy to the cyborg body of the twenty-first century, displacing accounts prone to accept purely rational–scientific ways of understanding its trajectory.

Chapter 5 shifts from seeing clothing as a theoretical object to treating dress as composed of concrete objects existing in the material world, and looks specifically at how items circulate and are exchanged in the case of the family. This is the most 'anthropological' chapter in the book, and proposes the existence of a gift-based family-clothing economy existing inside a commodity-based general economy. It also suggests a revision of some of the conventional understandings of the power relations characterizing the gift relationship.

Chapter 6 picks up the circulation and exchange theme of Chapter 5, but sets it in the virtual world of the Internet newsgroup alt.fashion. Demographic details on apparent location, presented gender and presented age are considered, and are followed by a more qualitative analysis of the message contents of threads concerned with the key concepts that emerged from an overall analysis of the sample: community, temporality and exchange. Participation rates per poster are analysed, as well as the ways in which the community constructs a sense of itself and how it responds to threats to the idea of what it ought to be. Different forms of internal stratification are also discussed. The temporal nature of the community is considered in the context of the construction of a sense of daily togetherness for the posters. Patterns in the exchange of objects show that the members of the newsgroup relate in highly structured ways, and six different forms of exchange-based social solidarity at work within the group are discovered and explained.

Chapter 7 sums up some of the general conclusions of the book, and proposes a hermeneutics of dress.

2

The Dangers of Dress: Utopian Critiques

Introduction

Utopias are of sociological interest for two main reasons. First, they are of interest in a very general sense: as Krishan Kumar (1991: vii) remarks, 'utopia deals with many of the same issues as more conventional social theory, but in its own way'. Utopian texts form a sort of parallel universe to conventional sociological and political theories, commenting upon the contemporary societies in which their authors lived through engagement with an imaginatively constructed society located in another place or another time. The Marxist who wishes to criticize society generally opts for sociological, economic and political accounts of that society, while the utopian writer generally accomplishes the same thing through narrative fiction. Similarly, Thomas Hobbes' *Leviathan*, which appeared in 1651 as an ordered solution to the disorderly problems of the English Civil War, was matched by the more utopian form of James Harrington's *Oceana* in 1656. The critical impulse leads here to more or less systematic accounts of the functioning of society, the one through social scientific discourses and the other through literary discourses. Indeed, there seems to be an approximate correspondence between periods of social unrest and the production of Utopias, which may be why most of the eighteenth century seems to have produced little while the rise of working-class movements and socialism in the nineteenth century may be related not only to the major social scientific texts of Karl Marx, Emile Durkheim and Max Weber but also to the major utopian texts of Etienne Cabet, Edward Bellamy and William Morris. The shifting status of women with respect to the public world gave rise to the publication of feminist utopian texts during the campaigns for women's rights in the late nineteenth century (many of which are collected in Kessler [1984]) and in the last third of the twentieth century, where the efforts of feminist researchers in the social sciences were paralleled by the feminist science fiction of the 1970s. More generally, a quantitative study of utopian literature produced in Britain and the United States between 1883 and 1975 found that the production of such texts increased significantly during periods of economic contraction and hegemonic breakdown (Kiser and Drass, 1987).

The two different forms taken by social criticism here seem intended for two different audiences: Kumar (1991: 89) notes that

> Most social theory shows the systematic basis of social problems. However, its appeal is limited – at least in the eyes of the populace at large – by its reliance on abstract principles. Utopia reverses, in form at least, the a priori, deductive method of most social theory. Its method is commonly rather of the concrete, inductive sort – unfashionable with contemporary philosophers of science but greatly appealing to the common sense of mankind.

Utopia criticizes and analyses contemporary society by showing the good society in action, usually doing this through a form – narrative fiction – that is accessible to all. Utopian texts, then, may be approached as social–scientific texts of an engaged nature marked by their own peculiar rhetorical structure.

The second reason for considering utopian texts concerns the fact that most do indeed include discussions of the place of dress (or undress) in their imagined societies. These range from very clear, explicit and systematic accounts such as those of François de Fénelon (1994 [1699]), Denis Diderot (1966 [1796]) or Cabet (1848) to the rather more inexplicit and inferential writings of feminist science fiction authors of the 1970s such as Esmé Dodderidge (1988 [1979]), Marge Piercy (1979 [1976]), Sally Miller Gearhart (1985 [1979]), Ursula Le Guin (1975 [1974]) or Joanna Russ (1985 [1975]). Texts of the latter type may be interpreted in a multitude of different ways, of course, and the author must apologize for the limitations of viewing them through explicitly sociological spectacles.

How were the utopian texts discussed below selected? If we include all texts dealing with imaginary societies then we would have to include the whole of science fiction, but that is clearly impossible. Even if we do not, there are still great numbers of texts queuing for consideration. Ruth Levitas (1990) spends much of her book discussing various ways of defining what a utopian text is, opting in the end for a very open approach:

> The solution cannot be to pursue agreement on a narrow definition of utopia. Such agreement will not be achieved, since it cannot encompass the range of questions that are already being asked; and if it were to be achieved, the result would be a thoroughly undesirable repressive orthodoxy. The only solution to these problems lies not in a descriptive definition of utopia, but in greater explicitness about the principles governing the choice of empirical material in particular studies. (Levitas, 1990: 199)

This seems wise advice, and so I now specify my criteria of selection.

Utopias are written with an eye to the society in which the author lives and hence it is likely that the topics of interest to utopian texts will change over time, so a sample of texts spread across a wide historical period seems appropriate. The present sample consists of the text from the sixteenth century that gave the genre its name, More's *Utopia*, seven from the seventeenth century, five from the eighteenth, fifteen from the nineteenth and thirteen from the twentieth.

A second criterion of selection includes writings conventionally considered important elements of the canon of utopian texts by writers in English: Bacon (1924 [1627]), Bellamy (1986 [1888]), Cabet (1848), Campanella (1981 [1602]), Harrington (1992 [1656]), More (1965 [1516]) and Morris (1912 [1890]). On a somewhat less exalted level we find Andreae (1916 [1619]), Gott (1902 [1648]), Lawrence (1981 [1811]), Lytton (1871) and Wells (1967 [1905], 1976 [1923]). Huxley (1994 [1932]), Orwell (1984 [1949]) and Skinner (1976 [1948]) are also included as important twentieth-century accounts of imaginary societies. Relatively familiar to Francophone if not to Anglophone readers are d'Allais (1966 [1702]), Diderot (1966 [1796]), Fénelon (1994 [1699]), Foigny (1990 [1676]), Mercier (1974 [1771]) and Morelly (1970 [1755]).

Levitas (1990: 32) remarks that women's utopias 'are conspicuously absent from the tradition as it emerges in the first half of the twentieth century', and this provides another important criterion of selection: texts by women writers. Relevant works include Appleton (1984 [1848]), Cavendish (1992 [1666]), Cooley (1984 [1902]), Corbett (1984 [1869]), Cridge (1984 [1870]), Dodderidge (1988 [1979]), Gearhart (1985 [1979]), Gilman (1979 [1915]), Griffith (1984 [1836]), Haldane (1926), Howland (1984 [1874]), Lane (1984 [1880–81]), Le Guin (1975 [1974]), Mason (1984 [1889]), Piercy (1979 [1976]), Russ (1985 [1975]) and Waisbrooker (1984 [1894]).

Satirists who are perhaps more dystopian than utopian are represented by two of the best known in English: Butler (1932a [1872], 1932b [1901]) and (briefly) Swift (1967 [1726]).

The main clothing-related themes discoverable in the sample are indicated in Table 2.1, and the existence of a limited number of recurring themes across the texts would suggest that the sample is appropriately representative of utopian works in general. It is clear that the theme of clothing is variably present across the sample: several writers treat dress in only one particular context, while H.G. Wells in the two works considered here covers a great number of contexts: each writer has their own utopian-dress 'fingerprint' corresponding to the ways in which key aspects of their ideal societies translate into concerns with apparel. It will hardly surprise, for example, that indication of the social status of the characters populating these worlds seems to be an almost constant concern across the historical period chosen, for, as we shall see below, it is typical of utopias that the social function of individuals or groups is immediately readable from their dress: not only does everyone have their proper place in utopia but this place is visible to all. Wells (1967 [1905]: 227) writes of the 'translation of the social facts we have hypotheticated into the language of costume': social structure in utopia is worn on the sleeve. Unlike the near-constant presence of social status, aesthetic qualities, as Aileen Ribeiro (1992: 229) has also noted, really only begin to matter from the middle of the nineteenth century onwards, reaching a peak in William Morris's *News from Nowhere* in 1890. We shall consider the reasons for this later.

Table 2.1 *Principal clothing themes in utopian literature, authors ordered chronologically*

Author	Year	Power	Cost	Social status	Nudity	Fashion	Circulation	Body	Division of labour	Gender/ Sexuality	Practicality	Aesthetics
More	1516		•	•		•		•		•	•	
Campanella	1602			•				•		•		•
Andreae	1619		•	•			•			•		•
Bacon	1627	•		•								
Gott	1648		•	•						•		
Harrington	1656	•		•								
Cavendish	1666	•										
Foigny	1676				•							
Fénelon	1699		•	•		•						
d'Allais	1702											
Swift	1726	•		•	•	•		•				
Morelly	1755	•	•	•								
Mercier	1771		•				•	•			•	
Diderot	1796									•		
Lawrence	1811											
Griffith	1836		•						•			•
Appleton	1848											•
Cabet	1848	•	•	•		•		•	•		•	•
Corbett	1869											•

Author	Year	1	2	3	4	5	6	7	8	9	10	11
Cridge	1870	•		•								•
Lytton	1871	•		•		•						•
Butler	1872/1901	•	•	•		•	•					•
Howland	1874			•								•
Lane	1880					•						•
Bellamy	1888	•	•	•				•				•
Mason	1889											•
Morris	1890	•	•	•		•		•				•
Waisbrooker	1894											•
Cooley	1902											•
Wells	1905/1923	•	•	•	•	•	•	•	•	•	•	•
Gilman	1915			•				•		•	•	•
Haldane	1926			•				•				•
Huxley	1932		•	•	•	•		•	•	•		•
Skinner	1948		•		•			•	•	•		•
Orwell	1949	•		•	•	•		•		•		
Le Guin	1974	•	•	•	•	•	•	•	•	•	•	•
Russ	1975	•	•	•	•			•	•	•	•	•
Piercy	1976	•		•	•	•	•	•	•	•	•	•
Dodderidge	1979											•
Gearhart	1979			•	•			•	•	•		•

The following analysis is concerned less with how individual authors orchestrated their themes in individual works than with how particular themes are treated across the sample generally. A small number of writers who figure in Table 2.1 are therefore not discussed further. The point is to explore utopian discourse, not utopian authors.

The remainder of this chapter considers social status, relations of power and ruling, body–clothing relations, aesthetics, the gendered division of labour, gender differentiation and sexuality in dress, and the historical shift from the dangers of luxury to the imperative of consumption.

The primary sign: social status

One of the simplest functions of dress is its role in signalling the social status of the wearer. This will be familiar from the work of writers such as Bogatyrev, Enninger and Sahlins, to mention but the semiotically inspired. For Bogatyrev (1971 [1937]: 83), 'In order to grasp the social function of costumes we must learn to read them as signs in the same way we learn to read and understand different languages.' Enninger (1984: 78) distinguishes between the weak symptomatic codes of fashion and the strong codes of full signs such as the uniform, with the latter being highly institutionalized and thus easy and unambiguous to read. For Sahlins (1976: 179), 'a series of concrete differences among objects of the same class [here, dress] . . . correspond[s] [to] distinctions along some dimension of social order . . . the set of manufactured objects is able to comprehend the entire cultural order of a society it would at once dress and address'. Utopian texts do not tend to go for many languages or weak codes, which leave too much room for interpretative work and would risk some uncertainties about the match between appearances and realities. Instead, there is a single language, code and settled social order: clothing in imaginary communities is usually coded in such a way that all the social distinctions relevant to a particular society are clearly indicated through apparel. The colour of the material worn, for example, may indicate a particular age class (d'Allais, 1966 [1702]: 55), craft (Campanella, 1981 [1602]: 105), or other occupational category: 'The colour appropriate for religion is white, that of statesmanship red, of scholarship blue, of the working class green' (Andreae, 1916 [1619]: 253). In Orwell (1984 [1949]), blue overalls are the attire of Outer Party members while black overalls mark the member of the Inner Party. The caste of each citizen of *Brave New World* is instantly readable by colour: Alphas wear grey, Betas mulberry, Gammas green, Deltas khaki and the Epsilons are all in black (Huxley, 1994 [1932]). Gender, marital status and season of the year are other distinctions that may be made manifest through dress. The general point is best made by Cabet:

> Not only are the two sexes dressed differently, but within each of these categories the individual switches clothing frequently according to age and

social condition, for the particularities of clothing indicate all the circumstances and positions of the members of society. Childhood and youth, the ages of puberty and majority, the condition of being married, single, widowed or remarried, the different professions and various functions – everything is indicated by clothing. Everyone sharing the same social condition wears the same *uniform*; but thousands of different uniforms match thousands of different conditions. (Cabet, 1848: 58, my translation)

'Everything is indicated by clothing': by a mere inspection of dress, everything socially important about a person may be determined. There is no room for ambiguous appearance in utopian texts where social status is continuously broadcast. We always know with whom we are dealing. But there is more to it than that. Writing of uniforms in contemporary Japan, Brian McVeigh (1997: 198) remarks that ritualized dress is a way of expressing one's commitment to the dictates of the group. Similarly, the dress of utopians serves to give the impression that they are fully engaged in the utopian social project. Utopian clothing both enacts the social structure and embeds its carrier within it.

That social structure was made transparent through dress may have appeared to be a very positive thing in the period before the rise of individualism, when confused appearances led to a confusion of social rank. If different ranks are treated very differently, as was the case particularly in pre-bourgeois societies, then it is of vital importance that one can class one's interlocutors with confidence: that one can trust appearances. Indeed, the classes that were to put an end to feudal relations provoked many sixteenth- and seventeenth-century complaints from those who wished that sumptuary laws were followed: the rising classes no longer dressed according to their old station, and it began to appear as if the social order, which sumptuary laws on dress translated into the realm of the visible, was about to enter an age of confusion. William Prynne (1628: unpaginated preface), for example, asks: 'what outward difference can you finde betweene many young Gentlemen, who professe Religion and the deboistest Ruffians? between many Grave Religious Matrons, or Virgins, who pretend devotion, and our common Strumpets?'. Neither class nor sexual status could any longer be read reliably from garments in the 'real world', and thus many of the earlier utopias with their ever-reliable signs may be read as a conservative reaction against classes of person with rising social aspirations. In the epoch of the individual, however, clothing saturated with the signs of society may be interpreted rather differently. Far from reassuring the reader, the rigid categories of dress in *Nineteen Eighty-Four* or *Brave New World* are more likely to appear as nightmares of the destruction of the individual. Earlier generations might have found such visions rather comforting, but then one historical epoch's utopia is another historical epoch's dystopia.

Our initial point, then, is a semiotic one: in most utopian texts, social structure is made manifest through clothed appearance. Let us now pursue this semiotic point in its sociological implications.

Relations of power and ruling

Power, the sovereign, rank and the state

Utopias may be read as fantasies of the perfectly ordered society written by those who live in societies marked by disorder of various sorts. But what is the source of order and how is it maintained? Seventeenth-century utopias tend to have a rather Hobbesian cast, with a sovereign or sovereign-equivalent ruling legitimately over an ordered society. Utopias of this period generally abolish the distinction between the public and the private good, and also, indeed, between public and private goods. The only good is the public good, and there are no private agendas to trouble the world: nobody has their 'own' interests. Social actors thus resemble the bees and ants in Hobbes' example of those societies that are unlike human communities because members work harmoniously and entirely for the good of society, undisturbed by the war of all against all brought about by the belief in the equality of sovereign individuals (1991 [1651]: 141–2). At a time when feudal societies were beginning to come to grips with the bourgeois societies that were about to replace them, it is perhaps not surprising that utopias of the period sometimes took the form of feudal fantasies about the harmoniously unequal society: the sovereign at the top, and the rest happy to be in a hierarchy of clearly separated grades readable from their dress. Indication of social rank can be found, for example, in Samuel Gott's Nova Solyma of 1648, where 'the chief marks of honourable rank consist not in gorgeous and expensive robes, but in the colour and length of their ordinary dress, and the law is that each one's dress is to differ according to his rank and dignity' (Gott, 1902 [1648]: 106, Vol. I). The clearest statement, however, is to be found when Fénelon's Mentor proposes a very detailed system to the King of Salente in *Telemachus, Son of Ulysses*:

> Let those of the highest rank next to yourself [the king] be dressed in white with a gold fringe at the bottom. They will have a gold ring on the finger and a medal of the same metal hanging from the neck, impressed with your image. Let those of the second rank be clothed in blue with a silver fringe, and a ring, but no medal: those of the third class in green, with a medal, but neither fringe nor ring: those of the fourth in deep yellow: of the fifth in a pale red, or rose color: of the sixth in a gray-violet color: of the seventh, constituting the last and lowest class, in a mixed color of white and yellow. These are the dresses for the seven different ranks of freemen. As for the slaves let them be clad in gray-brown. (Fénelon, 1994 [1699]: 162–3)

The legitimacy of the sovereign or sovereign-equivalent in seventeenth-century utopias is taken for granted, then, and everybody knows their place. Social order in utopias of all periods is translated directly into dress, and this is of course the case here. The dress of the ruler(s) displays their power, and the dress of the other members of society displays their place in it. The Duchess of Newcastle, Margaret Cavendish, provides a detailed description of the clothing of the empress in her *Description of a New World Called the Blazing World* of 1666:

> Her accoutrement after she was made Empress, was as followeth: on her head she wore a cap of pearl, and a half-moon of diamonds just before it; on the top of her crown came spreading over a broad carbuncle, cut in the form of the sun; her coat was of pearl, mixed with blue diamonds, and fringed with red ones; her buskins and sandals were of green diamonds: in her left hand she held a buckler, to signify the defence of her dominions; which buckler was made of that sort of diamond as has several different colours; and being cut and made in the form of an arch, showed like a rainbow; in her righthand she carried a spear made of a white diamond, cut like the tail of a blazing star, which signified that she was ready to assault those that proved her enemies.
>
> None was allowed to use or wear gold but those of the imperial race, which were the only nobles of the state; nor durst anyone wear jewels but the Emperor, the Empress, and their eldest son. (Cavendish, 1992 [1666]: 132–3)

The clothing and accessories of the empress display overwhelming wealth and show that her dominions include the sky (half-moon, sun, blazing star, rainbow), the sea (pearls) and the earth (diamonds); and that these dominions will be defended and her enemies assaulted. A simple hierarchy of power is expressed by Cavendish in the limitation of gold to the 'imperial race' and of jewels to the ruling and ruler-in-waiting members of the imperial family.

The Father of Salomon's House, ruler of Francis Bacon's *New Atlantis* of 1627, impressed the onlooker through distinguished clothing such as 'a Roabe of fine black Cloath', an 'under Garment . . . of excellent white Linnen', 'shoes of Peach-coloured Velvet', 'a rich Cloath of State over his head' (1924 [1627]: 33–5). Dress for Cavendish expressed imperial splendour in a ruler, but for Bacon it seems to express something closer to an ecclesiastical splendour still evident in the Catholic Church of today. The ecclesiastical construction of ruler–ruled relationships through clothing is quite clear when the visitors to New Atlantis gain an audience with the Father of Salomon's House: 'we bowed Lowe at our first Entrance; and when we were come neare his Chaire, he stood up, holding forth his Hand ungloved, and in Posture of Blessing; And we every one of us stooped downe, and kissed the Hemme of his Tippet' (1924 [1627]: 35). Indeed, the model of the religious community lies at the base of several utopias of this period, Johann Valentin Andreae's *Christianopolis* of 1619 suggesting as much through its very title. Bacon's clothed world is more complex than that of Cavendish, for it also indicates the place of those who surround the ruler. The Father of Salomon's House is

> With two Horses at either end [of his chariot], richly trapped in blew Velvet Embroydered; and two Footmen on each side in like Attire . . . He had before him fifty Attendants, young men all, in white *Satten* loose Coates to the Mid Legg; and Stockins of white Silk; And Shoes of blew Velvet; And Hatts of blew Velvett; with fine Plumes of diverse Colours, sett round like Hat-bands. Next before the Chariott, went two Men, bare headed, in Linnen Garments downe to the Foote, girt, and Shoes of blew velvett; Who carried, the one a Crosier,

the other a Pastorall Staffe like a Sheep-hooke . . . [the next day] He was alone, save that he had two Pages of Honour, on either Hand one, finely attired in White. (Bacon, 1924 [1627]: 33–5)

The power of the ruler is echoed through the attire of his attendants. The vestimentary echo of ruling seems restricted to those who immediately surround the ruler here, but in more elaborate utopias, as we shall see below, the sounds ripple down to those quite distant from the centre.

The dress of power in Harrington's Commonwealth of Oceana encompasses still further social categories. The various members of the Senate are attired according to their function after the manner of feudal nobility or professions:

the orator, adorned with scarlet robes, after the fashion that was used by the dukes in the aristocracy . . . the three commissioners of the seal [and] . . . the three commissioners of the treasury, every one in a robe or habit like that of the earls . . . the secretaries of the senate . . . with their tufted sleeves in the habit of civil lawyers . . . the censors in the robes of barons . . . the two tribunes of the horse [and] . . . the two tribunes of the foot, in their arms; the rest of the benches being covered by the judges of the land in their robes. (Harrington, 1992 [1656]: 119–20)

The lower orders are dressed more directly in what Harrington terms the livery of the commonwealth. This 'for the fashion or the colour, may be changed at the election of the strategus according unto his fancy' (1992 [1656]: 176). Clearly, this demonstrates the subordination of these orders to the arbitrary fancies of the chief ruler, so not only do the likes of trumpeters, ballotines, guards, postilions, coachmen and footmen dress to show their relationship to the state in general, but also to a ruler in particular. There is a double subordination at work here quite in keeping with royal rather than democratic traditions: each particular 'reign' is marked by distinct lower-order clothing, but the continuity of ruling is expressed through the enduring institution of the livery of the commonwealth. The fact that the strategus is elected changes nothing of the feudal character of the relationship.

The government of Emporium, capital city of Oceana, is based on the companies residing in particular wards, every ward having 'her wardmote, court or inquest, consisting of all that are of the clothing or liveries of companies residing within the same'. A company is 'a brotherhood of tradesmen professing the same art, governed, according unto their charter, by a master and wardens' and 'such are of the livery or clothing as have obtained unto the dignity to wear gowns and parti-coloured hoods or tippets, according unto the rules and ancient customs of their respective companies' (Harrington, 1992 [1656]: 185). These companies 'are the roots of the whole government of the city; for the liveries that reside in the same ward . . . have also the power to make election' (Harrington, 1992 [1656]: 186). That is, the electorate is organized according to the dress of the companies. So the political structure of Oceana is visible through clothing: the members of the Senate and the trade-based electorate retain the dignified appearances of ancient feudal nobility, professions and guilds; while the appearance of the servant members of the state apparatus may change according to the fancy of the strategus. Although democratic elements such as elections mark what Kumar (1991: 68) calls Harrington's 'constitution for a property-owning democracy . . . [with] a separation of powers within the state [and] elaborate checks and balances to prevent the concentration of power in any one part', looking at Oceana through the lens of dress shows the continuation of feudal relations of appearance. Written during the century of civil war clashes between monarch and parliament, it is unclear if Oceana is to be read as a democracy in feudal guise or a feudal system in democratic guise.

Cabet devotes a specific chapter to clothing in his *Voyage en Icarie*, originally published in 1840 (references here are to the fifth edition of 1848). Inheriting ideas from the French Revolution, Cabet has a socialist-style Republic clearly in the place of the sovereign and seems to follow the tendency, noted by Zygmunt Bauman (1982: 40–1), of post-sovereign forms of power to regulate ever more areas of life, ideas made familiar to us through Michel Foucault's various accounts of disciplinary mechanisms and, in a different tradition, Norbert Elias's (1994 [1939]) work on the civilizing process. In the case of both food and clothing, the law decides everything. A committee examined the clothing of all countries and indicated those to be adopted and those proscribed, classifying them according to their necessity, utility and decorative nature. Not only does the Republic design, make, and distribute clothing, but it also banishes bad taste and the bizarre, replacing them with grace and elegance, simplicity and practicality (Cabet, 1848: 56). Clearly, there is no room in Icaria for the competing versions of taste that mark struggles in class societies (see, for example, Bourdieu, 1984 [1979]): here, the citizens display themselves as members of the Republic by adopting only the one set of tastes in dress that the Republic has set down. Everyone is at all times in the livery of the commonwealth, as Harrington might say, although Cabet's committee consults and discusses rather than acting in the arbitrary manner of the strategus of Oceana. Nevertheless, the power of the State over everyday life is clearly on show. Cabet attempted to transfer his utopian schemes from the printed page to the actually existing community, and set up Icarian societies in the United States. These were not a success: Kumar (1991: 70) remarks that 'for most of their time they lived a most unutopian existence marked by dissension, disease and physical and financial hardship'. The great plans for clothing came to nothing, and in practice everybody continued to wear what they had brought with them originally, patching up the garments as time went by (Petitfils, 1982: 181–2). Kate Luck (1992: 202) suggests that this was the case with many nineteenth-century American utopian socialist communities, and that the style prevalent at the time of the community's inception became fossilized and thus eventually recognizable as the sign of the community. So over time, such dress could be seen as evidence of the enacting of and engagement with the local utopian project.

With the increasing influence of the Romantic reaction against industrial societies, it became more and more difficult simply to accept with equanimity the notion of a utopia populated by creatures of the state. Colin Campbell (1983; 1987) argues that Romanticism replaced the old idea of the individual with a new one. The pre-Romantic individual 'emphasized the commonality of mankind, the sense in which all men shared a common status leading to possession of common rights' (Campbell, 1983: 285). The Romantics saw the individual as a distinct and autonomous being, and so the uniqueness rather than the generalizable side of the individual came to dominate views of what it was to be a person. If in pre-Romantic times the individual was seen as linked to society in formal ways and perhaps only *was* an individual through these links, the Romantics saw an opposition, rather than a continuity, between the two: self and the nasty society outside came to be understood as opposing, rather than complementary, concepts. The individual appears as something divorced from society, and its job comes to be the development of its own uniqueness. This, indeed, becomes a duty. Such a shift in the status of the individual can clearly be discerned in the utopias written even by socialists towards the end of the nineteenth and the beginning of the twentieth centuries: where the state or sovereign once dressed the population, now this is considered an illegitimate area for the exercise of public power. Bellamy's Doctor Leete, speaking from the perspective of the year 2000, remarks that 'A government, or a majority, which should undertake to tell the people, or a minority, what they were to eat, drink, or wear, as I believe governments in America did in your day, would be regarded as a curious anachronism indeed' (Bellamy, 1986 [1888]: 141), while Morris (1912 [1890]: 87) draws an explicit distinction between matters which affect the welfare of the community and matters which are personal and therefore free of regulation, the latter echoing and supplementing Bellamy's list: 'how a man shall dress, what he shall eat and drink, what he shall write and read, and so forth'. Such a distinction between person and community would be impossible to draw in Cabet's ideal society, or indeed any earlier utopia. Wells (1967 [1905]: 67, 92–3) explicitly opposes Cabet's model where 'everyone shall do nothing except by the consent of the savants of the Republic, either in his eating, drinking, dressing or lodging', proposing instead that items such as clothing are extensions and expressions of the personality and are thus inalienably private property. One even has the right to dress foppishly or inartistically (Wells, 1967 [1905]: 227), deviations impossible in Icaria with its single Republican taste. But as is often the case in utopian literature, writers may have been reacting against what was going on in the 'real world'. Elizabeth Wilson (1992: 10) writes that 'the enormous growth of uniforms in the nineteenth century would also contribute to this "regime" of discipline' analysed by Foucault and, we may suspect, sensed by the utopianists.

The idea of a private space in utopias seems to come about at the same time as the idea of private space in capitalist industrial societies, and marks the end of ideal societies where the state is all-regulating. With individual personalities and private property in consumption (if not production), utopia turns bourgeois-romantic.

Power and gender

Explicit discussions of the relations between dress, power and gender are fairly rare and seem to occur only in utopian texts written during periods when the rights of women were on the broader political agenda.

Cridge (1984 [1870]) uses the simple device of reversed conventional roles in an imaginary society in order to make her point that aesthetics (in the guise of dress) and politics are gender-specific mutually exclusive domains: clothing renders one sex fit for public office and public life generally and the other both unfit and uninterested. Women are the rulers in this society, and their plain, substantial and flowing robes are seen as granting dignity to the wearer – a point made three times between pages 84 and 92. Such clothing grants to women and women alone both dignity and a legitimately active place in public life:

> As I looked upon these women in the colleges, as students and professors, as lawyers, judges, and jurors, as I looked upon them in the lecture-room and the pulpit, the house of representatives and the senate-chamber, – yea, everywhere, – I observed their quiet dignity, clothed in their plain flowing robes; and I was almost tempted to believe that Nature had intended – in this part of the world at least – that woman, and only woman, should legislate and govern; and that here, if nowhere else, woman should be superior to man. (Cridge, 1984 [1870]: 84)

Men lack the dignity granted by such dress, and this renders them unfit for political life. Their obsession with how they look in their pretty hats and coats of flimsy, insubstantial material leads one elderly lady to say 'What does it look like to see a parcel of men pretending to make speeches, in their tawdry pants and fly-away coat-tails, covered with finery and furbelows?' (Cridge, 1984 [1870]: 89), while another woman commenting on men's apparel remarks 'How would they look in the senate-chamber in their style of dress, so lacking in dignity? Why, we should have them quarrelling and pulling hair very soon! . . . No, no, gentlemen! you can discuss fashion and money-spending far better than national affairs' (1984 [1870]: 93). Wells (1967 [1905]: 204) remarks similarly that the 'barbaric adornments, the feathers, beads, lace, and trimmings' of, in his case, women, prevent their wearers from participating 'in the counsels and intellectual development of men'. For these writers, then, it is not the case that apparelled appearances do not count or ought not to count in political and public life, but rather that they count very much indeed. The fabrication of a dignified appearance is essential to legitimate participation in these domains, and clothing practices that render an entire class of person 'undignified' function to maintain political exclusion. 'Dignity' seems to require clothing that does not draw attention to the body of the person as such, and so the finery and furbelows of Cridge and the feathers and beads of Wells are essential elements in the gendered algebra of political inequalities.

Power relations are further marked by the dominant ones (women) making a practice of telling the dominated ones (men) how pretty they look, and the 'weak-minded men' responding by taking much pleasure in the compliment (Cridge, 1984 [1870]: 85). The compliment as rhetorical device imposes a particular definition of the situation, the dominated one indicating acquiescence with the inequality of the relationship through happily accepting it. Any reciprocity in compliments is presumably impossible here, for to return a compliment of similar ilk would be to claim a relationship of equality. Lord Lytton (1871: 235), indeed, remarks on the embarrassment of the complimented man in his account of the underground world of the Vril-ya: 'In the world I came from, a man would have thought himself aggrieved, treated with irony, "chaffed" . . . when one fair Gy [woman] complimented me on the freshness of my complexion, another on the choice of colours in my dress . . .'. If the unreciprocated compliment *form* indicates inequality in general between persons (or categories of person if one category, such as 'women', systematically compliments and the other, such as 'men', is systematically complimented), the compliment *content* indicates the particular acceptable areas of excellence of the complimented one. In the above example from Cridge, the man's domain is restricted to the prettification of personal appearance and the senate chamber remains unthinkable. It is the content of the compliment that ensures that inequality is preserved even when the parties are able to trade them. For example, if one of Cridge's women tells a man that his outfit is pretty and the man replies by telling her that she is a great senator, then the 'proper' domain of each maker/receiver of compliments is confirmed. If the man were to tell the woman that she, too, is pretty, then her reaction would be similar to Lytton's aggrieved man. The compliment, then, may be added to the inequality equation.

Women of Russ's (1985 [1975]) Whileaway or Gearhart's (1985 [1979]) Wanderground live in all-female communities, and discussions of the power elements in dress are confined to accounts of the old world that the utopian women have escaped. Russ presents the mirror image of Cridge's world, for here 'pretty clothes' are seen as exclusively the area of females (Russ, 1985 [1975]: 65, 67, 135, 151) and go with the exclusion of women from the worldly activities that are considered properly masculine: 'you can wear pretty clothes and you don't have to do anything; the men will do it for you', 'the pretty clothes . . . and how I did not have to climb Everest, but could listen to the radio and eat bon-bons while my Prince was out doing it' (Russ, 1985 [1975]: 65, 151). Outside Russ's utopia, being female *means* being dressed up in 'pretty clothes', and thus prevented from participating in the broader world. Writing more than a century apart, Cridge and Russ both see in 'pretty clothes' the index of exclusion.

Russ and Gearhart indicate the existence of a further dimension of power that women meet outside Whileaway or the Wanderground, namely dressing specifically for men – even, in Gearhart's case, according to very explicit dictates. On page 29, Russ lists ten different things that women did 'for the Man', headed by 'dress for the Man'. Her second list of seventeen on page 66 includes 'being perpetually conscious of your appearance for The Man'. Gearhart (1985 [1979]: 67–8) describes the appearance of the 'man's edition' of woman, 'streamlined to his exact specifications, her body guaranteed to be limited, dependent, and constantly available'. This particular status of the female body is attained through particular forms of clothing: 'her body encased in a low-cut tight-fitting dress that terminated at mid thigh; on her legs the thinnest of stockings, and the shoes ... How could she walk in those spindly things? And with the flimsy straps that fastened them to her ankles and feet?'. Dress regulations banning women from wearing trousers are introduced: 'Any woman caught wearing pants went to a behaviour modification unit; she emerged wearing a dress and a very scary vacant smile' (Gearhart, 1985 [1979]: 165).

Dress, then, seems an important element in the creation and preservation of a bipolar world of gendered inequality. The Russ and Gearhart solution to this problem is to be found in societies consisting of women only, a position clearly in tune with the separatist strand of the women's movement of the last quarter of the twentieth century.

Establishing and disestablishing power relations: circulation and exchange

Readers familiar with the anthropological literature on the gift relationship (e.g., Cheal, 1988; Codere, 1968; Gouldner, 1960; Gregory, 1982; Mauss, 1969 [1925]; Schwarz, 1967), which is discussed in detail in a later chapter, will know that power relations may be established through the ways in which goods circulate. For example, if A gives B a gift and B cannot reciprocate, then A has established a relationship of power over B. If B can return a gift of higher value, however, the tables are turned. Wherever something remains 'owing' in this system, a power relationship exists.

Earlier utopias exploit the powerful qualities of the gift relationship by using it to establish the state, the sovereign, or the father as dominant over citizens, subjects or sons. In Icaria, the Republic designs, makes and distributes clothing to its citizens (Cabet, 1848: 56); in the Paris of the year 2440 (or 2500, as the English translation somewhat bizarrely insists), the King grants a specially embroidered 'honourable hat' to those who excel in their art and thereby ensures that signs of excellence in subjects are dependent upon the approval of the sovereign (Mercier, 1974 [1771], Vol. I: 33); while in New Atlantis a father may give to sons of eminent virtue and merit a jewel 'made in the Figure of an eare of Wheat, which they ever after weare in the front of their Turban, or Hat' (Bacon, 1924 [1627]: 30). There seems to be no mention of reciprocation in any of these cases, and so a one-way relationship of power is established. Much later, Piercy (1979 [1976]: 364) shows how the same technique can be used to indicate class dominance: 'Adele also gave her a beige cardigan with embroidered flowers, shrunk in the wash, a pair of panty hose, and a pile of old *Vogues* and *New Yorkers*. It reminded her of the sort of things people gave you when you cleaned for them'. So cleaning for somebody here is not a pure money transaction between formal equals on the market, but infused with a form of power relationship that far predates capitalism: the cleaner is constructed as subjugated person, not as an impersonal economic actor performing a service in return for market rates of reward. We shall see below that Piercy extends the principle of the unreciprocatable gift beyond the personal to the institutional level.

The nineteenth-century growth of the realm of the personal touched upon earlier downplays the power elements in circulation and accentuates the ways in which items are used to indicate relations of affection between lovers and family members. In Butler's Erewhon, for example, the protagonist gives two buttons from his coat to Yram and appropriates the boots of his son to be kept as keepsakes (Butler, 1932a [1872]: 55; Butler, 1932b [1901]: 204, 321, 353, 364). Le Guin's *The Dispossessed* of a century later continually contrasts life on the planets Annares and Urras: on the former, handmade items such as a scarf, hat, or shirt are offered to loved ones, whereas Urras is entirely based on a capitalist economy and such a personalized pre-capitalist relationship does not seem to exist (Le Guin, 1975 [1974]: 161, 212, 216). The gift establishes a link between persons *through* inequality, but Butler and Le Guin seem to see only the link and not the inequality. In a later chapter, we shall see how the gift operates in the real world of family relations and in the virtual space of the Internet.

Rather like Le Guin's contrasting planets, Piercy's *Woman on the Edge of Time* of 1976 switches back and forth between contemporary New York and the future utopian society of Mattapoisett. Much of the contemporary part of the novel is set in a mental hospital, where there is a tension between institutional dominance as represented by hospital-issue dress and personal autonomy as represented by having one's own clothes. Autonomy is recognized for those who register themselves and for middle-class white people (Piercy, 1979 [1976]: 21, 340), as these categories retain their own garments. Others, however, become the clothed creatures of the institution through the imposed gift of hospital dress. Dominance is indicated by the lack of fit between the institutional dress and the physical characteristics of the wearer: 'they gave her a pair of blue pyjamas three sizes too big'; 'The coat was so long it hung to her midcalves and the sleeves concealed her hands, but she knew better than to complain' (Piercy, 1979 [1976]: 21, 142). Here the person is obliterated under the sign of the institution, a phenomenon well captured in the cry of 'I'm not going to meet a bunch of strangers in this filthy bughouse dress. I'm not!' (Piercy, 1979 [1976]: 71), uttered when the protagonist Connie is to meet people in Mattapoisett. Connie's fear seems to be that the strangers would see only the 'bughouse', not the person. Even for wearers of their own clothes, the institution can mark some limits: 'She had her own clothing, for sure. Some attendant had made her sew up the front a couple of inches with the wrong colour thread, but the dress was still shorter and fit better than anything else around'

(Piercy, 1979 [1976]: 145). The proper fit and (presumably) appropriateness to current fashion here guarantee autonomy, even if this is nuanced by the wrong colour thread. Even when Connie gets her own clothes she has lost so much weight that they fail to fit anyway, and so she still cannot appear as a properly autonomous woman (Piercy, 1979 [1976]: 218).

The power elements in the circulation of dress in Mattapoisett are quite different. There appear to be three classes of dress here: (a) clothing for everyday use such as 'warm coats and good rain gear. Work clothes that wear well' (Piercy, 1979 [1976]: 248); (b) items for once-only wear at party-type festivals called 'flimsies'; (c) more enduring 'costumes' for special occasions such as birthings, namings or dyings. Anybody can design a flimsy for themselves, and they are worn to express whatever one feels like at a given time. They are, then, the highest form of expression of the person in dress, indicating moods and desires of the moment. Such autonomy is unattainable for Connie in the mental hospital, or even for those wearing their own well-fitting and fashionable clothes: although indicating control over one's person, they cannot match the evanescent quality of the flimsy destined to last only a single evening and are tied to the social fact of fashion rather than the free flights of fancy that take material form in the flimsy. One can give to oneself in designing a flimsy, which would seem to avoid some of the problems of circulations with others. One still relates to others, but through display of one's momentary self rather than material exchanges: 'At a festival, why not be looked at?' (Piercy, 1979 [1976]: 171).

Costumes, unlike flimsies, are tied to exchange relations, but these relations are again quite different to those of the non-utopian world. 'The costumes are labours of love people give to the community when they want to make something pretty' (Piercy, 1979 [1976]: 248). We have seen instances above of the community imposing its appearance upon people in utopian societies, but here the relationship is reversed: the people give the costumes to the community. These costumes then circulate: 'Costumes you sign out of the library for once or for a month, then they go back for someone else' (Piercy, 1979 [1976]: 171). The villages of Piercy's utopia are also tied together through circulation: 'Circulating luxuries pass through the libraries of each village . . . some is always on loan to our village. And always passing on' (Piercy, 1979 [1976]: 175). There seems to be no imbalance of 'owing' between the villages and therefore no relationship of inequality, while for individual borrowers (who, of course, 'owe' for the duration of the loan), the power elements in exchange relations are reduced to the democratic level of the lending library.

Body–clothing relations

There are two main themes in utopian texts that touch upon body–clothing relations: nudity and comfort.

Nudity

Utopias where nudity is the normal state are uncommon. This is probably due to the great advantage of clothing in indicating social status in the hierarchical or otherwise differentiated societies that dominate the imaginations of utopian writers. For Christians, nudity indicated either the state of grace and innocence before the Fall or the state of sin after it: in the appropriately named Christianopolis they 'fear the temptations of nudity' and the body is described as 'How unclean, how polluted, how moist, how sweaty, how decayed, how filthy! And yet it pleases the soul, dictates to it, wears it out, and at last crushes it!' (Andreae, 1916 [1619]: 270). In Nova Solyma (subtitled *Jerusalem Regained*), the 'obscene ground-pattern of naked men and women' on a bedroom wall in a dream served to entice visitors into a trap where only captivity or death awaited (Gott, 1902 [1648] [Vol. I]: 115). So it is not surprising, then, that many utopias of nakedness have a strong Edenic tinge. Even in the not obviously Christian feminist science fiction of the 1970s, we find contrasts between the easy innocent nakedness of utopias and the complications of desire and domination (sin) that characterize nudity in contemporary societies.

It was difficult for writers of Christian tradition to posit naked utopias, because there was little point in showing perfect societies of naked bodies to readers who knew that such perfection could only be attained by those untainted by original sin. As a model for reform of contemporary society, this was asking for an impossible return to the state before the Fall. Christian sects like the Adamites or Anabaptists that attempted such a thing were considered heretical (Clarke, 1982: 47). But European colonialist expansion led to contact with very differently organized cultures where nudity was not understood in the same way. It became clear that there were actually existing societies where people did not necessarily wrap-up on an everyday basis. One reaction to this was to force them into European dress, thereby constructing them as just as originally sinful as the European Christians (as well as providing large profits for clothing manufacturers, as Perrot [1977: 193] suggests in the case of the French in Africa). However, it was also possible to argue that here indeed were people living in a state of innocence with respect to their nakedness, free of the corruptions that marked European society. Thus it became possible to use them to criticize European society in return: the 'naked savage' becomes the 'noble savage'. The theme of the natural innocence of, in this instance, Tahitians and the corrupting influences of Europeans is especially clear in Diderot's *Supplément au voyage de Bougainville*, written in 1771 and finally published in 1796. Character B remarks that the Tahitian 'touches the origin of the world and the European touches its old age' (Diderot, 1966 [1796]: 421, my translation), while the old Tahitian man's speech (Diderot, 1966 [1796]: 422–8) is an extended criticism of Europeans for destroying the natural innocence of his home island, where the point of life was to reproduce and those eligible to procreate could present themselves naked. But not everyone is naked in Diderot's Tahiti, for there is a clothing system based on sexual status that we shall consider in a later section.

An Edenic text of the colonialist expansionary period that has no place for clothing whatsoever is Gabriel de Foigny's *La Terre Australe Connue* of 1676. Here, dress is seen as the enemy of nature and contrary to reason.

Foigny's utopia is a land free of serpents, populated by naked hermaphrodite Australians. The explicit absence of serpents suggests that there is nothing to tempt any Australian Eve or Adam to fall in the familiar manner, and the reference to hermaphrodites is presumably meant to remind the reader of the state of the sexes before the splitting into two suggested in Plato's *Symposium*. So Foigny produces a doubly innocent utopia that is located before both the Judeo-Christian Fall and the classical Greek splitting. In case we are in any doubt about the innocence of the Australians, the narrator Sadeur is the only one who displays the physical signs of sexual arousal and never manages to discover how the Australians reproduce. As Sadeur also happens to be hermaphrodite, this rules out the possibility of arousal due to differently sexed beings, and becomes a comment on the different cultural approaches to nakedness: same bodies, different codes. The explicit comparison between nakedness in Sadeur's European homeland and *Terre Australe* is to be found on pages 102–6 of the 1990 reprint. Sadeur explains dress in Europe by invoking custom, climate and modesty, but his (?) Australian interlocutor has difficulty in accepting this and wonders how it is possible that a whole people could embrace a practice so contrary to nature: 'We are born what we are, and we cannot be covered without believing that we are unworthy of being seen' (Foigny, 1990 [1676]: 102. My translation, as are the remaining citations from Foigny). From an Australian perspective, Europeans place themselves lower than beasts if they cannot look at one another naked without becoming sexually aroused, and indicate inferior reasoning capacities if they cannot 'see' what lies behind clothing: 'If it is true that garments can keep them unaroused, then they are like young children who cannot tell what an object is once it has been covered up' (Foigny, 1990 [1676]: 104).[1] Sadeur is completely convinced by this, seeing in dress the mark of sin. But looking at the Australians 'one could easily say that in them Adam had not sinned, and that they are what we would have been without that fatal Fall' (Foigny, 1990 [1676]: 105). Eden exists on earth, then, and it is populated by Australians. Colonialist expansion makes Eden thinkable and attainable in a way it would not have been before, and over the next centuries many practical attempts were made to found utopian communities in various parts of the 'New World' (see Kumar, 1991: 73–6).

There are echoes of the French writer in Jonathan Swift's *Gulliver's Travels*. Part IV, 'A Voyage to the Country of the Houyhnhnms', is the most utopian part of the book. Gulliver provides a Foignyesque explanation of clothing to his master the horse, citing climate and 'decency', and the master echoes the Australian puzzlement: 'he could not understand why Nature should teach us to conceal what Nature had given . . . neither himself nor family were ashamed of any parts of their bodies' (Swift, 1967 [1726]: 283). Both the dominant houyhnhnms (horses) and the dominated Yahoos (humans) go naked, but Gulliver spends a lot of time trying to retain his dress because it is the only thing preventing him from being revealed as a Yahoo himself. Swift may well be satirizing attempts to return to an Edenic state of innocence, suggesting that humans without garments are no more than animals and may indeed be dominated by other animals. It is only wisps of material and his master's indulgence that save Gulliver from this fate.

Two discourses that became of greater importance in the nineteenth and early twentieth centuries were those of natural science and the equality of persons. These come together in Wells's 1923 book *Men Like Gods*, where the utopians are scientists and experimentalists who combine 'chemistry – and nakedness' and are described in such terms as 'stark Apollos' who live in a world of 'Olympian nudity' (Wells, 1976 [1923]: 30, 31, 51). The body for natural science *is* the naked body, and it is thus entirely logical for this sort of utopia to practise nudity. The scientific cast of the utopia would seem to preclude a return to Eden (where science is not practised), hence the references to the world of classical Greece (where science was founded). Nakedness was associated with Greek culture anyway, and Magnus Clarke (1982: 45–6) maintains that 'twentieth century nudism in European society owed almost all its origin to the nineteenth century "discovery" of Greek culture'. If the classical civilization of Greece contained nudity as part of its essential nature, then nakedness was peculiarly suited to a utopia of experimentalists. Clothing is associated by the utopians with their own Age of Confusion, which resembled closely the situation on earth at the time the novel was written (Wells, 1976 [1923]: 55). Dress was bound up in social difference and the unscientific morality of religion, as evident from the Earthlings who find themselves in the new world: top hats, frock coats, clerical collars, the professional uniforms of chauffeurs, the 'grey-clad' American and 'smartly dressed' Frenchman (Wells, 1976 [1923]: 27, 33, 39, 100). Wells here seems to have produced a novelistic version of the argument proposed by nudists that 'The universal and widespread practice of nudity would involve the obliteration to a large extent of class and caste distinctions' (Parmelee, 1929: 13). Thoreau makes the same point in *Walden* (1980 [1854]: 33), and Clarke, in his empirical study of nudism in Australia, reports that such 'nudist egalitarianism' forms a central part of nudist ideology (1982: 12, 13, 18, 50). The natural scientific attitude to the body, then, would seem to promise greater social equality through nudity. This assumes, of course, that all bodies were perceived as equally perfect in their nakedness, which indeed seems to be the case in Wells's world of 'Beautiful People', as Chapter 3 is titled. It soon becomes evident that this perfection springs from selective breeding based on the principles of eugenics (Wells, 1976 [1923]: 64, 74). The naked utopia of the 1920s becomes possible through the application to human societies of a branch of natural science that was soon to become discredited through its adoption by the fascist movements of the following decade. If the price of the naked utopia requires payment in the currency of eugenics, then it may suddenly begin to appear not as a utopia, but as a dystopia.

B.F. Skinner, writing in 1948 after the political discrediting of eugenics, continues with a 'scientific' approach to the body, but seems to confine everyday nudity to babies and children under three or four in *Walden Two*. The explanations are in terms of comfort, efficiency and control of the environment:

'But why don't you put clothes on them [babies]?' said Barbara.

'What for? It would mean laundry for us and discomfort for the child. It's the same with sheets and blankets. Our babies lie on a stretched plastic cloth which doesn't soak up moisture and can be wiped clean in a moment . . . Clothing and blankets are really a great nuisance', said Mrs. Nash. 'They keep the baby from exercising, they force it into uncomfortable postures B'. (Skinner, 1976 [1948]: 88)

Temperature and humidity 'were controlled so that clothes or bed-clothing were not needed' (Skinner, 1976 [1948]: 91) until the child entered a regular dormitory. Presumably, nakedness ends because children of that age do not pose the same efficiency problems for the adults that those less in control of their bodies do and because it is not practical to control temperature and humidity over the entire area of Walden Two – unless there is a residual Edenic myth at work, where naked innocence is granted only to very young children. It may be that Skinner avoids the problems of adult nudity by not permitting the technological level of his utopia to allow temperature and humidity control over the whole environment. There is no explicit discussion of this point, however.

There seems to be no suggestion of nudity in the nineteenth and early twentieth-century utopias written by women, even though, as we shall see in a later chapter, the relationship between clothing and the female body became a much-discussed topic among the dress reformers of the 1870s and 1880s. The concern was with clothing that properly fitted, not no clothing at all: as Frederick Treves (1883: 499) put it, the reformers operated within 'the strictest dictates of modesty'. But the feminists of the 1970s saw that nudity could mean different things depending upon the setting. In the all-female utopia of Whileaway indoor work takes place in the nude 'until your body's in a common medium with theirs and there are no pictures made out of anybody or anything' (Russ, 1985 [1975]: 95). The body as something that can be objectified visually and therefore judged invidiously is abolished in this account, becoming instead a medium of being together. Here, nakedness is part of social solidarity rather than social distinction. But the display of flesh on Earth can be dangerous because of its duosexed and gender-unequal nature: 'Her skirt was too short and that provoked him' (Russ, 1985 [1975]: 193). The partial or full display of the body in Mattapoisett seems to be a very relaxed thing at festivals, swimming and birthings (Piercy, 1979 [1976]: 172, 184, 222, 250), promising pleasure or ceremony for both women and men rather than domination of one by the other. The contrast with the United States of the 1970s is expressed through a comment on a book being read by a ticket clerk: 'On the cover two naked women embraced while a man about eight feet tall dressed all in black leather cracked a whip around them' (Piercy, 1979 [1976]: 256). Only the women are naked, and they are clearly constructed here as being under male dominance. For both Russ and Piercy, then, nudity in utopia means a relaxed way of being together, but on Earth the display of female flesh is caught up in gendered relations of dominance and submission.

Comfort

One of the peculiar aspects of clothing is that it indicates social status generally while being worn by a very particular body. It is perfectly possible for these two aspects to be in contradiction rather than harmony, and very frequently the necessity to display status overrides any consideration of bodily comfort. Indeed, in Veblen's familiar argument (1975 [1899]: 167ff.), it is necessary for the 'leisure classes' that clothing indicate incapacity to engage in any form of manual work and thus dress *must* in some degree be uncomfortable. A dress that would allow free play of the body would mark its wearer as lower class. It is always likely that display of social status will prove to be of greater weight than bodily considerations, for social status locates the wearer actively as part of the social world while dressing solely for the comfort of the body reduces the wearer to the compass of their physical self. They are not oriented to the social world, and can easily be perceived as not counting for much: physical bodies rather than proper social actors. But we all have bodies, and dress seems to be partially locatable as a resultant of the shifting balance of tensions between orientation to status display and the limits of the physical body.

The demands of the body play a frequent role in utopias, which would seem to indicate that the clothing worn in the authors' own societies had tipped too far away from the physical comfort zone and was instead concerned simply with the indication of status. In More's *Utopia* (1965 [1516]: 127), clothing is 'convenient for bodily movement, and fit to wear in heat and cold', garments in The City of the Sun are neatly fitted and adjusted to shape and size (Campanella, 1981 [1602]: 51), while the principle of elasticity allows a relatively small number of standard sizes to fit the many sizes and shapes of Icarian bodies (Cabet, 1848: 59). In Mattapoisett, clothes are of an adjustable size so a 'woman would not outwear them if she gained or lost twenty pounds' (Piercy, 1979 [1976]: 72). Louis-Sébastien Mercier makes an explicit contrast between pre-Revolutionary French dress and the Paris of 2440. A citizen of the future Paris is taken aback by the narrator's awkward and unhealthy eighteenth-century clothing, with arms and shoulders imprisoned, the chest laced tight thus impairing breathing and legs exposed to weather in all seasons (Mercier, 1974 [1771], Vol. I: 21). The narrator observes that the citizen's

> neck was not tightly bound with muslin; but surrounded with a cravat more or less warm, according to the season. His arms enjoyed their full liberty in sleeves moderately large; and his body, neatly inclosed in a sort of vest, was covered with a cloak, in form of a gown, salutary in the cold and rainy seasons. Round his waist he wore a long sash that had a graceful look, and preserved an equal warmth. He had none of those garters that bind the hams and restrain the circulation. He wore a long stocking, that reached from the foot to the waist; and an easy shoe, in form of a buskin, inclosed his foot. (Mercier, 1974 [1771], Vol. I: 22–3)

Clearly, clothing that paid little attention to the comfort of the body was a major problem of the dress of Mercier's time. Forty years later we find the same complaint in *The Empire of the Nairs*:

> Both men and women enjoyed the perfect use of their limbs. No restraint proceeded either from the materials of fashion or their habits; the same spirit of liberty, which had inspired all their laws and manners, seemed to have presided at the toilets of the Nairs – no unnatural ligature repressed agility of the men; no whalebone imprisoned the shape of the women, no hoops impeded their motions, no high heel gave them a tottering step – they moved as nature had designed them. (Lawrence, 1981 [1811]: 36, quoted in Sargent, 1981: 91)

Less than another half century after this Bellamy (1986 [1888]: 41) saw the bustle as dehumanizing the form and Morris (1912 [1890]: 14) sketched the women of his utopia as 'decently veiled with drapery, and not bundled up with millinery . . . they were clothed like women, not upholstered like arm-chairs, as most women of our time are'. In the twentieth century, Wells's Mr. Barnstaple was distressed at the prospect of being forced to leave his comfortable utopian dress of sandals and light robe to return to the home world where he would 'struggle into socks and boots and trousers and collar; the strangest gear. It would choke him he felt' (Wells, 1976 [1923]: 217).

But it is the feminist writers of the twentieth century who have paid most attention to the relationship between clothes and the body, beginning with Charlotte Perkins Gilman's *Herland* of 1915. *Herland* describes an all-female world into which wanders a group of three men. Dress here is clearly meant to be what women would design for themselves if there were no men around, and the leitmotiv of Herlandish garments is comfort. The term repeatedly recurs in the men's own reactions to the only available dress: 'undoubtedly comfortable', 'absolutely comfortable', 'they were quite as comfortable as our own – in some ways more so', 'I felt very comfortable. When I got back to our own padded armour and its starched borders I realized with acute regret how comfortable were those Herland clothes' (Gilman, 1979 [1915]: 25, 26, 73, 84).

Russ and Gearhart tax non-utopian women's clothing in particular as uncomfortable, because it is designed to appear for men rather than for the physical comfort of women. The theme crops up in Russ several times, with 'ridden up' bras, hampering party dresses, tortuous undergarments, winter coats with no way of holding them shut, broaches that catch on things, and the like (Russ, 1975: 33–4, 39, 40, 63, 83–4). Gearhart (1979: 67, 94, 152, 158) makes similar remarks about the 'man's edition' of women. For these feminist writers, dressing for men means not dressing for bodily comfort but for the particular display of the social status 'proper female' as read by the male gaze. The problem disappears in all-female societies. The steady principle in utopian writings, then, concerns the problem of the display of social status through dress overriding the desire for physical comfort: if social status is to be indicated, it should not be at the expense of the body.

Aesthetics

If we look at earlier utopian texts, we find very few comments indeed on the aesthetic elements of dress. This is not surprising, for where a principle function of clothing is the indication of rank or social status then questions of beauty are of no great import. By the nineteenth and early twentieth centuries, however, aesthetics had clearly become a major concern. In particular, variations on the term 'grace' recur with striking regularity across texts of this period such as those by Appleton (1984 [1848]: 53), Bellamy (1986 [1888]: 41), Cabet (1848: 57), Cooley (1984 [1902]: 207), Griffith (1984 [1836]: 33), Haldane (1926: 39), Lytton (1871: 96, 163), Morris (1912 [1890]: 143) and Wells (1967 [1905]: 52, 109, 226, 228, 316; 1976 [1923]: 39). Morris was particularly taken with the notion of 'gay' attire (1912 [1890]: 23, 24, 34, 138, 180, 200, 208), and variations on 'harmony' can be found in Morris again (1912 [1890]: 138) and in Wells (1967 [1905]: 227, 228; 1976 [1923]: 39). This is not the place to pose philosophical queries such as 'what is beauty?', and so instead we ask the rather more mundane sociological question: what ends do aesthetic elements serve in utopian accounts of dress? There is some evidence that they are meant as a criticism of the class-based nature of beauty that prevailed at the time. Indeed, Veblen (1975 [1899]) considered that we perceive something as beautiful to the degree that it indicates the wealth of the owner/wearer. In this view, wealth guarantees beauty while poverty ensures ugliness. But beauty can belong to all classes in Wells (1967 [1905]: 226): 'The dress is varied and graceful . . . and the clothes, even of the poorest, fit admirably . . . There is little difference in deportment between one class and another; they are all graceful and bear themselves with quiet dignity'. Morris actively dissociates wealth and class from beauty: the dustman Boffin is one of the most richly and elegantly dressed of all the people he meets, those who work in the hayfields are still elegant, and the narrator is puzzled that everyone can afford beautiful clothing (1912 [1890]: 20–1, 138–9, 143, 154, 162). The liberation of aesthetics from wealth is clearest in his comment on the stream of elegantly dressed people he sees going into the market-place: ' "Elegant," I mean, as a Persian pattern is elegant; not a rich "elegant" lady out for a morning call. I should rather call that *genteel*' (1912 [1890]: 100 footnote). Aesthetics here is autonomous and we are quite mistaken to confuse wealth and elegance. Artistic beauty of the craft type permeates the utopia of Morris, and is part of his protest against mass industrial society and the 'cheapening of production' (1912 [1890]: 93) it entailed.

Aesthetics in the nineteenth century was considered by some to have a directly moral influence on people, moulding their behaviour in certain desired directions. Mass art was not for art's sake, but had social duties to perform. Adrian Forty (1986: 109) quotes the journalist Loftie who wrote in 1879: 'A few bare walls hung with pictures, a few flowers in the window, a pretty tile on the hob, would, in my opinion, do more to keep men and women at home, and to promote family love, than libraries of tracts and platforms full of temperance lecturers'. So here beautiful house produces happy family, and keeps people off the streets, where they could cause all sorts of troubles. Note also in this passage a conviction that beauty in the house can be a much more powerful moral influence on people than the more conventional weapons of moral reformers, such as tracts and lectures slamming the demon drink. Aesthetics has a *moral* purpose here: the pictures on the wall are not there just to give idle pleasure, they fulfil the greater purpose of family solidarity and a life led in the private sphere rather than on the public streets. Forty (1986: 110–12) also shows how morality was built into the very design of furniture of the same period. So it is possible to suggest that the strong aesthetic component of nineteenth- and early-twentieth-century utopias is linked to the more general concern with the social disorder that threatened capitalism at the time. Social order in utopias of the period, then, is at least partly dependent upon the civilizing influence of aesthetics as applied to the dress of the masses. Societies where beauty 'belongs' only to a particular class are deeply and fundamentally divided, but grace, harmony and beauty for all demonstrate unity in a very visible way. The social divisions of actually existing societies are overcome through the aestheticization of the utopian masses. It is the belief in the autonomy of art with respect to social relations, a belief shared by figures as far apart as Morris and Marcuse (1979 [1977]), that makes this way of thinking possible. Today, following Bourdieu (1984 [1979]), we might wish to suggest that different classes might hold quite different notions of what beauty is, and that any society marked by just one version is either under the complete ideological hegemony of one class or has no classes whatsoever. In either case, society will appear consensual on the aesthetic level. Whose 'grace', 'elegance' and 'harmony' triumph in utopias? Utopians would answer that art itself provides the laws for such things, but this view may itself be typical of a particular class. There is clearly scope for research that would map nineteenth- and early-twentieth-century aesthetic terms onto social class.

The gendered division of labour

Students of sociology will be familiar with the notion of the Great Transformation, which refers to the large number of economic, political and social changes that accompanied the process of capitalist industrialization in nineteenth-century Europe. Before the Great Transformation, many productive activities took place at home: people engaged in their crafts or trades there, and merchants did their buying and selling. Capitalist industrialization brought about a concentration of paid labour in the factory, and a draining of recognized labour from the home. Where once the home was also the site of productive activities, now many activities were taken out of the home and placed in the factory, and those that remained were degraded to the level of non-work. Home activities once understood as vital to the economy became invisible, and women's work, which was once highly valued, was transformed into a devalued chore.

This degrading can be seen in the shifting evaluation of the clothing-related gendered division of labour across utopian texts. In two seventeenth-century works, tasks related to clothing not only formed part of the world of women but were also understood as forming an integral part of the economy. Andreae makes a direct link between human industry in general and women's arts in particular:

> For whatsoever human industry accomplishes by working with silk, wool, or flax, this is the material for women's arts and is at her disposal. So they learn to sew, to spin, to embroider, to weave, and to decorate their work in various ways. Tapestry is their handiwork, clothes their regular work, washing their duty. (Andreae, 1916 [1619]: 260)

The work peculiar to women is presented in a very positive and active light here as artfully skilled and of acknowledged importance. For Fénelon, women's work was an integral part of the great commerce of the city of Tyre, while the wool spun by the women of the land of Bétique was both used for their family's needs and appreciated throughout the world (Fénelon, 1994 [1699]: 36, 109–10). Women's clothing-related work contributed both to the global economy and the domestic one and there was no sense of a negative evaluation of such labour. There was clearly a gendered division of labour, but it did not necessarily resonate with inequalities or with alienation from the broader socio-economic world.

By 1836, the positive aspects of the work had been reduced in Griffith's (1984 [1836]: 44–5) utopia to the particular class of poor women to whom 'it is of great advantage . . . that they can cut out and make their husbands' and children's clothes'. In Icaria, the repair of clothes was the job of the women in the family – but this required only minimal effort and washing was a nationalized affair (Cabet, 1848: 60). Socially, the range and importance of women's clothing labour becomes ever narrower. By the time we meet the 1870 utopia of Cridge, all positive aspects of clothing-related labour have disappeared and nothing remains but the oppressive drudgery of the chore. Cridge's role-reversal, where it is the men who undertake domestic labour, perhaps brought the negative aspects into clearer relief to a readership accustomed to associating men with heroic, satisfying and important deeds. Instead of the triumphant picture of active colonial–industrial man, we find long weary days of depressing tasks:

> It was wash-day, and I watched him through that long and weary day. First at the wash-tub, while baby slept; then rocking the cradle and washing at the same time; then preparing dinner, running and hurrying here and there about the house: while in his poor disturbed mind revolved the thought of the sewing that ought to be done, and only his own hands to do it.

> It was evening: the lamp on the table was lighted, and there sat the poor husband I have described, in his rocking-chair, darning stockings and mending the children's clothes after the hard day's washing. I saw that it had rained; that the clothes-line had broken, and dropped the clothes in the dirty yard; and the poor man had had a terrible time rinsing some and washing others over again; and that he had finally put them down in wash-tubs, and covered them with water he had brought from a square distant. (Cridge, 1984 [1870]: 76)

Even where there is some hint of a positive role for work such as embroidery or fancy knitting, these are dismissed as mere 'delicate nothings' (Cridge, 1984 [1870]: 83).

In the similarly role-reversed utopia of Dodderidge (1988: 171–2), clothing-labour is again portrayed as a depressing and endless task. Outside Whileaway, Jeannine's simple attempt to leave the house is retarded and frustrated by the score of clothing chores she feels compelled to undertake as part of the gendered division of labour (Russ, 1975: 105–7).

Utopian texts, then, trace the shift of women's share of the gendered division of labour from a recognized positive contribution to both the domestic and broader economy to a series of oppressive, endless, unsatisfying, frustrating tasks that imprison women within the home for long periods. Alienation in the factory came to be accompanied by alienation, for women at least, in the home.

Gender differentiation and sexuality in dress

Clothing in utopian texts is more often gender-specific than not. In a manner similar to the shift in meaning of the gendered division of labour traced above, earlier texts note the differences between the garments of women and men without necessarily implying any inequalities, while later writings see the gendered nature of dress as inherently expressing the non-egalitarian nature of society. A lesser degree of differentiation or no differentiation is sometimes proposed as a solution.

For Andreae (1916 [1619]: 171), Campanella (1981 [1602]: 41) and More (1965 [1516]: 127), gender indication is one function of clothing among others. There is no special discussion of this point, and it is plausible to assume that this meant that gender was just another social status that was important enough to signal clearly. Suggestions that there may have been problems in the non-utopian societies of the time begin with Gott's (1902 [1648]: 106) comment that the 'distinction of dress between the sexes' is *strictly* enforced (my emphasis) in Nova Solyma and become very pronounced in Fénelon's tirades (1994 [1699]: 6, 41, 50, 162, 332) against what he calls 'effeminacy'. For example, Mentor, who is in fact the goddess of wisdom Minerva in the guise of an old man, warns that 'A young man who delights in gaudy ornaments like a weak woman, is unworthy of wisdom and glory' and Telemachus replies by proclaiming that 'the son of Ulysses shall never be vanquished by the charms of a base effeminate life' (Fénelon, 1994 [1699]: 6). In Salente itself, 'All foreign merchandise that might introduce luxury and effeminacy was prohibited' (Fénelon, 1994 [1699]: 162). Gender confusion in dress was not an uncommon theme in the non-utopian writings of the sixteenth and seventeenth centuries: for Philip Stubbes (1836 [1585]: 68), for example, 'Our apparell was given as a signe distinctive to discern betwixt sexe and sexe; and, therefore, one to weare the apparell of an other sexe is to participate with the same, and to adulterate the veritie of his owne kinde', while John Evelyn (1951 [1661]: 24–5) complains of the gender confusion brought about by French clothes: 'Behold we one of our Silke Camelions, and aery Gallants, making his addresses to his Mistress, and you would sometimes think yourself in the country of the Amazons, for it is not possible to say which is the more Woman of the two coated Sardanapalus's'.

Masculinity of a certain type seemed to be under particular threat from what appeared to such writers to be an unmanly interest in dress, but the 'proper' type could at least still be found in Fénelon's utopia. The properly masculine qualities of wisdom and glory are to be found neither in the enchantments of the wardrobe nor in those of the looking glass.

The mapping of gender differences in dress onto broader gender inequalities is most pronounced in the feminist science fiction of the 1970s, and has already been touched upon in the section on power: for both Russ (1985 [1975]: 29) and Gearhart (1985 [1979]: 68, 91) non-utopian women's clothing is specifically designed to please men and, for Russ in particular (1985 [1975]: 65–7, 122, 135, 151), an intense preoccupation with these man-pleasing 'pretty clothes' almost makes up the whole of what being a proper non-utopian woman is. Men's suits, by contrast, 'are designed to inspire confidence even if the men can't' (Russ, 1985 [1975]: 138) and permit one's version of events to be taken seriously. Piercy (1979 [1976]: 381) suggests the latter in quoting from the medical report on her protagonist Connie: 'Mr. Camacho [Connie's brother] is a well-dressed man (grey business suit) who appears to be in his 40's. He operates a wholesale-retail nursery and has a confident, expansive manner. I would consider him to be a reliable informant . . .'. Strongly gendered dress codes, of course, make successful disguise easier: in Nova Solyma, Phillipina manages to pass herself off as the male Philander thanks to her masculine dress (Gott, 1902 [1648], Vol. II: 48, 91), and Gearhart's *Ijeme* (1985 [1979]: 69–70) is taken for a man by a woman through the same device.

Lack of gender differentiation in dress seems more common among children than among adults in Utopian writings: Morelly (1970 [1755]: 147) describes the clothing, food and first lessons of five-year-olds as everywhere uniform, 'Boys and girls wear much the same sort of costume' in Wells' *Utopia* (1967 [1905]: 226–7), and the Parsons' girl and boy in *Nineteen Eighty-Four* are described as both 'dressed in the blue shorts, grey shirts, and red neckerchiefs which were the uniform of the Spies' (Orwell, 1984 [1949]: 24). Adults in Piercy's Mattapoisset seem to know no gender differentiation in dress, but here the men are physically capable of breast-feeding children and birthing does not take place through the body. This would appear to suggest that sexuality in utopias is an important factor in gender differentiation in dress: no obviously marked sexuality in children and a sort of semi-shared sexuality in Mattapoisset. In Gearhart's novel, the sexually non-threatening 'gentles' were 'dressed much like the hill women, in soft shirts, work pants and boots' (1985 [1979]: 183). In Diderot's reproduction-happy Tahiti, on the other hand, the entire clothing system seems tied to a precise and explicit expression of sexuality: the boys are dressed in tunic and chain until age 22 when they demonstrate the frequent effusion and high quality of their semen, while pre-nubile girls wear a white veil. A black veil indicates sterility, and a grey veil menstruation (Diderot, 1966 [1796]: 444, 452, 456). In Huxley's Brave New World, sex is encouraged where 'everyone belongs to everyone else' (Huxley, 1994 [1932]: 38) but reproduction takes place in laboratories and the few non-sterile women are the ones who wear 'Malthusian belts' stuffed full of contraceptives (Huxley, 1994 [1932]: 45–7, 49, 69, 107, 175, 178).

Wells tends to see the expression of sexuality in the women of his time in an entirely negative light, complaining that

> The education, the mental disposition, of a white or Asiatic woman, reeks of sex; her modesty, her decorum is not to ignore sex but to refine and put a point to it; her costume is clamorous with the distinctive elements of her form.

> The contemporary woman of fashion who sets the tone of occidental intercourse is a stimulant rather than a companion for a man. Too commonly she is an unwholesome stimulant turning a man from wisdom to appearance, from beauty to beautiful pleasures, from form to colour, from persistent aims to brief and stirring triumphs. Arrayed in what she calls distinctively 'dress', scented, adorned, displayed, she achieves by artifice a sexual differentiation profounder than that of any other vertebrated animal. (Wells, 1967 [1905]: 202)

Hence he recommended that 'the sexual relation [be] be subordinated to friendship and companionship' in his modern utopia, ensuring that 'the costume of the women at least would be soberer and more practical [than in contemporary Europe], and less differentiated from the men's' (Wells, 1967 [1905]: 204, 227).

But where a diminished level of differentiation in dress among adults is seen less as an appropriate and desirable lowering of the sexual temperature and more as a form of sexual repression, as in *Nineteen Eighty-Four* with its uniform of overalls for Party members and its red sash of the Junior

Anti-Sex League, a craving for differentiation is considered both a proper expression of the sexed self and a subversive political act, more subversive even than the simple casting-off of the overalls that 'seemed to annihilate a whole culture, a whole system of thought, as though Big Brother and the Party and the Thought Police could all be swept into nothingness by a single splendid movement of the arm' (Orwell, 1984 [1949]: 31). Alone with Winston, Julia in her short hair and 'boyish overalls' operates a 'much more surprising' transformation by painting her face: 'With just a few dabs of colour in the right places she had become not only very much prettier, but, above all, far more feminine'. But Julia intends to go even further: 'And do you know what I'm going to do next? I'm going to get hold of a real woman's frock from somewhere and wear it instead of these bloody trousers. I'll wear silk stockings and high-heeled shoes! In this room I'm going to be a woman, not a Party comrade' (Orwell, 1984 [1949]: 126, 127).

The links between male sexuality, dress and power have been treated very briefly by Russ and at more length by Dodderidge. Where men are dominant overall, there is a simple link between display and power: '. . . his crimson epaulets, his god boots, his shaved head, his sky-blue codpiece, his diamond-chequered-costume attempt to beat up the whole world, to shove his prick up the world's ass. She looked so plain next to him' (Russ, 1985 [1975]: 168).

But where women are dominant overall, as in Dodderidge's role-reversed utopia, the display of male sexuality through dress means something very different. Here, the women dress plainly in 'an unbecoming tubular garment which concealed completely those parts of the female form wherein my sex [male] is wont to take most delight and to view with most pleasure' (Dodderidge, 1988 [1979]: 41), and it is they who have the right to look, to stare and to evaluate.

Costly garments: from the dangers of luxury to the imperative of consumption

In the non-utopian world of the seventeenth and eighteenth centuries, luxurious and costly dress posed quite serious problems of national economy to those Europeans who lived outside France, which was the main source of fashionable innovations. John Evelyn (1951 [1661]: 6–7) complained that imports of French clothing strengthened the French economy at the expense of the English, while an anonymous English text of 1715 aimed

to dissuade my Country-men from the Use of French Fashions, and from apply-ing to Foreigners in Matters of this nature, where we have a Right, and Power, and Genius to supply our selves. Which if I can prevail on them to do; The End of that will be, a flourishing Trade, vast Sums of Money spent within the Kingdom, which are now sent Abroad into France to buy the commodities of that Country; perpetual Liberty, Plenty, and the Spirit of Elegance and Politeness which need then not be deriv'd from Foreign Nations, but will be the Natural and Genuine Product of our Own. (Anonymous, 1715: 3)

Bringing this argument to its ultimate conclusion, Gustav III of Sweden (1778) introduced a national dress for his subjects in order, among other things, to avoid the high costs and customs fraud to which the importation of French garments led, hoping thereby to put an end to the drain on both state revenues and those of individuals. It is hardly surprising, then, that the cost of clothing was a theme picked up by utopian writers. As we shall see below, there has been a long-term shift from a preoccupation with the problems posed by luxury and the need to limit it to an acceptance, and even promotion, of luxury as essential to the economy.

The economic dangers of luxury mentioned above are echoed by Mercier (1974 [1771], Vol. II: 188), where foreign commerce in the Paris of the future is abolished because of the destructive luxury of such imports as 'the gaudy stuffs of India', while clothing for Morelly (1970 [1755]: 137–8) is 'sans luxe extraordinaire' and in accordance with what the Republic can afford. In Salente, Mentor reduced the number of merchants handling foreign materials and taught the Salentines to 'despise that wealth . . . which exhausts the state' (Fénelon, 1994 [1699]: 165). The love of such wealth is not just a danger to the national economy, but also to the whole social order:

> luxury poisons a whole nation . . . [which] comes by degrees to look upon superfluities as necessary to life, and to invent such necessaries every day; so that they cannot dispense with what was counted superfluous thirty years before. Such luxury is called good taste, the perfection of the arts, and the politeness of a nation. This vice, which draws after it an infinite number of others, is extolled as a virtue, so that the contagion extends at last to the very dregs of the people. The near relations of the king want to imitate his magnificence; the grandees, that of the royal family; those in the middle ranks of life, that of the grandees; for who is it that keeps within his own sphere? And those in low life will affect to pass for people of fashion . . . A whole nation goes to wreck; all ranks are confounded. (Fénelon, 1994 [1699]: 297)

The love of luxury spells ruin for the nation, social classes and individuals. One utopian solution in times when feudal distinctions were still dominant was to disconnect the link between social rank and the display of wealth through such items as expensive dress. In Nova Solyma, for example, 'luxury is subject to public censure' and 'the chief marks of honourable rank consist not in gorgeous and expensive robes, but in the colour and length of their ordinary dress, and the law is that each one's dress is to differ according to his rank and dignity' (Gott, 1902 [1648], Vol. II: 133, Vol. I: 106), while in Salente the 'different ranks among your people may be distinguished by different colors, without any necessity to employ for that purpose either gold, silver, or precious stones' (Fénelon, 1994 [1699]: 162). More radical utopians seemed to abolish social rank anyway, so the display of wealth in this Veblenesque manner would have been pointless. More's Utopians dress unpretentiously in the same design and colour and hold expensive dress in contempt (1965 [1516]: 133–5, 153–5), in Christianopolis the inhabitants 'have only two suits of clothes, one for their work, one for the holidays; and for all classes they are made alike . . . none have fancy tailored goods' (Andreae, 1916 [1619]: 171), nothing in Morelly's deliberately modest dress could lead to any special consideration (1970 [1755]: 138), and in the Paris of the future 'everyone is dressed in a simple modest manner; and in all our walk, I have not seen either gold clothes or laced ruffles . . . "When a man is known to excel in his art, he has no need of a rich habit . . . to recommend him"' (Mercier, 1974 [1771], Vol. I: 32). Rank conservers and rank abolitionists are united in their concerns about the ill effects of luxury.

With the expansion of capitalism in the direction of consumerism, vast numbers of new goods came on the market and more and more classes of persons possessed a freely disposable part of their income. For the British and French middle classes of the late nineteenth century, the consumer society had arrived. It was perhaps this development that made it possible no longer to think in terms of being forced to choose between having, say, either good food or good clothing. With the ever-increasing profusion of goods, furthermore, luxury in clothing would have appeared less of an economic problem than in a period when it was relatively much more important to the overall economy. Expenditure on dress was now less likely to be ruinous to either the individual or the state. Morris (1912 [1890]) reflects the tensions in the transition between a society of want that was still real for many people and a society of plenty that more and more could reach. His narrator is puzzled that everyone can afford costly garments, and receives a rather indignant reply:

> Of course we can afford it, or else we shouldn't do it. It would be easy enough for us to say, we will only spend our labour on making our clothes comfortable: but we don't choose to stop there. Why do you find fault with us? Does it seem to you as if we starved ourselves of food in order to make ourselves fine clothes? or do you think there is anything wrong in liking to see the coverings of our bodies beautiful like our bodies are? (Morris, 1912 [1890]: 139)

Here, the problem of cost has been abolished in two senses: there is no longer an actual economic problem, nor is there any problem about the 'costly' aesthetic step of going beyond mere comfort. Everyone in Morris's aesthetopia can afford to be a member of the aesthetocracy. He may have preferred to see a craft-based community as the one that would allow this to be possible, but consumerist capitalism may have been what was, and still is, laying down the practical bases of such a future society.

But who controls consumption? For Morris, it seemed to be an aesthetically informed populace. In real-world capitalism, however, needs are to greater or lesser degree shaped by the economic imperative to expand consumerism, and we are all familiar with the role played by advertising in seeking to direct our consuming desires in expansive directions. The apotheosis of this form of consumerism is Huxley's *Brave New World*. Instead of advertising, however, we have something far more efficient: a direct education of the young to consume through the hypnotic technique of sleep teaching.

Over and over again they are fed the same slogans: ' "But old clothes are beastly", continued the untiring whisper. "We always throw away old clothes. Ending is better than mending, ending is better than mending, ending is better . . . The more stitches, the less riches; the more stitches . . . I love new clothes, I love new clothes, I love . . ." ' (Huxley, 1994 [1932]: 43, 46). Consumption is no longer ruinous, but enriching.

Conclusion

Our analysis of utopian literature has shown that

- social structure is made manifest through clothed appearance and clothed appearance embeds its carrier in social structure;
- relations of power may be expressed through both the appearance and circulation of dress;
- aesthetic elements of dress may function to include or exclude wearers from the world of public life and political responsibility;
- in the nineteenth century, aesthetics also came to be seen as a way of overcoming class differences;
- the act of complimenting a person on their dress may be related to the establishment and maintenance of relations of subordination and domination;
- accounts of nudity show the continuing influence of the Edenic myth even in feminism;
- nudity plays the contradictory roles of social solidarity and egalitarianism on the one hand and gender-based relations of inequality on the other;
- there is a continual tension between treating the body as primarily physical in quality and using it as a base for the display of social status;
- the progressive degradation of the value of women's clothing-related labour can be traced historically across utopian texts;
- gender differentiation in dress is seen as desirable where gender confusion might undermine the social order or where the social order seems to use undifferentiated dress not only to exclude expressions of sexuality, but also to undermine social relations where hyperdifferentiation is found;
- the cost of dress has shifted from threatening ruin in earlier economies to promising increased riches in later, consumer-orientated formations.

Utopian texts address the problems of the worlds in which their writers lived, and thus provide a privileged critical source for a socio-history of the roles of dress in society. These roles, as we have just seen, turn out to be fundamental to senses of what society is and how it works.

Note

1 Diderot (1966 [1796]: 430) makes a similar point when the Tahitians instantly recognize one of Bougainville's crew as a woman, although she had managed to hide this completely from everyone else during the long months at sea. This may not have been unusual, for there was quite a tradition of female transvestism in early-modern Europe, as Dekker and van de Pol show in their book on the

matter (1989). Faced with the stark choice of becoming either a prostitute or a man, potentially destitute women in countries where soldiers and sailors were always in demand apparently had little difficulty in considering the latter option. The frequent success of such enterprises would seem to confirm a tendency to take clothed appearance on trust: if the dress says 'man', then the body carrying it is assumed to be male. Foigny and Diderot are no doubt satirizing a European tendency to judge the world by appearances, but if such a stance was worth satirizing it must have held some currency at the time.

3

More than the Times of Our Lives: Dress and Temporality

Introduction

The other main chapters of this book are concerned with analyses of circumscribed empirical materials. This chapter is different. Where the empirical chapters attempt to come to a series of conclusions and thus close down the analysis, this chapter tries to open up concepts of temporality in clothing more generally. It is exploratory and theoretical where the others are methodically analytical, and thus roams across a wide range of disparate texts and writings with the aim of coming up with an account of the different possibilities that might be thinkable in the context of dress-mediated temporalities. Although one can say a lot about utopia by looking at utopian texts, a lot about families by sampling families and a lot about Internet newsgroups by sampling actual Internet newsgroups, there is no obvious place to go when one wishes to say even slightly more than a little about time. As we shall see, examination of the contents of a widely cast net leads to accounts of two different aspects of temporality in dress: the time units involved and the shapers of certain facets of time. The former are composed of the year, the season, the week, the day and the now; the latter of the body, politics, dominant class and dominant culture. We begin, however, with some general considerations.

Time has not always been with us – at least, not in the familiar form of the universally coordinated chronological time that regulates most of the lives of the vast majority of people living in industrialized societies. Time, in other words, has a history. For Norbert Elias (1993 [1987]), our present clock-sense of time is a result of a long drawn-out process of civilization and neither exists prior to experience nor inheres in nature. Instead, it results from the demands of increasingly larger and more urbanized and mechanized human settlements for coordination at ever-higher levels coupled with the decreasing efficiency of natural rhythms, such as the seasons or the tides, in accomplishing this coordination. Clock time is highly abstract and highly social, although, in a typical example of the Eliasian civilizing process (Elias, 1994 [1939]), we have internalized it as entirely 'natural' to complex societies. Clearly, some forms of time are linked to natural rhythms and others to demands that require more autonomy with respect to nature, with the former looming large in smaller settlements and the latter dominating greater ones. The bulk of this chapter explores the complexities of both natural and social times as revealed through the analysis of dress.

In order to grasp temporal complexities, we must go beyond Elias's complaint (1991: 30) that 'our present mode of thinking, the structure of our categories, is attuned to relatively short time distances' – as short, even, as the commodity-driven instantaneity noted by David Harvey (1990) in his account of postmodernity. It is not, however, merely a question of choosing between the *longue durée* and the *histoire événementielle* of Fernand Braudel (1958) nor, in the reformulation of Anthony Giddens (1987: 144–5), between the interlacing *durées* of day-to-day life, the lifespan of the individual and of institutions, nor between the instantaneous and glacial times discerned by Scott Lash and John Urry (1994: 242). Barbara Adam (1990: 16) gives an indication of the complexity at work when she writes that 'It is not either winter or December, or hibernation time for the tortoise, or one o'clock, or time for Christmas dinner. It is planetary time, biological time, clock and calendar time, natural and social time all at once'. Even a time-unit as apparently simple and clear-cut as the day can be very complicated: in the Indonesian week-calendar, for example, each day belongs to nine weekly cycles and the 'same' day can be called by any of nine different names depending upon its position in a particular cycle (Zerubavel, 1989 [1985]: 55–6). When the day begins can vary within the very same institution: in the hospital he studied, Eviatar Zerubavel (1979: 31) found that the 'same' day could begin at midnight, 6 A.M., 7 A.M., 8 A.M., or 11 A.M. depending upon the institutional activity one was considering. Furthermore, each social group within the hospital (such as nurses and physicians) had its own rotational cycle of a specific length that often neither matched nor was synchronized with the cycles of the other groups (Zerubavel, 1979: 14–15). Zerubavel's analysis is considerably more intricate than these examples indicate, but the general point should be clear: it would be a mistake to assume that each social institution has a single time that is its own. As the example of the hospital shows, there is a multiplicity of times at work within the same institution, so even such apparently simple and unified concepts as 'day' or 'institution time' turn out on inspection to be unexpectedly complex.

Adam (1990: 67–8) contrasts the understandings of time in the social and physical sciences, maintaining that the former associate 'time in events' with traditional societies and 'events in time' with industrial societies, while the latter seem to have evolved in the reverse direction: 'events in time' are associated with classical physics and 'time in events' are associated with modern physics. Similarly, Heidegger maintains that entities do not merely exist in time but that time expresses the nature of what objects are (Giddens, 1987: 141). If we substitute 'object' for 'event', take the stances of modern physics, traditional societies and Heidegger, and furthermore accept that the linear time of industrial capitalism (Thompson, 1967) may apply only to a restricted part of our lives, then we can see that a relevant question to ask would be: what times are there in objects, and how – if at all – do they relate to each other? This question may obviously be posed of any object in the world, but here will be addressed only to clothing. Zerubavel (1979) tried to identify the socio-temporal structure of the hospital, so here we try to identify the socio-temporal structuring of dress. We begin by considering clearly temporal concepts, such as the times of the year and the cycle, the season, the week and the day, as well as the notion of 'nowness', and then examine dress in the light of the times of the body and age, political time and the times of dominant cultures and classes.

The year: chronological time and cyclical time

Gathering years

Some of our time distinctions are based on a tendency to gather years together in bunches of ten: we say that a given outfit is 'very fifties' while another may stand in for the eighties as an entire decade, even though it may have been prominent in only a few of those years. Further multiples of ten, such as centuries and half-centuries, lie at the base of the organizational pattern of certain clothing histories (Boehn, 1971 [1932]; Cunnington and Cunnington, 1952; Cunnington, 1981; Laver, 1964). This is an artefact of the dominant number system and the attempt to grant social significance to mathematical divisions: if it is possible to order the world according to numbers then, in a fine example of alienated thought, the world must follow the logic of the numbers. Even if this criticism holds true at the level of many fashion histories, Christopher Breward (1995: 184–5) suggests that such alienated numbering has been turned to advantage by recent sellers of fashion through the deliberate use of the notion of the decade as a promotional device. It is as if terms such as 'the sixties' or 'the nineties' have taken on cultural reality thanks to our numbering system, and so the numbering system drives 'reality' instead of being driven by it.

The (generally) arbitrary relationship between decade, half-century or century and particular events does not apply to the notion of year, with its definite relation to earth and sun. This will be taken up again in the section on seasonal time, but the year may be pressed into service for covering periods shorter than decades ('the year of...') or discrete years may be gathered together to project a history of any institution. Take the examples of the Australian designer label Jag and the fashion house Balenciaga in the September 1992 issue of *Vogue Australia*: an advertisement for Jag consists of seventeen black and white photographs of people in Jag dress organized in photo album style, each with a caption and a year (from 'It all started with great jeans... 1972' to 'Celebrating 20 years. 1992'), while the feature article on Balenciaga includes photos and sketches of Balenciaga fashions, each of which is accompanied by a caption and date. This dates-and-events style of history means that events are made meaningful by being assigned a date, and dates are made meaningful by being assigned their events, each legitimizing the other and thereby creating a simple kind of 'historical' significance. Collecting different sets of date/event mappings provides legitimation for the different institutions. Thus, Jag and Balenciaga claim to be historically significant. We can see the same principle at work in the dated photographs of the family album – this is one way in which families construct a history for themselves.

The fashion year

Bunches of years are not always gathered together in particular ways, but can stand as units on their own. This, for Roland Barthes (1983 [1967]), is essential if the systematic character – the here-and-nowness – of fashion is to be established. For one year all is system, all diachrony expunged. 'This year's' items are infused with fashionability, although it seems unlikely that all items worn will necessarily carry this modish charge: certain items of apparel may be thus privileged while others remain out of play, but the determination of which ones are so marked in a particular year is a matter for further research. A naïve structuralist approach would include all items, but this is not appropriate here: items 'of the year' may be detachable from a relatively neutral (not necessarily unfashionable, as binary thought might imagine) background of other items. From the point of view of Venetian lace makers, for example, lace is considered a durable beyond the caprice of fashion (Sciama, 1992: 122). The mode in fashion magazines, which was the subject of Barthes' research, would encourage the 'all elements' approach, but actually worn clothing differs in not (normally) being all of the one year, except perhaps for those who change their complete wardrobe with every revolution of the earth about the sun. The structure evaporates at the end of the year and a new one is put in its place. Fashion, in this sense, is a series of synchronicities of 1-year duration. However, to remain at the level of the fashion year would be to miss regularities operating on much greater time scales.

Long cycles and short cycles

Even if we go no further than what Barthes (1983 [1967]: 295) calls 'memorable duration', that is, the time each of us can personally cover through our own life experience, we may notice a tendency to recurring cycles: the mini-skirts of the sixties seem to return at regular intervals, if not in quite the same guise, and the flared trousers of the seventies also return, in slightly altered forms on occasion. If we position ourselves as surveyors of the past few centuries, then some much longer wavelengths start to become visible in both formal evening wear (Kroeber, 1919; Richardson and Kroeber, 1940) and more typical everyday dress (Young, 1966 [1937]). In her study of illustrations of women's street and daytime dresses from 1760 through to 1937, Agatha Young (1966 [1937]) notes that the shape of the skirt goes through three mutually exclusive cycles in quite regular order: back-fullness (such as the bustle) is followed by a bell shape, which in turn is superseded by a tubular type, each shape dominating for about one third of a century. This fundamental cycle is seen to be quite independent of political, economic and cultural events that might otherwise be taken as having an influence over clothing. Rather, these latter categories operate at a different time level and on other aspects of dress, a point that will be addressed below. This particular cycle appears absolutely rather than relatively autonomous, but that is far from arguing that all clothing cycles possess the same degree of autonomy. Some details, such as colour, type of material or various accessories and attachments may change quite rapidly without having any impact on the rate of change of the skirt shape itself, and it is these aspects that are more directly shaped by political, economic and cultural influences. The rapid rate of change seems to be a way of characterizing fads rather than long-cycle fashion change, but rate of change is not all that is involved: Herbert Blumer (1968: 344) suggests that 'fads have no line of historical continuity, each springs up independent of a predecessor and gives rise to no successor'. It appears, then, that there are aspects of clothing specifically open to the carrying of relatively ephemeral political, economic and cultural significations and other aspects that remain immune from rapid change.

It is possible that the skirt length cycle has become more rapid for everyday dress today but retains a slower periodicity for formal evening dress which, as Jane Richardson and A.L. Kroeber (1940: 111) point out, 'has fulfilled a fairly constant function for several centuries'. Their study, which covered fashion plates of women's evening dress from 1787 to 1936, found skirt length cycles of 144 (maximum to maximum), 53 (minimum to minimum), 109 (maximum to maximum) and 94 (minimum to minimum) years, averaging out to 100 years. The average cycle for skirt width was also 100 years, while waist length and décolletage length were 71 years, waist width was 93 years and décolletage width was 154 years in the same period. This raises the possibility that different parts of the very same item are caught up in different time cycles, and even in different positions with respect to their 'own' maxima and minima. If this is the case with a single item, then there are many more cyclical times at work in a given outfit than one may have imagined hitherto. We tend to see an outfit or an item as an integrated whole, a Gestalt, not suspecting the quite different time scales simultaneously at work in the synchronic snapshot we get by glancing at someone in the street. In our new view, however, a given garment begins to appear not as the solid product of the here and now, but rather as the meeting place of a number of different historicities.

Fred Davis (1992: 157ff.) suggests that dress now moves in microcycles rather than classical macrocycles, with no single overall look but a multiplicity of looks tied to the disparate identities encouraged by consumer culture. However, it is not easy to discern a long-term cycle if one is living through it, and it is likely that work dress in certain occupations and formal dress generally still changes at a slower pace than leisure or informal dress. Our work identities as producers usually remain within much stricter bounds of variation of our multiple identities as consumers, and it is the increasing importance of the latter that leads to the perception that classical fashion in the sense of one dominating look has come to an end. To put this another way: long-wave cycles are associated with the self as a public participant in the culture of production, shorter waves with the self as a private participant in the culture of consumption. However, the recent institution of 'casual Fridays' on Wall Street (Kauffmann, 2000) may indicate the beginning of the collapse of these separate identities into one another. If work comes to be understood as a lifestyle choice like any consumer commodity (a possibility in advanced consumer societies), then the macrocycle may indeed cede its place to the short-term, episodic, fragmentary time that Zygmunt Bauman (1995: 91) sees as typical of postmodernity.

It was suggested above that variations in skirt shape have become less important than variations in skirt length. This is because the present female body is not the same body as the female bodies of other centuries. The nineteenth-century dress reformers, who will be discussed in more detail in Chapter 4, were the first to maintain that the natural shape of the body should be revealed by clothing, rather than an artificial shape imposed upon it by dress. If this is generally accepted, then the shape of a dress would not vary very much, because to do so would be to offend against the philosophy of the 'natural' body shape – but this would have little effect on variations in length once legs are made visible. In other words, the legacy of the dress reformers inhibits change in dress shape, but has little effect on skirt length, which can vary according to all sorts of other criteria. There have been great changes in women's relation to the labour market in the twentieth century, and so it is probable that the utilitarian values of the workplace have also had some effect on shifting skirt shape periodicity into the background.

Seasonal time

The time of fashion magazines

The fashion year may be broken down into a succession of moments, each a different inflection of the overall 'look' of the year: 'every season has its own Fashion', as Barthes (1983 [1967]: 250) remarks of his analysis of 1950s fashion magazines. As we shall see in Chapter 4, seasonality remains important in the magazines of the 1990s.

There is, then, a solar discourse of seasons against the backdrop of the overarching 'nowness' (synchronicity) of the year in fashion magazines. This may be clearer if we contrast the time of the fashion magazine with the time of utopian texts. For example, Andreae (1916 [1619]: 171) sees a simple summer/winter distinction in his Christianopolis, while in the City of the Sun 'Four times each year, when the sun enters Cancer, Capricorn, Aries, and Libra, the people change to other outfits' (Campanella, 1981 [1602]: 51).

Where each year is different to the next in fashion societies (this spring will be different to last spring but resemble the rest of this year in some ways), utopians do not necessarily see each year as different to the next (this spring will be the same as last spring but differ from the rest of this year). Such change would threaten the stability of utopian societies, which need to be atemporal at the level of successive years (or successive rulers, as we saw in Chapter 1), whereas the 'natural' change associated with the seasons can only confirm the 'naturalness' of the societies. 'Spring' in fashion societies is a continually varying constant because it manages to non-paradoxically combine cyclical return (the constant) with linear shifts over a series of successive years (the variation). 'Spring' in our utopian examples is simply a cyclically recurring constant with no linear variations.

Dressing for and against the season

We are accustomed to the idea of a harmonious relationship between season and fashion, but the explicit *opposition* of fashion to season was recognized in debates preceding the 1778 dress reform of Gustav III of Sweden. A competition was launched for a new design in 1774, an important consideration being that the reformed dress would be both suitable for the Swedish climate and end the continual changes in fashion which were costing the economy dearly (Bergman, 1938: 15). Respondents such as Adolph Modéer (1774: 65) complained that fashion, designed in the warmer climes of southern Europe, seemed to prevail over what he considered the health and seasonal imperatives of the cold Nordic climate, but perhaps J.B. Méan has a more subtle understanding of the almost ironic links that did exist between fashion and season when he writes that 'This mania for changing fashions so frequently has even affected men; hence these puerile distinctions between winter, summer, autumn and spring cuffs: embroidery and braid in gold for the winter and in silver for the summer, as if one was hotter or colder than the other...' (Méan, 1774: 117, my translation). Here, fashion certainly marks the season but not in a way that pays any practical attention to varying temperatures: a colour on a sleeve cuff may switch from gold to silver, but keeping one warmer or cooler is not the point. Fashion here absorbs the seasons, and they re-emerge as connotations of clothed fashionable discourse, devoid of any independent reality. This eighteenth-century postmodernist stance is what scandalizes Méan and others who would see season as the reality to which clothing should submit, and not the reverse. The principle of seasonal dressing, then, may also act in opposition to the principle of fashionable dressing, and may do so again in future. But can linear and seasonal vestimentary times coexist in the same society?

The link between seasonal change and clothing change has been documented in the case of agricultural societies (Maslova, 1984: 110–25), but industrial societies appear, unsurprisingly, more complex. Gender appears to be an important variable here: Doris Langley Moore (1929: 217–18) writes that 'To take one great instance of the curious apathy of men towards their own comfort, it is strangely absurd to wear practically the same clothes (in town at least) during all the seasons of the year', while Virginia Woolf (1938: 36) once remarked on 'whole bodies of men dressed alike summer and winter – a strange characteristic to a sex which changes its clothing according to the season'. Industrial society saw not only the elaboration of a linear time of industrial production alongside the more traditional cyclical time of agricultural production, but also a mapping of these very different sorts of time onto men's and women's clothes respectively. Although this has more recently been mapped onto work and leisure clothes respectively for both women and men (which is not to argue that the earlier mapping has completely disappeared), Moore and Woolf were not the only pre-Second World War writers to see the matter in gendered terms. J.C. Flügel (1930: 204) lists 'much greater adaptability to varying seasons' as one of his no less than thirteen reasons why women's clothes in 1930 were 'superior to man's in nearly every respect'. This may have given rise to some practical problems that are still evolving. First, the association through clothing of women with seasonal change and men with 'man'-made linear time would appear to strengthen the dichotomizing links between women with nature and men with culture. Second, the split between the linear and the seasonal would certainly not hinder the marginalization of women with respect to paid labour: from an industrial point of view, their clothing marked them out as being of quite another time (agricultural) and therefore of quite another place (the private sphere). To admit the presence of the agricultural–feminine private–cyclical into the temple of the industrial–masculine public–linear would be to subvert the latter even more than its own cycle of economic boom and bust, which lay it open to charges of irrationalism. The adoption of occupational uniforms is one solution to this problem, and it may be noted that women in certain occupations (e.g., banking) are sometimes required to wear uniforms particular to a specific institution while the men are not, the latter already wearing the international work uniform of their sex, namely the suit. It seems as if women still need to be put into clothing marking the firm's time, whereas men prove their solidity by an apparently spontaneous adoption of the dressed sign of the linear time of industrial society. It has been argued that women in executive positions have faced problems due to the lack of an accepted equivalent to the masculine suit, and the skirted suit has been recommended as a solution by 'wardrobe engineers' such as John Molloy (1980). 'Time dressing', where women take on masculine linear time, may be of more fundamental importance than 'power dressing'. One could speculate, however, that the increasingly widespread influence of ecological myths of living more in tune with 'nature' may eventually lead to the more general acceptance of seasonality in the clothing of many sections of the population, at work or not. Furthermore, the recent return to prominence of consumption encourages a more playful orientation to goods and signs than an ethic of production ever would, and may begin to undercut linear time. Seasonal time, no longer agricultural but both post-industrial and 'ecological', seems as neat a way as any of tying down the floating clothing signifiers of the postmodern. The meeting of ecological ideas with consumption would seem to render unlikely the older form of conspicuous consumption where it was 'by no means an uncommon occurrence, in an inclement climate, for people to go ill clad in order to appear well dressed' (Veblen, 1975 [1899]: 168). Indeed, if individuals 'regard all those objects which advertise their taste as also indicating their moral standing', as Colin Campbell (1987: 153) remarks of the classically consuming Puritan classes, then seasonal clothing may become the mark of the proper ecological consumer, virtue to the fore.

Hebdomadal time

Although filtered to varying degrees through culturally specific spectacles, units such as the year or season clearly derive from natural phenomena. The decision on where the year begins may be determined according to entirely social criteria (European cultures have usually used 1 January, but the French Republican calendar chose 22 September [Zerubavel, 1977: 870]), but the actual duration of a year is a matter for the solar system. Although the beginnings and endings of seasons may be unclear and relate to several different discursive fields, so that, for example, an Australian may decide that summer begins on 1 December (Gregorian calendar time), 21 December (solstice time), when light cotton dresses first appear in the shops (fashion time), when the percentage of men in shorts rises over fifty per cent in the supermarket on a Saturday morning (positivist sociologist's time), or whenever it becomes comfortable to walk barefoot across the kitchen tiles (body-centred time), and the Nuer decide on the season by drawing upon the socio–spatial notion of whether they are residing in the village or the camp (Evans-Pritchard, 1940: 95–6), there is, nevertheless, a link to sun–earth relative positioning. The week is an entirely different matter. The familiar seven-day cycle appears rooted in Judaeo–Christian creation myths: God created the world in six days and rested on the seventh. The intrinsically religious nature of this type of week was recognized by both the French Republicans and Joseph Stalin, who attempted – and failed – to abolish church influence by adopting weeks of ten and five days duration respectively (Zerubavel, 1977: 870–1). Other weeks have been organized according to the rhythm of the local market. This

> market week still flourishes in developing countries around the world. The three-day market weeks of ancient Colombia and New Guinea, the five-day market weeks of ancient Mesoamerica and Indochina, and the ten-day market week of ancient Peru all serve to remind us that such *weekly market cycles* have not always been seven days long. (Zerubavel, 1989 [1985]: 45)

There is nothing 'natural', then, about a week. But is there a hebdomadal rhythm to be found in clothing? Evidence would suggest that there is, although it may be in the process of transformation. The importation of the time of the factory into the home in the nineteenth century led to an increasingly strict regulation of domestic time, and this had implications for the mapping of particular days of the week onto particular domestic tasks. Drawing upon the researches of Anne Martin-Fugier (1979) and Odile Arnold (1982), Alain Corbin writes of the French case that

> A *Manuel des domestiques* published in 1896 recommended soaping and washing on Wednesday, ironing on Thursday and mending on Friday. In lower-class households, however, the linen was seen to by the housewife on the Sunday and Monday. Among the women's congregations, it was on Saturday that the clean linen for the week was distributed. (Corbin, 1995 [1991]: 20)

There is a long association between Mondays and washdays in the English-speaking world, but it is likely that the availability of automatic washing machines to many social classes coupled with the greatly increased participation of women in the labour force has weakened this traditional link: the chances of neighbours meeting while hanging out the washing in the suburbs of the 1950s may have been high, but current home technology and labour market changes facilitate privatization and the idea that any day can be wash day, de-privileging the social coordination possible when everyone hung out their clothes at the same time. The clothes line remains, however, what Ronald Klietsch (1965: 78) called, in his study of clothes line behaviour, a 'detached collective presentation', where the positioning of clothing items is deliberately designed to convey certain impressions about their owners. We may no longer meet our neighbours on our uncoordinated washdays, but they give us plenty to read as, expert suburban semioticians, we furtively glance into their back yards. Our families may be different: Jean-Claude Kaufmann (1992: 54) mentions the tendency of men not living as part of a couple to bring their washing back home to mother at the weekend. The weekly wash consolidates mother–son ties of a certain type. This is true even when the man lives as part of a couple, for 'the couple' did not become constituted as such in Kaufmann's sample of twenty French heterosexual partnerships until their own washing machine had been obtained. The machine seems central in the shift from the hebdomadal time of washing with mother to the more diffuse, everyday time of the couple.

If Mondays were for washing clothes, Sundays in the Christian world were for special clothes. Petr Bogatyrev (1971 [1937]: 36) refers to the church dress of a valley in Slovakia, 'where the women have as many as 52 different aprons, which they wear according to what the priest's vestments will be on a particular Sunday'. There was clearly a tight and detailed link between clothing and the religious calendar here, but other cultures also distinguished Sunday clothes from other clothes, if not at the level of a special apron for every Sunday of the year. Wilfred Webb (1912: 154) remarks on a simple Sunday/weekday distinction among the clothes of agricultural labourers in Britain, while Rosemary Harris (1972: 26), in her study of Ulster farm families carried out in the 1950s, found distinctions between working clothes and Sunday clothes for men; and work, Sunday and shopping clothes for women. Children's new suits and dresses were kept for church on Sundays. In an ethnographic study of dress in Dublin families, the present writer (Corrigan, 1988) found that similar distinctions were drawn in urban Ireland by women talking about their experiences of growing up in the 1950s, but that things had now altered. Technological change having made available many more and cheaper clothes, the identification of certain garments with Sunday appears to have weakened. But it is also possible that the religious 'Sunday' has been replaced by the secular 'weekend': if particular leisure pursuits have replaced churchgoing as a major Sunday activity, then there may still be 'Sunday' clothes but they may have little to do with religion as generally understood. Barthes (1983 [1967]: 250), indeed, regards the weekend as one of the privileged moments of the fashion discourse. The hebdomadal cycle, then, still exists, but it has been reorganized around the quite different principles of contemporary consumer societies. Just as Christian societies absorbed non-Christian feast days and changed their significance, so consumer societies are absorbing Christian feast days and altering their meaning to suit advanced industrial conditions. Christmas and its associated gift-giving is a good example, as also is the increased tolerance given to Sunday shopping in many large towns in nominally Christian countries: in both cases, our relations with commodities transform Christian concerns into something else. This absorption of the seven-day religious cycle into commodity discourse may prove longer lasting than the French Republican or Stalinist attempts to undo religion by changing the cycle itself: commodities may triumph where politics has failed.

Diurnal time

Like the year, the day, understood as the period during which the earth rotates once about its axis, is tied to the sun–earth relationship, but it is also like the year in that the periods into which the day is divided are open to wide cultural variations. Even the obvious day/night or dawn/dusk distinctions, which we may think of as 'natural' boundaries, are not always available in human settlements. In the Arctic summer, for example, social activities lack the 'natural' day/night punctuation:

> People come and go at all hours of the day. Men routinely hunt seals for 20, 30, or more hours at a time; women prepare food for their families when they get hungry, and everyone sleeps when they are tired. Children frolic quite happily outside at 4 A.M., and adolescents play softball games that can last for a week. (Goehring and Stager, 1991: 667)

The day/night distinction in the Arctic is really a seasonal one, and Marcel Mauss (1978 [1905]) shows how social activities in winter (darkness) differ in almost all respects from those in summer (light). In less extreme climes, finer distinctions are made at certain points of the day than others. E.E. Evans-Pritchard (1940: 101) remarks that Nuer timekeeping makes 'almost as many points of reference between 4 and 6 A.M. as there are for the rest of the day', explaining this principally by the fact that there are many more distinct social activities in play between these particular hours than at any other time. Pitirim Sorokin and Robert Merton (1937: 615) see this as generally true: 'social phenomena are frequently adopted as a frame of reference so that units of time are often fixed by the rhythm of collective life', and Emile Durkheim (1915 [1912]: 440) also considered that the rhythms of social life were at the basis of time distinctions. Time distinctions, then, often seem to have more to do with social activities than either 'natural' or mathematical divisions.

So is there a relationship between clothing, social activity and time of day? It would appear that there is. The upper-class dress of the Victorian period and the early part of the twentieth century seems to represent the most developed form of costumed punctuation of the day. In the case of men, Penelope Byrde (1979: 142) writes that 'The Victorians developed the idea of wearing different clothes for different occasions to an almost unprecedented degree and a man might be obliged to change his clothes several times a day', while Margaret Oliphant remarks rather acidly that

> it is a most gratuitous assumption on his part, making half-a-dozen changes of costume in the course of the day, and having a different toilette for every act of his life, that it is the other half of humanity [women] which wastes its time and occupies its mind with the cares of dress. (Oliphant, 1878: 45)

But women's clothing divided the day in just as complex a manner, as can be seen from Moore's quotation from an unnamed fashion paper:

> There are clothes for early morning, clothes for shopping, clothes for every type of luncheon party, the early afternoon or sitabout dress, the dress for receiving at home in the afternoon, the dress for going out to tea, with its special coat; a cocktail time dress, a little dinner-dress, the grand dinner-dress, the theatre-going-dress, all with their special coats; the quiet evening dress, the dance dress, the ball dress, and the full regal grand evening dress, all with their special wraps. Apart from all these, which may represent the average chic and wealthy woman's day in town, there are also the various complete and distinct sports, outdoor, and country costumes, and the sports, the day, and the evening fur coat. (Moore, 1929: 242–3)

By the 1950s, matters had become scarcely less complex, at least in the world of fashion magazines: fashion had 'a very complete timetable of notable moments throughout the day (nine o'clock, noon, four o'clock, six o'clock, eight o'clock, midnight)' (Barthes, 1983 [1967]: 250). Barthes makes it appear here as if clock time is determinant, but it is much more likely that the social activities associated with these periods are the most central: one does not dress in a particular way because it is eight o'clock, but because at eight o'clock one is going to engage in a particular activity. In Corrigan's (1988) ethnographic study, distinctions drawn by working-class respondents were simpler: the mother (housewife) of one family drew distinctions between house clothes for working at home, day clothes for shopping and night wear for an evening out, while her daughter saw day clothes, night clothes for going out and work clothes as the main contrasts. The principle of the link between activity, time of day and clothing seems common to several classes and historical periods, then, but the level of complexity varies. Of course, the same item may indicate different times of day depending on its position within its own particular life course: 'Don't you ever feel a little sorry for a gown that had a success at afternoon affairs, when you see it forced to do duty in its old days during the working hours of the morning?' (Concannon, 1911: 67). However, a considerable amount of further research would be required to provide an accurate picture both of the variations in diurnal dressing practices across classes, genders, ages and ethnicities today and the points in its passage from new to old at which a garment begins to indicate different sorts of time.

'Nowness'

The notion of 'now' or 'the present' is very hard to pin down: as Jean-François Lyotard puts it with reference to Aristotle,

> it is no less impossible to grasp any such *'now'* since, because it is dragged away by what we call the flow of consciousness, the course of life, of things, of events, whatever – it never stops fading away. So that it is always both too soon and too late to grasp anything like a 'now' in an identifiable way. (Lyotard, 1991 [1988]: 24–5)

This little philosophical difficulty does not prevent 'now' from cropping up frequently in all manners of discourse. Clearly, one will draw upon contextual cues in order to grasp such an indexical concept. So: how is 'nowness' constructed through the contexts of clothing? It may come about either through the relatively rapid changes of fashion or through change so slow as to be barely noticeable. Consider the first: we have already seen that nowness in the world of fashion magazines (Barthes, 1983 [1967]) stretches over a single year, that the 'nows' of styles, fashions and fads indicate increasingly shorter periods as we move from style to fad (see also König, 1973 [1971]), and that the mapping of particular garments onto particular time-bound occasions led to several changes of clothing per day for upper-class Victorian women and men. For writers such as Georg Simmel (1957 [1904]: 547), Gilles Lipovetsky (1987: *passim*) and Mike Featherstone (1991: 74), fashion change provides us with more of a sense of the present than most other phenomena, for it shows us through our own clothing that we are somewhere other than where we have just been. Present-day clothes always appear somehow 'right', and it is hard to disagree with Moore (1929: 212–13) when she writes that 'Each era prides itself on its impeccable taste, its discovery – at long last – of the true harmonies of form, colour, and fabric, its complete knowledge of fitness and comfort. And each era is the laughing stock of the next!'. The same writer (1929: 201) notes that 'the shorter the period which has elapsed since the discarding of a style, the more ludicrous it invariably appears'.

The most elaborate statement of this position is by James Laver (1937: 255), who claims that the same costume will be:

Indecent	10 years before its time
Shameless	5 years before its time
Outré	1 year before its time
Smart	
Dowdy	1 year after its time
Hideous	10 years after its time
Ridiculous	20 years after its time
Amusing	30 years after its time
Quaint	50 years after its time
Charming	70 years after its time
Romantic	100 years after its time
Beautiful	150 years after its time

Although one might disagree about the choice of adjectives or the exact number of years, most readers will probably feel intuitively that Laver has indeed grasped something essential about time and aesthetic judgement. But why do we think like this? Last year's clothes connote the near immediate past, a version of our everyday life that no longer quite matches the way we live and look today. We see from last year's clothes that everydayness, despite appearances, can be and is organized around arbitrary signifiers that we accept without much thought: but at the same time we desire an 'authentic', immanent, self-evident, obvious everydayness well-captured in Moore's (1929: 202) observation that 'an enormous majority of people . . . maintain that we have reached the very summit of elegance combined with commonsense, from which we will never depart to any material extent'. Last year's clothes remind us that this is a utopian aspiration. They may also recall a whole set of relationships that may now no longer hold, relationships to both the world in general and other people in particular. But the further removed the clothes are from us in time, the less they connote aspects of our personal histories, and the more they exist as clothes for themselves. They will of course recall historical periods, but periods in which we have decreasing personal involvement and eventually none at all, and so we can more or less dispassionately judge these clothes according to increasingly pure aesthetic criteria culminating in 'beautiful'.

Next year's clothes also show that our present life as constructed through fashion is indeed a short-lived thing: we know we are going to change our appearance, and any desire for a nicely settled authentic identity, where our clothing would transparently display our true selves, as Thomas Carlyle (1908 [1831]: 50), Joanne Finkelstein (1991) or Henry David Thoreau

(1980 [1854]: 34) would wish, is simply unattainable in fashion societies. Although the notion of an ever-changing clothed identity may seem indecent or shameless to some, to others it appears to be what life is about. Davis (1992) sees our identities as ambivalent and shifting in contemporary society, needing continual fashion change as an always-provisional solution to the problem of stabilizing our uncertain selves. However, it is the existence of more and newer clothing commodities that permits this uncertainty in the first place.

Change and commodity society

Campbell (1987) places the desire for novelty, which he sees as a consumerist ethic essential to complement the Weberian Protestant ethic of production, at the very centre of the fashion process. The aesthetic of societies where the consumer is the sovereign actor lies in the about-to-arrive commodity that is just around the corner: this is where the most advanced version of nowness lies, and it is only by striving to attain it that we can claim to be fully synchronized as consumers with the most essential characteristic of the present state of advanced industrial societies – the production of the Next Commodity. This has less to do with psychological desires for the pleasures of the new, as Campbell (1987) seems to think, and more with social actors being at one with what we might call 'consumer time'.

If a sense of presentness can be attained through continual rapid change, it can also be reached through no change at all or through a change, which compared to fashion, is slow. The first is appropriate to commodity-driven ever-changing societies where 'all that is solid melts into air' (Marx and Engels, 1968 [1847]: 38), the second to non-commodity societies and to certain institutions within commodity society that align more with ideals aspiring to longer life than that provided by evanescent consumer nowness. Examples of the latter include church, military, hospital and school dress. Although moving at a slower rate than fashion change, these institutions do not necessarily alter at the same pace. Church dress, for example, may take centuries to change and therefore give the impression to relatively short-lived humans of not changing at all, but nurses' uniforms may shift a little more rapidly (see Lhez [1995] on uniform changes in French nursing). Rates of change are the rough product of the tension between serving the public understood as ever-changing consumers and serving enduring ideals such as God, the Law, medicine or whatever. The closer serving the public as customers comes to be seen as the primary task, the more rapid will be the change in institutional uniforms. Elizabeth Ewing (1975: 56, 135) shows that the dress of maidservants, who served commodity-consuming families, changed in tune with fashion, while that of female flight attendants was updated approximately every seven years – slower than fashion, but still relatively quick. The latter are very directly servants of passengers, yet also represent the enduring reliability of the airline and their own established skills that may be called on in an emergency. The rate of change in their uniforms, then, can be understood as the product of these tensions. Similarly, nurses need to not only respond to the public, but also must represent the unchanging notions of caring and the enduring characteristics of an institution that may have been in the community for a very long time. Military and police uniforms must also face in more than one direction, and change according to how these tensions are resolved. Even the Catholic Church admitted that it had to serve the changing public as well as an (in principle, at least) unchanging transcendent God when it allowed reforms of religious dress in the 1960s. School uniforms are a permanent battle-ground between the aspiration to the unchanging values of the school and the changing fashions espoused by schoolchildren who also consume as groups and individuals. Amish dress (Enninger, 1984), however, which belongs to a culture that rejects consumerism, remains frozen – the time of the Amish is not that of modern commodity society.

Body time and age time

Time springing from the body versus time as imposed by fashion

The notion of the body as a machine is a metaphor that is currently very influential in discourses such as dieting (Turner, 1992), medical conceptions of women's bodies (Martin, 1987) and sports science. This appears to be quite a modern way of looking at the body, and hardly existed before the eighteenth century. The shift to the use of chronological time seems important in this 'machinization' of the body, but how was time measured before chronology? In a famous passage, E.P. Thompson writes:

> in seventeenth century Chile time was often measured in 'credos': an earthquake was described in 1647 as lasting for the period of two credos; while the cooking time of an egg could be judged by an Ave Maria said aloud. In Burma in recent times monks rose at daybreak 'when there is light enough to see the veins in the hand'. The Oxford English Dictionary gives us English examples – 'pater noster whyle', 'miserere whyle' (1450), and (in the New English Dictionary but not the Oxford English Dictionary) 'pissing while' – a somewhat arbitrary measurement. (Thompson, 1967: 58)

The important point to note here is that time had to do with certain forms of activity that had their basis in the body: the saying of a prayer, the visibility of a hand or the process of urination. In other words, the sense of time came from the body and the world was encompassed in these terms. So here, the body makes sense of the temporality of the world. With the advent of chronology, the relationship between body and the world is reversed: instead of the body being a subject that measured the world, chronological time with its clocks and watches turns the body into an object of measurement. It then becomes possible to coordinate bodies to the same 'objective' chronological time, something that was clearly rather useful in the organization of factory production. The objectively coordinated body can then be matched to the objectively coordinated machine – machine time takes over from body time, or rather the latter is subordinated to the former.

There has been a similar tension in discourses around dress: sometimes clothing is understood in terms of the time of body, at other times the reverse is considered to hold and the time of fashion dominates bodily concerns – we become clothes horses, changing our apparel when the mode dictates. As an example of the first, we may consider the nineteenth-century link between giving birth and wearing a cap (Gernsheim, 1963: 29), the special clothes often worn during the period of pregnancy or sanitary products for the appropriate time of the month. The anthropological literature also provides evidence for links between the time of the body and dress: in Moravian Slovakia, for example, 'we find gradual development of signs which distinguish various age levels of childhood: the youngest child, the girl up to age fourteen, then the adolescent maiden' (Bogatyrev, 1971 [1937]: 77) and like distinctions apply to boys. Danielle Geirnaert (1992: 68) writes that 'in East Java, to each generation of women, "from marriageable daughter to grand-mother past child-bearing age, corresponds an array of skirt and shoulder cloths with specific colours and patterns" (Heringa, 1988: 55–61)'. Other examples include the growing elaboration of dress as one ages in the Naga Hills of northeast India (Barnes, 1992: 32), the increasing darkening of colours in clothing as men age in Thailand (Lefferts, 1992: 52), and the case of Kalabari dress in Nigeria, where 'greater amounts of the body are covered and more cloth and adornment are added' (Michelman and Ereksima, 1992: 180) as men and women rise in status through age (men) or physical and moral maturity and reproduction (women). Not all societies draw such clear distinctions: several writers (Ariès, 1962 [1960]: 48; Jackson, 1936: 16; Laver, 1951: 1–2; Moore, 1953: 11–12) have remarked that special dress for children in European societies was unknown before the seventeenth or eighteenth centuries, while Moore (1953: 55) places the beginning of adolescent dress in the 1860s. It is likely that the increasing complexity of industrial society, and the concomitant increase in the time necessary to form its members before full entry to the labour force, led to the invention of such categories as 'child' or 'adolescent' through institutional forms like the school. The vastly increased numbers of consumer items (including clothing) available today to display one's belonging to social categories may make differentiation according to age ever more subtle and precise, as each social group anchors down its own special combination of the signifiers floating about in the postmodern ocean. Clearly, advertising addressed to peculiarly gendered, aged and classed bodies will help in forming these special combinations. Such points, however, must be explored elsewhere.

The shift over the last century to less cumbersome sports clothing, especially for women, would also seem to privilege the body. According to Alison Gernsheim (1963: 54), women used to climb mountains in crinolines, a practice that would certainly seem to privilege clothing over the body. This could be turned to advantage when particular statuses of the body were to be hidden: 'social reformers objected that the wearing of crinolines encouraged concealment of pregnancy' (Gernsheim, 1963: 47). So where maternity clothes openly indicate a particular time period in the history of a female body, crinolines render this period invisible to onlookers. Similarly, the 'chic abdominal swell' (Hollander, 1978: 109) which was in fashion for women in fifteenth-century Europe made everybody look pregnant, and again it was impossible to tell whether a given body was gravid or not. Indeed, it might be possible to learn something about the general status of the female body at various historical periods by considering whether the prevailing clothing styles rendered the pregnant body visible as pregnant or made it impossible to distinguish from the non-pregnant body. If the shifting statuses of the female body are clearly indicated at all times, does this mean that the power of the actual and potential birth-givers is highly honoured by society, or that women are simply rendered easier to control by inspection, or both? If all women look pregnant at all times, is that a way of controlling their own body states without anyone knowing, or is it an indication that all women are expected to be mothers, or both? Or are women commenting ironically through their dress on their expected bodily functions? Clearly, this chapter cannot hope to answer such questions.

Body rhythms and fashion rhythms matched and mismatched

The time of (women's) fashion has been understood in terms of a succession of attention shifts across different parts of the body. Flügel (1930) perceives fashion as the product of the dialectic of modesty and display – or prudery and seduction, as Laver (1969: 38) more brashly expresses it – applied to body parts, so that, for example, breasts may be exposed yet legs covered modestly at a given moment, but legs may subsequently be rendered visible and breasts hidden. In other words, fashion in clothing follows the rhythm of bodily display and concealment – which may itself, of course, be understood as a fashion operating on the body. Fashion in clothing shadows fashion in the body in this case: they are not quite the same thing. Laver sees fashion in a very similar manner:

> The erogenous zone is always shifting, and it is the business of fashion to pursue it, without ever actually catching it up. It is obvious that if you really catch it up you are immediately arrested for indecent exposure. If you almost catch it up you are celebrated as a leader of fashion. (Laver, 1937: 254)

Fashion in clothing is therefore by definition slightly out of phase with shifting fascinations with various body parts, change in the latter being understood in terms of the exhaustion of the 'accumulation of erotic capital' (Laver, 1969: 97).

Clothing histories may also be written according to the different ages of the human body, although the only example of this seems to be

Alison Lurie (1981). For her, each stage of fashion may be distinguished by the age of the 'ideal women' (or man) that contemporary dress appears to construct. For example, 'In 1810, the ideal woman was a toddler; in 1820 she had grown into a child; and by the mid-1830s she had become a sensitive adolescent...' (Lurie, 1981: 63). However, this may be a product of how we differentiated between toddler, children, adolescent and various types of adult clothing when Lurie was writing her book, rather than an appropriate account of how the clothes were perceived at the time. It is likely, nevertheless, that if political, economic or cultural power (which may not always coincide, as Pierre Bourdieu [1984 {1979}], has shown) is held by particular generational groups, then the distinguishing characteristics of these groups may be promoted as standard and 'normal'. For example, if people between the ages X and Y have more disposable income than those aged between A and B, then it is likely that advertisers will promote bodies and images associated with the first group rather than the second, and the former will therefore appear to define the ideal consuming body of the time.

Political time

It was remarked above that some fashion histories organize their narratives in terms of centuries or half-centuries. For a writer such as Lyotard (1991 [1988]: 25–6), however, periodization has less to do with this sort of time than with the modernist desire for nice, clean unambiguous units of time with clear beginnings and endings. For him, 'diachrony is ruled by the principle of revolution...Since one is inaugurating an age reputed to [be] entirely new, it is right to set the clock to the new time, to start it from zero again'. Such revolutions may be religious (Christianity and Islam both have their Year Ones), political (the French Republican Calendar [Zerubavel, 1977]), or even aesthetic – Geoffrey Squire (1974) organizes his clothing history into such periods as Mannerism, Baroque, Rococo, Neoclassicism and Romantic. Many fashion histories are organized according to a version of political time that may be captured in the phrase 'The King is dead, long live the King!', that is, the succession of monarchies: each reign in Britain is deemed to have its own matching clothing (Bradley, 1922; Brooke, 1949; Calthrop, 1934; Planché, 1900). Daniel Roche (1991 [1989]: 31–2) notes a similar tendency in slightly older French fashion histories, citing Quicherat (1879) in particular. We do not normally think about clothing in this way any more: speaking of 'Elizabethan dress' may conjure up images of the late sixteenth century, but the adjective could hardly be applied in a meaningful way to post-1953 apparel. Nevertheless, the 'Diana look' of the early 1980s hinted at some life in the old association, and the 2006 fascination of Australian women's magazines with the appearance of the originally Tasmanian Princess Mary of Denmark suggests that the light has not yet completely dimmed.

There were rather more direct links, however, between politics and clothing in other systems. As John Evelyn (1951 [1661]: 15) put it, 'Let it be considered, that those who seldom change the Mode of their Country, have as seldom alter'd their affections to the Prince.' A certain fixity of dress, then, indicated political constancy: in a manner analogous to the fashion year, with its synchronicity of one year duration, time was to be frozen for the duration of a reign. But where there is political competition, different times can clash. Let us now explore this in the context of Islamic dress.

Ever since the Iranian revolution of 1979, Westerners have been aware of debates around the veil and Islamic dress for women in general, although the beginnings of the controversy can be traced back to Qassim Amin (1976 [1899], as quoted in Ahmed, 1992). What versions of political time do we find in such discussions? If we consider the relevant literature available in English (Afetinan, 1962: 60; Amin, 1976 [1899]: 54, 69, 71, 72, 78, as quoted in Ahmed, 1992, Chapter 8; Anonymous, 1983 [1981]: 94; Azari, 1983: 43, 45, 51; Fischer, 1980: 186; Khomeiny, 1985 [1943]: 171–2; Maududi, 1988 [1939]: 20, 178–9; Minai, 1981: 64–5; Pahlavi, 1961: 231; Tabari, 1982: 13; Taheri, 1985: 95; Taleghani, 1982 [1979]: 104–5), a very restricted set of time-related discourse terms emerges. Terms like 'advancement', 'modern' and 'progress' form one set (nineteen occurrences) and those such as 'backwardness', 'old fashioned' and 'tradition' form an opposed set (eighteen occurrences).

For colonizers and indigenous Westernizers such as Ataturk in Turkey or the Shah of Iran, Islamic dress represented all that was traditional, backward and old fashioned, all that was preventing efficient industrialization and the advance of Western ways of doing things. The unveiled woman represented progress and civilization. Their opponents contested this mapping, and saw as properly traditional what the Westernizers considered merely backward. Ayatollah Khomeiny wrote that

> they regard the civilization and advancement of the country as dependent upon women's going naked in the streets, or to quote their own idiotic words, turning half the population into workers by unveiling them...We have nothing to say to those whose powers of perception are so limited that they regard the wearing of European hats, the cast-offs of the wild beasts of Europe, as a sign of national progress. (Khomeiny, 1985 [1943]: 171–2)

Ayatollah Taleghani describes the Shah's reform of 1935–6 in similar vein:

> [Reza Shah] thought if he shortened dresses, if people wore coats and trousers and put on hats, if our women went without veils, then we would become progressive; he thought these things were the criteria of progress. He thought if the West had advanced in science, industry, power, economy and politics, that these are the results of women going unveiled and men wearing hats and suits, and the Iranians lack these things. (Taleghani, 1982 [1979]: 104–5)

Westernization in Iran meant a repressive state and a bourgeoisie 'heavily and crudely dependent on the West, [which] simply scoffed at the notion of hejab [Islamic modest dress] and the idea that it could be anything but a sign of backwardness' (Azari, 1983: 51). It is hardly surprising, then, that Westernization came to be seen as 'Westoxication' (Hashemi, 1982 [1980]: 193), and wearing a veil became a way of rejecting this whole way of life (Tabari, 1982: 13). Progress versus backwardness – a discourse that belonged to colonizers and Westernizers – was reinterpreted as meaning decadence versus tradition: Western dress and hejab retained their opposi-tional places, but they were differently valued. Leila Ahmed (1992: 164) makes a similar point with respect to Egypt. See Vahdat (2003) for a detailed discussion of the philosophical underpinnings of 'Westoxication'.

Political time in clothing is not restricted to broad level changes such as the succession of monarchies or revolutions in the political system such as happened in Iran (or France, to use the reference of an earlier generation of writers on dress). Apparel may also be caught up in lower-level tensions between cultures and classes, as we shall now see.

The times of dominant cultures and dominant classes

Reactions to the domination of French dress

A question that can be posed of nowness is: whose nowness is it anyway? So far we have implicitly answered this in terms of a tension between institutions and consuming subjects. But the nowness of fashionable dress can 'belong' to particular cultures or classes. In the seventeenth and eighteenth centuries, English and Swedish writers complained of the dominance of foreign – particularly French – time over their dress, which both seemed to threaten their national identity and ruin their national economies. For example, Henry Peacham writes:

> I have much wondered why our *English* above other nations should so much dote upon new fashions, but more I wonder at our want of wit, that wee cannot invent them ourselves, but when one is growne stale runne presently over into *France*, to seeke a new, making that noble and flourishing Kingdome the magazin of our fooleries. (Peacham, 1942 [1638]: 73)

Evelyn also complains about French domination of English appearance, hinting that it leads to effeminacy and weakness in English men while at the same time '*La Mode de France*, is one of the best Returnes which they make, and feeds as many bellies, as it clothes Backs' (1951 [1661]: 6). Gustav III's reform wanted to replace French time with a national Swedish time: 'be Swedish: be what you were under your ancient kings...in a word, let us be what other nations are ceasing to be: take on a national spirit, and I dare say that a national dress contributes more to that aim than anyone imagines' (Gustav III, 1778: 27–8, my translation). In the early twentieth century, French dress was seen as inimical to patriotic Germanness among certain youth groups (Guenther, 1997: 30).

Gustav maintained (1778: 37) that keeping up with ever-changing foreign modes led to the ruin of a poor country, while Modéer (1774: 65) claimed that it led to increased embezzlement, fraud, corruption, poverty and higher national debt. Similarly, the British infatuation with Indian calicoes posed a serious threat to the wool trade which, 'By mercantilist doctrine, meant that they were imperilling the entire development of their country' (Mukerji, 1983: 169). Such were the dangers when the definition of nowness in dress belonged to a foreign country. Fashion capitals such as Paris, Milan, New York and London may continue to set agendas, but they do not threaten the much more diverse national economies of the present day. But it is perhaps dominant class rather than dominant culture that begins to define fashionable dress in industrial societies.

Class struggles through imitation as creating class-specific dress times

In 1883, the aristocrat Lady Paget remarked that 'The reason why fashions change so rapidly now is because they at once spread through every stratum of society, and become deteriorated and common' (Paget, 1883: 463). This is an early statement of one of the classical sociological theories of fashion change in commodity society: emulation of the dress of a higher class, followed by a change once the lower class had appeared to catch up with the higher – in other words, fashion time results from class competition on the level of appearances. The sumptuary laws of medieval societies indicate a similar problem (Baldwin, 1926), but now much larger numbers of people could afford to imitate higher social classes. Featherstone (1991: 18) expresses this neatly when he writes that, in capitalist societies, 'The constant supply of new, fashionably desirable goods, or the usurpation of existing marker goods by lower groups, produces a paperchase effect in which those above will have to invest in new (informational) goods in order to reestablish the original social distance'. This position is shared by Bernard Barber and Lyle Lobel (1952), Quentin Bell (1976), Edmond Goblot (1925) and Simmel (1957 [1904]), and has its highest explanatory power when there is general agreement on the fact that a higher social class ought to be imitated. But more recently, commodity societies have tended to become less organized in terms of smooth hierarchies and more organized as relatively disconnected status groups such as the 'tribes' of Maffesoli (1996 [1988]). Status groups may differ from one another, but it is not obvious that their members always see other groups as 'higher' or 'lower' and therefore to be imitated or kept at a distinguishing distance – they may merely be different, and accepted (or rejected) as such. The vastly increased number of consumer goods allows a status group to create its own meaningful existence: its goods may need to be different from the commodities of other groups in order to stake out its own social space, but this does not necessarily mean that they are 'better' or 'worse'. Competition is possible when we all desire the *same* types of goods, but means little when we do not. Indeed, it is perfectly possible for the same individual to engage in competitive emulative behaviour in a work context and in non-competitive difference after hours, for at work one may be forced to live within a hierarchical model, but one may be free to belong to the great fracturing of disconnected status groups outside it. Further research is required on how the tension between class-based competitivity and status-group-based (in)difference is lived by various social categories. Davis expresses this well:

On the one hand, we see the emergence of very powerful, highly integrated corporate units creating and propelling a global marketplace for fashion commodities. On the other hand, we encounter a veritable cacophony of local, sometimes exceedingly transient, dress tendencies and styles each attached, however loosely, to its own particularity, be it a subculture, an age grade, a political persuasion, an ethnic identity, or whatever. (Davis, 1992: 206)

The relation between these is uncertain, but it seems a useful starting point for research into clothing at the current stage of advanced (post)industrial society.

Conclusion

The significances of the principal forms of time identified in this chapter may be summarized as follows:

The century (or, better, centuries) is more useful to the analyst of social appearances than to actual wearers of dress, limited as they are to the temporal boundaries of the individual lifespan and its associated meaningful changes. It makes visible long-term cycles and continuities that would otherwise be obscured underneath the appearance of perpetual rapid change, and makes it easier to recognize fundamental discontinuities when they do occur.

The decade de-emphasizes the significance of the times of bodies or processes through the promotion of the significance of the peculiarities of a particular numbering system. Instead of simply using the numbering system to measure the duration of a phenomenon, the phenomenon comes to be meaningful in terms of the ways in which the base ten system divides up the world. Here we have the construction and consequent recognition of decennially-bounded socio-cultural nows. History becomes a series of cross-sections, each of 10-year duration: certain social, political, economic and cultural phenomena of a 10-year period are stretched and compressed so that all together they come to express what the decade meant. Thinking of history in this way persuades us that it is nothing more than a jumble of happenings held together by the notion of the decade. Any decennially indifferent proper temporalities of phenomena and processes become invisible and unthinkable. The decade becomes the significant unit of history. Despite its analytical insufficiencies, the decade offers us a convenient way of seeing our lives intersecting with history: if we consume in decennially typical ways, then we are visibly a full participant in the broader world rather than simply an individual living in his/her own time.

The year turns each natural rotation about the sun into a socially significant phenomenon through the device of the fashion of the year. Participation in fashion time of any sort frees the body from the limitations of its own compass to become part of the greater body social, a series of years permitting the accumulation and exploration of different socially sanctioned identities by allowing an individual to be part of the same shifting now for an agreed time. Year-based fashion time accomplishes presentness: we are now, for twelve months. Access to this particular nowness does not necessarily entail changes in entire wardrobes: a single, small inexpensive item recognizably of the year can do this. The time of the fashion year stresses the sameness rather than the difference of social actors at the broadest level, although levels of apparent participation in this now will vary according to the number of items of the year one possesses. If fashion time is a nowness index, then we can individually be high or low on it.

The season permits regular differentiation within the overall look of the year, and gives socially clear boundaries to the fuzzy boundaries of nature. Indeed, it permits persons to be simultaneously natural and social beings under the domination of the social, as the time of nature gives us seasons but we in turn signify the reality of seasons through dress.

The week Dress in the week shows how work and non-work days are differentiated, and the degree of separation between work and non-work in a given society.

Similarly, appearance can indicate the levels of differentiation of separate social activities and events during the day. Dress here is event or activity-centred rather than simply body-centred.

The now allows one to be present in social worlds of varying duration: to be 'of one's time', to exist unquestionably.

Body time The ways in which age classes and different corporal states are differentiated through dress indicate those aspects of *body time* that are salient in a given society.

Political time may display the continuity of regime (or an ideology) through establishing unchanging dress, embedding the wearers symbolically within a particular politically defined society. It may also differentiate the values of a particular political formation from those of other formations through the organization of appearance.

Dominant cultural time constructs a world of dominant and subordinate cultures where a periphery follows the shifts of a centre, and assumes a time lag between the two: the peripheral is always at least slightly behind those at the centre of the world.

Dominant class time Formally, dominant class time is similar, with the dominated classes attempting to follow the shifts of the dominant one, again with a time lag. This time is, of course, familiar from the classical theories of fashion change, where emulation of upper classes by lower leads to subsequent change in the practices of the former, followed by further emulation and so on. With the recent shift of identity to the relative fragmentation of consumption rather than relative unity of production, class may however have been replaced by status group and by no obvious structure of domination and subordination.

It has been remarked that 'a substantial amount of sociological work has flatly refused to participate in the conceptualization of time', and that work that did attend to temporality rarely went beyond simple linear time, because this was the sort of duration with which statistical analysis could best cope (Maines, 1987: 304–6). Sociology generally seems to have suffered from what Michael Herzfeld (1990: 305) calls the 'structural nostalgia' for the time before time came along and complicated matters. This chapter has demonstrated that even one of the simplest items in the social world – a garment – is caught up in webs of multiple temporalities. Clearly, timeless analysis of social phenomena will no longer do. Time is at least as much the business of the sociologist as it is of the philosophers and theoretical physicists who have hitherto tended to be the ones to take it seriously.

4

The Fabricated Body: A New History

Introduction

Much recent attention has been paid to the place of the body in sociological theory, particularly with respect to the notion of the body as a machine, factory or signalling system, the disciplined body, the body in religious culture and the body in consumer culture (see, for example, Corrigan, 1997; Featherstone, 1991 [1982]; Foucault, 1977 [1975]; Martin, 1987; Mellor and Shilling, 1997; Shilling, 1993; Turner, 1984; 1992). However, 'the body' is as yet far from being a coherent object for a discipline, a state of affairs recognized in the very first word of the title of a large three-volume edited collection: *Fragments for a History of the Human Body* (Feher, 1989). This chapter presents some more fragments on the human body, but, with the exception of brief diversions into anatomy and the role of the body in Marx, fragments fractured from the same mosaic at least: that depicting relationships between the body and appearance. First, we look at the links between nature, aesthetics and health in the eighteenth and nineteenth centuries, paying special attention to the dress reform movement of the 1880s; second, we consider the body of the producer through an analysis of Soviet Constructivist texts on clothing of the early part of the twentieth century; and, finally, we examine the versions of the body constructed in the 1990s through a sample of issues of the magazine *Vogue Australia*.

The 'classical' body: nature, aesthetics and health

Ever since C.P. Snow's famous essay on the two cultures (1974 [1964]), there has been a consciousness in the English-speaking countries that science and art tend to tread separate paths destined never to meet. This separation has been institutionalized through the organization of universities, and strengthened by a tendency for the 'artist' and the 'scientist' to devalue each other's cultural capital in a middle-class struggle worthy of the attentions of a Bourdieu. Science and art were less reticent in each other's company in earlier times, and sociologists, never too sure about the side of the art/ science divide on which they are supposed to stand, should we be well-placed to appreciate this. Snow, indeed, seems convinced that sociology and similar disciplines may actually form a 'third culture' capable of speaking to each of the other two (Snow, 1974 [1964]: 70–1). The human body in particular was, and still is, the privileged site where art and science meet: flesh and bone provide material for the anatomist and the corset-maker, the surgeon and the barber (once one and the same), the dermatologist and the make-up artist, the biologist and the couturier. Bryan Turner's argument that the Cartesian inheritance of the social sciences led to a state where 'The body became the subject of the natural sciences...whereas the mind or *Geist* was the topic of the humanities' (Turner, 1992: 32) may suggest that the body was the business of the natural sciences only, but it misses the fact that the body was also the business of the artist. This becomes particularly clear in the cases of eighteenth-century anatomy and nineteenth-century dress reform, both of which drew upon the aesthetic models of classical Greece and Rome as solutions to apparently 'scientific' problems.

Beautiful bones: anatomy springs from aesthetics

One might imagine that any curious citizen of the eighteenth century wishing to set up a science of anatomy would proceed in an inductive manner, studying a number of actual skeletons from actual cadavers and moving from these observations to the elaboration of a 'typical' or 'normal' model of our bony foundations. Indeed, this certainly happened to an increasing extent (Foucault, 1973 [1963]: 125). There are at least two problems here, however: first, one can never be entirely sure about the validity of the inductive leap and, second, one's newly minted science is struck from the coin of dead bodies – the symbolic stench of death lingers about the clean new discipline, while the ghosts of Burke and Hare haunt the back entrance to the anatomist's laboratory. Both of these problems can be overcome if we switch from an inductive to a deductive approach and if the model from which we deduce is already-existing and laden with high cultural value: we replace the (snatched?) dead bodies of eighteenth-century criminals and paupers with the marble statues of ancient Greece or Rome, and found our discipline in frozen aristocratic beauty instead of the rotting flesh of the hoi polloi.

Intentionally or otherwise, this appears to have been what happened. In her study of early illustrations of the female skeleton, Londa Schiebinger reports that Godfried Bidloo, a Dutch anatomist of the late seventeenth century, drew figures 'not from life but from classical statues'; Bidloo claimed these figures exhibited 'the most beautiful proportions of a man and woman as they were fixed by the ancients', while William Cheselden's 'female skeleton [of 1733] is drawn in the "same proportion as the Venus of Medicis"; his male skeleton is drawn in the same proportion and attitude as the Belvedere Apollo' (Schiebinger, 1987: 50, 58). The German anatomist Samuel Thomas von Soemmerring published an illustration of a female skeleton in 1796, also 'check[ing] his drawing against the classical statues of the Venus di Medici and Venus of Dresden to achieve a universal representation of woman' (Schiebinger, 1987: 58). As Laqueur (1990: 167) remarks, 'Anything that failed to meet the highest aesthetic standards was banished from [Soemmerring's] representations of the body'. The 'universality' of the body was to be founded in a peculiarly prestigious version of the beautiful, banishing any disquieting shadows of dismembered lower-class corpses of uncertain aesthetic value.

Foucault (1973 [1963]: 124–5) would consider the above account historically misleading, arguing that there was no real opposition to carrying out autopsies. However, there are at least two possible histories of the body writeable about the eighteenth century. Foucault seems to provide an official hospital–Enlightenment history, or at least privileges this 'rational' approach over what he sees as French historian Jules Michelet's mythifying tendencies. However, this is to ignore the views of a popular imagination avid, in England at least, for gothic novels and other such scarifying publications. For people such as these, cool Enlightenment logic might not have been so convincing: the macabre aspects of dead bodies would instead have retained their fascinated attention. The aestheticization of the body according to the canons of highly regarded art would have made the skeleton a 'respectable' thing when at any moment it risked falling victim to the lurid sensibilities of the mass public. Foucault's history does not seem to be able to account for the aestheticization we have seen, but our more 'gothic' history does.

Beautiful bodies: dress reform springs from aesthetics

The aesthetic foundations of eighteenth-century anatomy appear to have been inherited by the dress reformers of the following century. They also needed a model of the body of unquestionably high cultural value to set against the tightly laced and deformed bodies they wished to criticize, and again they found their model in the artistic products of antiquity. There was no acceptable body model to be found among middle-class ladies, for the 'normal' middle-class female body was tightly laced and hence 'deformed' in the eyes of the reformers. It might have been an overly risky strategy to suggest an alternative model based on uncorseted women of any 'inferior' classes still unseduced by whalebone, so the 'classical' body – readily available as a model, familiar and undoubtedly civilized – was called upon to do critical duty. As early as 1834, a Dr Combe argued that

> The statue of the Venus exhibits the natural shape, which is recognized by artists and persons of cultivated taste as the most beautiful which the female figure can assume: accordingly it is aimed at in all the finest statues of ancient and modern times. Misled, however, by ignorance, and a false and most preposterous taste, women of fashion, and their countless flocks of imitators, down even to the lowest ranks of life, have gradually come to regard a narrow or spider-waist as an ornament worthy of attainment at any cost or sacrifice. (Combe, 1852 [1834]: 182, as quoted in Newton, 1974: 23)

In the last-third of the nineteenth century, 'writers were repeatedly to call upon the art of the ancient Greeks to support their aesthetic and their sanitary theories', as Newton (1974: 41) remarks. Of the doctors, Frederick Treves gives perhaps the clearest account of the confrontation between classical and contemporary bodies in his 1883 article on the influence of dress on health:

> Now, in all the most excellent attempts that art has made to give expression to female loveliness, this outline of the healthy and perfectly constructed woman has always been reverently preserved... Such an outline is well represented by the famous Venus di Medici... There are some who would say that the Venus is coarse and unwieldy in outline, and maintain that the more modern figure gives a pleasant impression of trimness, and presents altogether a more agreeable configuration. Without discussing the matter at length, it can only be pointed out that the figure of Venus is the figure of anatomical perfection, of complete development, and of perfect health. If the outline be coarse and repulsive, then is nature coarse, and the expression of simple bodily vigour a thing to offend the eye. In the Venus there is a gentle sweep from the shoulder to the hip, all parts are in proportion, and the actual outline of the body precisely accords with the principles of beauty. In the modern figure there is an abrupt constriction of the waist; the shoulders and hips appear ponderous by comparison, the outline is pronounced and lacking in simple ease, and, so far as the anatomical eye can view it, the proportions of the body are lost. (Treves, 1883: 499)

To those who would object that 'nature' is coarse, Treves points out that the 'natural' Venus with its 'gentle sweep' 'precisely accords with the principles of beauty' and that it is the modern body which is ponderous and out of proportion, and hence, when compared to classical models, far from a thing of beauty. Among artists, Oscar Wilde (1920a [1884]: 64) in his dress reform period also lauds Greek proportion, maintaining that the costume of the future will come from 'a continuation of the Greek principles of beauty with the German principles of health', while the painter G.F. Watts (1883: 46–7) praises 'the innate taste of the Greeks' in contrast to the distorted shape of the 'accomplished lady' in his article on taste in dress. The 'natural' body in this context is not 'natural' in any scientific sense, but rather the construction of a reading of Greek and Roman art.

Once this 'natural' body has been constructed successfully through aesthetics, it is then possible to turn to science and medicine as ways of ensuring that our bodies manage to correspond to the ideal. It is not simply that the natural sciences laid unchallenged claim to the body and thereby excluded the humanities and social sciences, as in the Turnerian argument, it is rather that they may conceivably have *followed* what we can now see is the 'aesthetico-natural' body. They may subsequently have built their own technico-rationalist empire upon this body and eventually effaced the aesthetic elements, but such a body has not gone away. Indeed, cosmetic science and cosmetic surgery are predicated upon the aesthetico-natural model of the body, and they are likely to become more rather than less important in the consumerist epoch of what Arthur Frank (1991: 53) calls the 'mirroring body'.

Honesty aesthetics

Dress reform shared an obsession with the morally reforming virtues of honesty with some of the art of the nineteenth century. In the case of art furnishing, for example, moral virtues were embodied in the design of domestic objects. Everything had to be simpler, lighter and, above all else, more honest. Adrian Forty (1986: 111–12) writes that 'shams and deceits were forbidden: furniture which disguised the way it was made, or the materials of which it was made, was regarded as dishonest and therefore to be avoided'. But what was wrong with a piece of furniture that tried to appear that which it was not? A Colonel Eddis in 1883 wrote:

> If you are content to teach a lie in your belongings, you can hardly wonder at petty deceits being practised in other ways...All this carrying into everyday life of 'the shadow of unreality' must exercise a bad and prejudicial influence on the younger members of the house, who are thus brought up to see no wrong in the shams and deceits which are continually before them. (Quoted by Forty, 1986: 113)

So if your furniture lies, so will your children. For Keats, 'Beauty is truth, truth beauty' (*Ode on a Grecian Urn*): truth and honesty seem to be much the same thing so we could also say that beauty is honesty and honesty beauty – and it was the design of domestic furniture that was charged with the moral mission of inculcating these virtues in family homes. Civilized order could be imposed by art, no doubt saving on some of the more costly repressive measures that the enormous social upheavals provoked by capitalist industrialization brought in their train.

The honesty theme of art furniture was also to be found in dress. J.A. Gotch, for example, 'condemns without exception artificial flowers, birds stuffed or fabricated, and false bows, as used for trimming. He considers the employment of these to [be] "wicked" in the artistic sense, since they are meant to deceive' (Anonymous, 1882: 100), and Watts (1883: 48) maintains that 'it cannot be good sense and good taste to make by art any natural object look like something quite different. Good taste is shown by making the best of Nature's intentions, not by trying to subvert her intentions'. But perhaps one of the best representatives of honesty aesthetics is Mary Philadelphia Merrifield's *Dress as a Fine Art*, which appeared in 1854. For her, 'as a general principle...everyone may endeavour to set off or improve his or her personal appearance, provided that in doing so, the party is guilty of no deception' (Merrifield, 1854: 1). Dress may embellish the already given, then, but it must not mislead. We must start from 'our individual proportions, complexions, ages, and stations in society' and set them off as best we can, yet at the same time

> the most perfect honesty and sincerity of purpose may be observed. No deception is to be practised, no artifice employed, beyond that which is exercised by the painter, who arranges his subjects in the most pleasing forms, and who selects colours which harmonize with each other; and by the manufacturer, who studies pleasing combinations of lines and colours. (Merrifield, 1854: 2)

For Merrifield, the role of art generally is to display truth in an aesthetically pleasing form, not to bury it behind an aesthetically pleasing façade that promises the viewer something quite else. Our 'station in society' must not visually be fudged, and so the old idea of the sumptuary laws that our appearance must correspond to our reality (especially our social rank) is continued here. Rather than crude legalistic methods, however, we have a particular aesthetic: beauty is to strengthen truth, not to buttress falsehood. Age, for example, must not be hidden through the deceptive use of paint or false hair: from a moral point of view, this 'is worse than silly; it is adopted with a view to deceive; it is *acting a lie* to all intents and purposes, and it ought to be held in the same kind of detestation as falsehood with the tongue' (Merrifield, 1854: 3). Lady Paget (1883: 459) had similar views on paints and cosmetics, remarking that 'They are as fatal to health and beauty as they are misleading in effect'.

But age and 'station in society' are not the only social attributes that must faithfully be rendered, nor is 'acting a lie' merely an offence against some abstract code of morality:

> Yet as we have stated that we are at liberty to improve our natural appearance by well adapted dress, we think it our duty to speak out, lest we should be considered as in any way countenancing deception. We allude to those physical defects induced by disease, which are frequently united to great beauty of countenance, and which are sometimes so carefully concealed by the dress, that they are only discovered after marriage. (Merrifield, 1854: 4)

Potential spouses, too, are to be given an honest account of the state of the body. King (1882: 17) may have some similar deception in mind when she complains about the petticoat: 'it hides from our sight and knowledge the deformity which our evil style of dress produces'. Whether the bodily problems are caused by disease or by the actual types of garments worn, honesty aesthetics requires full disclosure.

Honesty at the theoretical level appears to translate into utilitarianism at the practical level in the case of the dress reformers. An 'honest' reading of dress would assume that everything that appeared corresponded to some 'truth' lying behind it, and so each and every part of a garment was to have a particular function. If it did not, it would mislead the viewer into thinking there was a solid truth where in fact there was nothing at all, except perhaps a playful ironic signifier dancing before the uncomprehending unamused. There were to be no 'meaningless excrescences' such as frills for Gotch (Anonymous, 1882: 99, 100), anything useless was 'against the principles of dress' for Wilde (1920b [1884]: 70), and Merrifield (1854: 85) insisted that all ornament be 'designed to answer some useful purpose. A brooch, or a bow of ribbons, for instance, should fasten some part of the dress; a gold chain should support a watch or eye-glass, or other object'. Paget (1883: 458, 462) understood the beautiful as the natural outcome of the practical, proposing that 'The wonderful dignity and finish we admire in medieval dress depends mainly upon all the ornamentation being based upon necessity'.

Ada Ballin, in her book *The Science of Dress in Theory and Practice*, goes further, claiming that 'Far from having no idea of the beautiful, we have what time will prove to be the highest and purest of all ideals. Beauty for us is the perfect adaptation of the means to the end' (Ballin, 1885: 3).

Wilde gives examples of what this practical beauty looks like, instancing the miners of the western United States as the only well-dressed men he saw in all his journeys through that country:

> Their wide-brimmed hats, which shaded their faces from the sun and protected them from the rain, and the cloak, which is by far the most beautiful piece of drapery ever invented, may well be dwelt on with admiration. Their high boots, too, were sensible and practical. They wore only what was comfortable, and therefore beautiful. (Wilde, 1909 [1882]: 164)

Wildean costume in general was to be functional and adaptable to circumstances: 'In a hat made on the right principles one should be able to turn the brim up or down according as the day is dark or fair, dry or wet; *The value of the dress is simply that every separate article of it expresses a law*' (Wilde, 1920b [1884]: 70, 74).

The proper body and the aesthetics of health

But where does all this aesthetico-utilitarian honesty lead? Honest dress is to reveal the truth of the body (among other things, of course, such as social class), for it must never mislead. But what sort of body is it? We already know from the above discussion that the 'truthful' body for the dress reformers is based on the artistic representations of antiquity interpreted as emmarblements of the 'natural' body. What happens when we try to translate from ancient stone to contemporary flesh? Treves (1883: 501) uses a drawing of the Venus de Milo to show the natural position of the internal organs, presumably because there were no acceptable models in actual life for the reasons already mentioned. The fact that statues rarely tend to have viscera does not seem to have bothered him, so convinced is he that the body of Venus represents the natural female body. He claims that a waist of 26 or 27 inches characterizes the perfect female figure, but 'The fashionable waist at the present time, is, I am told, from about 20 to 22 inches – a circumference that indicates no small amount of compression'. This compression appeared to him to have some serious consequences on the internal organs:

> It is no question merely of squeezing-in skin, and muscle, and bone – it is a question of squeezing-in lungs, and stomach, and liver. An examination of the body after death of those who have practised severe tight lacing shows forcibly the effect of the practice. The liver is found pushed down, and more or less dislodged from its proper place ... the stomach will be dragged out of position and is often structurally altered. The diaphragm is pushed up, the lung space is encroached upon, and the heart often suffers no inconsiderable displacement. (Treves, 1883: 502–3)

Treves then details the deleterious effects of tight lacing on respiration, circulation and the heart, the 'muscular apparatus of the trunk', and the general outline of the body. Similarly, King (1882: 5) complained about the effects of the compression of vital organs, writing that 'Almost from youth upwards the muscular and organic development of women has been checked, their health undermined, and their nerve power wasted by the clothes they wear'. Roxey Ann Caplin (1860: 38) also denounced 'the evils of tight lacing', and Merrifield (1854: 25) went so far as to ask 'Is it any wonder that persons so deformed [by tight lacing] should have bad health, or that they should produce unhealthy offspring? Is it any wonder that so many young mothers should have to lament the loss of their first-born?'

But what is tight lacing actually for? What services does it render? Such deliberate compression of the body by civilized European women of the late nineteenth century must have appeared irrational and incomprehensible to the dress reformers, and indeed both King (1882: 4) and Treves (1883: 497) consider tight lacing a sign that European women lie at a lower degree of civilization than European men, sharing an evolutionary level with 'savages' (King). Watts (1883: 46) also speaks of the 'savage' and the 'cultivated lady' in the same breath. David Kunzle (1982: 44), however, interprets tight lacing as an intentional and quite rational strategy, claiming that it could be considered 'as a protest against the total absorption of woman into a life of constant child-bearing and rearing, and the limitation of her sexuality to exclusively procreative ends'. This oppositional use of tight lacing seems to share with fasting practices and anorexia nervosa a tendency to use the body as a weapon with which to attain particular goals. Gordon Tait (1993), for example, shows that some medieval women used fasting as a way of reaching a state of piety because their bodies were the only readily available mechanisms they had that allowed them to practise the 'masculine' trait of discipline and thus demonstrate holiness. For Turner (1992: 221), anorexics manage to achieve 'personal power and a sense of moral superiority through the emaciated body'. So although tight lacing and fasting may appear strange at first sight, they are both interpretable as instances of the more general use of the body as a resource to attain particular ends where the 'owner' of the body has no alternative resources. In this perspective at least, tight lacing is a rational practice. For many other women of that period, of course, tight lacing may have been merely one more Durkheimian social fact that is neither rational nor irrational but just simply a given of the social world. If tight lacing is fashionable, for example, then one laces tight because if one does not one will be considered unfashionable and thus outside the pale of respectable company. On a Veblenian interpretation, tight lacing would increase the prestige value of the female body by rendering it clear that a husband had sufficient wealth not to have his wife engage in lowly productive work. The more hobbled a woman was, the greater the social value of the family. Kunzle's approach may account for the specific target-orientated use of tight lacing, but explains neither how tight lacing came to be something available to use in the first place nor whether everyone who tight laced saw matters in such a rational means–end way. In the Durkheimian model we may feel compelled to act in certain ways by the imposing facticity of social things and this could account for widespread relatively unreflective use of tight lacing, but again this tells us nothing about why particular social facts exist. Veblen seems closer to demonstrating the social functions of the tightly laced body and also shows why such a body is more likely to be female. He thus answers the question of Viscountess Harberton, founder of the Rational Dress Society: 'why should it be supposed that the male form came perfect from the hands of the Creator, while that of the female needs constant tinkering and screwing into shape to make it presentable?' (Harberton, 1882: 458). The 'constant tinkering and screwing' is necessary because a deformed female body forms an important element of male social value at this particular period in the history of consumptionist display.

Whether invoking antique statuary or not, dress reform writings shared an ideal model of the body as something natural and healthy. The aim of clothing was not to alter the natural form through the likes of tight lacing, but rather to *reveal* it. The theme recurs again and again in the texts of the period: for Mary Nichols (1878: 86), for instance, 'The perfection of costume is its fitness and adaptation to the beauty of the human form divine', while Caplin (1857: 1) wanted clothing to 'display the full beauty of the naturally well formed figure'. 'Let the human form command the clothing, and not be subservient to it', wrote Mary Eliza Haweis (1879: 21), and Bernard Roth (1880: 16) maintained that 'dress should not produce deformity, but should everywhere follow instead the natural lines of the human body'. Treves (1883: 494) was of the opinion that 'dress is the most becoming to women which the most accurately reproduces the exquisite outline of the nude figure', and for Gotch 'There is nothing more beautiful than the natural human figure, and therefore to spoil it by tight lacing, or by high heels . . . or by any kind of stuffing, padding, or meaningless excrescences is contrary both to common sense and art' (Anonymous, 1882: 99).

The natural body was also assumed to be a healthy one, and so for the first time the link between clothing and health was firmly established. Treves puts the position most succinctly:

> The perfect dress . . . should afford a proper protection to the body, and should preserve it in a proper degree of warmth. These ends should be effected without interference with any natural function, and without limitation of any natural movement. The material of the dress should be such as to exercise no injurious effects upon the parts of the body with which it is in contact. (Treves, 1883: 463)

The notion of free movement of the limbs was widely shared by critics of the dress of the time, with Merrifield (1854: 5), Gotch (Anonymous, 1882: 99) and Ballin (1885: 3, 100, 102, 173) all agreeing that clothing must allow for this.

The striving for the natural healthy body brought with it another aesthetic element to add to the already aestheticized 'natural' body discussed above. It was argued that in order to be beautiful one had first to be healthy (and of course wear what might be called, on an analogy with present-day health foods, 'health clothes' with properties such as those described by Treves above). For Merrifield (1854: 96), 'there can be no true beauty without health', King (1882: 7) asserts that 'true beauty and grace are the results of perfect health, perfect development, and perfect ease', Wilde (1920a [1884]: 60) believes that when 'the body is left free and unconfined for respiration and motion, there is more health, and consequently more beauty', in Nichols' (1878: 38) view 'True beauty may be found in inalienable relation to health', and an unknown member of the National Health Society proclaims that 'To plead the cause of *health* before our girls is, if they would only believe it, to plead the cause of beauty too' (Anonymous, ca. 1880: 14–15).

If clothing had once subordinated the body to itself and its social significance, the dress reformers wanted to subordinate clothing to their idea of the natural body. Their fascination with this type of body found its logical extension in the philosophy of nudism. They themselves were concerned with 'the strictest dictates of modesty' (Treves, 1883: 494) and shared the religious problem of shame, but a later generation were not quite so worried about this. Indeed, 'Away with shame!' was the slogan of the Russian nudists (Strizhenova, 1972: 21). The discovery of the natural body led to attempts to re-integrate with nature itself, a case argued by Maurice Parmelee (1929: 11): 'But the direct and personal enjoyment of nature can be attained at the highest possible degree only when unclothed, because then there is nothing artificial between man and nature, and he feels himself wholly a part of it'. An account of nudism and nudist movements, however, lies beyond the scope of the present work.

The body of the dress reformers, then, was the site at which particular notions of beauty, health and nature came together, a body that was to be clothed in the comfortable creations of the House of Aesthetico-Utilitarianism. At a period when unencumbering sports-style clothing is frequently worn outside strictly sporting occasions by great numbers of people, it appears that the revolutionary ideas of the nineteenth-century dress reformers have been transformed into the spontaneous dressed philosophy of the masses.

The body of the producer: Soviet Constructivism of the early twentieth century

Before considering the Soviet Constructivist solution to the problem of dress in a recently revolutioned society aspiring to communism, it may be helpful to sketch the model of the body that emerges from the work of the writer who provided many of the theoretical underpinnings of Soviet society, namely Karl Marx.

Production as the defining quality of the human

The body of the worker lies at the kernel of Marx's thought. It is what inspires his analysis of capitalism, and it is what inspires the revolutionary communist transformation of society. This idea stretches from the 1844 *Manuscripts* through to *Capital* itself, ignoring the early ('humanist') and late ('scientific') division in Marx's work that writers such as Althusser (1977 [1965]) have suggested. Far from being abolished by the often highly abstract and theoretical concerns of *Capital*, it remains obstinately present in that late text. Turner (1984: 187) points out that Marxists have paid little attention to the question of the body since 'revolutionary asceticism became opposed to bourgeois corpulence', and no doubt his later argument (Turner, 1992: 32) that the body was not conceptually visible to the mind-centred humanities and social sciences is also applicable. But a reading of Marx's own work shows the body unmistakably present. Where the dress reformers were concerned with the bodily deformities provoked by clothing and tight lacing and found their 'proper' body in an aestheticized version of the natural, Marx was concerned with the bodily deformities provoked by the logic of capital and found his 'proper' body in a philosophy of the species-being. In both cases, the notion of a 'proper' body that present conditions left twisted and deformed led to arguments for profound changes in these conditions. We have already seen this in the case of the dress reformers, so let us now look more closely at Marx's reasoning.

What is it that makes humans human? Marx and Engels answer this question as follows:

> Men can be distinguished from animals by consciousness, by religion or anything else you like. They themselves begin to distinguish themselves from animals as soon as they begin to *produce* their means of subsistence, a step which is conditioned by their physical organization. By producing their means of subsistence men are indirectly producing their actual material life... What [individuals] are...coincides with their production, both with *what* they produce and with *how* they produce. The nature of individuals thus depends on the material conditions determining their production. (Marx and Engels, 1989 [1846]: 42)

Humans, then, are essentially producers: labour is what makes us what we are. As C.J. Arthur (in Marx and Engels, 1989 [1846]: 21) points out, this idea is common to the *Manuscripts*, *The German Ideology* and *Capital*, and we can thus assume it to be one of the fundamental constants of Marxist reasoning. But what actually happens when 'labour' occurs in the world, and what has this to do with the body? Marx writes:

> While the labourer is at work, his labour constantly undergoes a transformation: from being motion, it becomes an object without motion; from being the labourer working, it becomes the thing produced. At the end of one hour's

spinning, that act is represented by a definite quantity of yarn; in other words, *a definite quantity of labour, namely that of one hour, has become embodied in the cotton.* We say labour, *i.e.,* the *expenditure of his vital force by the spinner,* and not spinning labour, because the special work of spinning counts here, only so far as it is the expenditure of labour-power in general, and not in so far as it is the specific work of the spinner. (Marx, 1974 [1867]: 184, my emphasis)

Being human means that the labouring activities of our bodies – our sweat and our blood, as Marx (1974 [1867]: 443) says – are externalized into objects. Furthermore, 'productive life is species-life. It is life-producing life. The whole character of a species, its species character, resides in the nature of its life activity, and free conscious activity constitutes the species-character of man' (Marx, 1975 [1844]: 328). To be properly human, then, means that we engage in free conscious production, embodying the work of our bodies in freely produced and conceived objects. This freedom also applies to the division of labour, as we can see in this ideal description of a communist society:

nobody has one exclusive sphere of activity but each can become accomplished in any branch he wishes, society regulates the general production and thus makes it possible for me to do one thing today and another tomorrow, to hunt in the morning, fish in the afternoon, rear cattle in the evening, criticise after dinner, just as I have a mind, without ever becoming hunter, fisherman, herdsman or critic; In a communist society there are no painters but at most people who engage in painting among other activities. (Marx and Engels, 1989 [1846]: 54, 109)

This is the 'proper' body, the body as it should be: free to produce what it likes, when it likes. In this vision, the economy and its objects are the pleasant emanations of the producer's body, a body entirely in control of what it does. Under capitalism, of course, things do not quite work like this. Indeed, instead of the economy and its objects being the emanations of a free body, the body becomes the deformed and stunted slave of that economy and of those objects. Labour becomes *estranged*, and the very body of the worker pays a terrible price.

Estranged labour, capital and the body

When the products of our labour are not ours, our labour – that which makes us human – is estranged into objects controlled by others. For Marx, this means that

In tearing away the object of his production from man, estranged labour there-fore tears away from him his *species-life*, his true species-objectivity, and trans-forms his advantage over animals into the disadvantage that his inorganic body, nature, is taken from him ... [Estranged labour] estranges man from his own body, from nature as it exists outside him, from his spiritual essence [*Wesen*], his *human* essence. (Marx, 1975 [1844]: 329)

In a sense, the body of a human becomes little different to that of any other animal. This may be bad enough, but under capitalism the body of the

worker is transformed into something that retains the organic vibrancy of
(mere) animality only in the most grudging way possible: 'the *worker* has
the misfortune to be a *living* capital, and hence a capital *with needs*, which
forfeits its interest and hence its existence every moment it is not working'
(Marx, 1975 [1844]: 335). As with any element of capital, the body of the
worker should be treated in such a way that maximum exploitation of
its potential takes place. The body is now reduced not only to an animal (by
estranged labour), but to a part of a machine (by estranged labour in concert
with capital). Marx's abhorrence of this double negation of the species-
being of humans does not disappear in *Capital*, but is transformed into
eloquent outrage at the effects of capital on actual, concretely existing
human bodies. Take the effects of the extension of the working day:

> [capital] usurps the time for growth, development, and healthy maintenance
> of the body. It steals the time required for the consumption of fresh air and
> sunlight. It higgles over a meal-time, incorporating it where possible with the
> process of production itself, so that food is given to the labourer as to a mere
> means of production, as coal is supplied to the boiler, grease and oil to
> the machinery. It reduces the sound sleep needed for the restoration, repara-
> tion, refreshment of the bodily powers to just so many hours of torpor as the
> revival of an organism, absolutely exhausted, renders essential . . . Capital cares
> nothing for the length of life of labour-power. All that concerns it is simply and
> solely the maximum of labour-power, that can be rendered fluent in a working
> day. It attains this end by shortening the extent of the labourer's life, as a greedy
> farmer snatches increased produce from the soil by robbing it of its fertility.
> The capitalistic mode of production . . . produces thus, with the extension of
> the working day, not only the deterioration of human labour-power by robbing it
> of its normal, moral and physical, conditions of development and function.
> It produces also the premature exhaustion and death of this labour-power
> itself. It extends the labourer's time of production during a given period by
> shortening his actual lifetime. (Marx, 1974 [1867]: 252–3)

Conditions in the factory are life threatening *because* the body is merely the
housing of what is essential to capital (labour-power), an essential that can
easily be bought on the market ready-housed. The housing can be used up
quite safely, so long as it is replaceable with another: the body is treated as
little more than another machine part, a point that recurs frequently in
Capital (Marx, 1974 [1867]: 321, 330, 364, 372, 397–9).

The transformation of this body into a healthy body is a main aim of
communist strategy, as is evident from this critique of Feuerbach:

> when, for example, [Feuerbach] sees instead of healthy men a crowd of scrofulous,
> overworked and consumptive starvelings, he is compelled to take refuge in the
> 'higher perception' and in the ideal 'compensation in the species', and thus to
> relapse into idealism at the very point where the communist materialist sees
> the necessity, and at the same time the condition, of a transformation both of
> industry and of the social structure. (Marx and Engels, 1989 [1846]: 64)

It is the capital-deformed body of the worker that demands revolutionary communism: such appears to be the moral motor at the core of
Marx's Marxism.

The body of the worker in the new Soviet Union

The Bolshevik Revolution promised an end to the morbid logic of capital, and one would expect a new worker's body to emerge. True to the Marx-Engels approach of *The German Ideology*, human beings were seen as producers above all else. The body embodied the producer, and the Russian Constructivists of the 1920s were marked by a twin inheritance from Marx and the dress reformers: 'production clothing' was designed that was also comfortable to wear.

The reader may be sceptical that the October Revolution would have ramifications for dress, but as early as 1919 we read: 'The great Russian Revolution must also prove its influence on the external coverings of people. The new clothing must be not merely comfortable and graceful, but also situated in full dependence on contemporary economic conditions and correspond with the demands of hygiene' (Anonymous, 1919: 1, my translation). This was not an unusual view, as Tatyana Strizhenova points out:

> Great significance was attached to the creation of new forms of clothes for the workers. In 1918...the Workshop of Contemporary Dress was set up. Its aims were formulated by Lamanova [a famous designer] herself at the first *All-Russian Conference of Art and Industry* in 1919. 'Art must penetrate all forms of daily life, stimulating the artistic taste and sensitivity of the masses. Artists in the field of dress, using basic materials, must create simple but at the same time beautiful clothes that are suited to the new demands of working life'. (Strizhenova, 1989: 9)

Beauty was to be returned to the worker, and this too is in accord with Marx: the ideally free person 'produces in accordance with the laws of beauty', but estranged labour 'produces beauty, but deformity for the worker' (Marx, 1975 [1844]: 329, 325).[1] In the new communist state of the USSR, it was 'the *artist's* job to unveil the new shape associated with contemporary man' (Exter, 1989 [1923]: 171, my emphasis).

The new dress was to be centred on notions of production and the body of the worker in two main ways. First, many of the fabrics used included industrial, agricultural and sporting motifs as their pattern (see Strizhenova and Organizing Committee, 1989: 59–167 for reproductions). These patterns played a very specific political role, for textile design

> is a vehicle for a new culture and a new ideology. It responds...to the use of textile products in an urban environment and to the role they play in the organization of a new ideology in the minds of the proletariat and working masses...only an extremely naive and primitive person would consider textiles simply as carriers of printed designs. (Fedorov-Davydov, 1989 [1928]: 181)

Second, dress was body-centred. For Alexandra Exter, for instance,

> clothing must be adapted to suit the workers, and the work which they are carrying out. The overcoat must not be too narrow, since it would impair movement, as would too big a hat or a close-fitting skirt...Clothing destined for physical work derives its movement from the conditions of work and from movements of the body, and must be structured in harmony with the proportions of the human body. (Exter, 1989 [1923]: 171)

Varvara Stepanova wanted clothing to be organized not only around the body as producer but also the body as a participant in sports. Indeed, according to Strizhenova (1989: 10), sports clothing was supposed to replace everyday dress completely because of Constructivist beliefs 'about the significance of gymnastics as a means of attaining a healthy and aesthetic life'. The sportingly clad bodies of the consumerist masses of the late twentieth and early twenty-first centuries might at first glance appear to have inherited some of these beliefs, but sports dress seems often to have less to do with healthy and aesthetic lives than with identification with the mass-marketed idols of Manchester or Madrid. Non-sports clothing was to indicate the specific type of producer: 'There is no dress in general, but clothing for any productive function...Production clothing [*prozodezhda*] individualizes according to occupation' (quoted in Strizhenova, 1972: 84, my translation). For example, the size, form and character of the distribution of the pockets on the clothing would vary according to the job.

The utilitarian aesthetic of the dress reformers was also taken up by Stepanova, but in a stronger form: 'The entire decorative and ornamental side of clothing is destroyed with the slogan: *"comfort and suitability to purpose of dress for a given productive function"*...Aesthetic elements are replaced by the process of production of the very sewing of the clothing' (Varst, 1923: 65, my translation). The aesthetic was to be an integral part of the make-up of the clothes, not something superadded. Due partly to the low level of development of the industry in the Soviet Union, none of these ideas bore fruit in terms of mass production, and the statements of the Constructivists remained programmatic.

Dress reform, then, focused attention on the relation between clothing and the (aestheticized) 'natural' body in the nineteenth century and between dress and the body of the producer in the early history of the Soviet Union. Now it is time to consider the body of the consumer as portrayed in the late twentieth century.

The body of the consumer: the *Vogued* body of the 1990s

More than a century after the heyday of the dress reformers, what is the status of the body in those discourses that frame it within the parameters of a concern with appearance? It was decided to approach this question through the analysis of a sample of eleven issues of *Vogue Australia* from 1993. The May issue proved unavailable, but the consistency of structure and content across the eleven remaining issues suggests that its availability would have made very little difference to the final analysis. *Vogue Australia* was chosen because it seemed to be the most clothing-oriented of the generally available mainstream 'women's' magazines on the local market at the time, and therefore promised insights into the constructions that a broad section of middle-class women were readerly consuming.

Before launching into more detailed analyses, an overview of the salient characteristics of the sample may be helpful. Table 4.1 shows both the

Table 4.1 *Table of contents entries,* Vogue Australia, *1993*

Issue	Fashion	Health & beauty	Features, people, ideas	Travel	Total (N)
January	12	10	17	6	45
February	12	9	21	3	45
March	16	8	19	3	46
April	11	10	18	4	43
June	15	7	18	7	47
July	16	7	18	3	44
August	15	8	21	3	47
September	14	11	19	2	46
October	12	9	22	3	46
November	13	9	16	3	41
December	18	7	22	3	50
Total (N)	154	95	211	40	500
Totals %	30.8	19	42.2	8	100

Table 4.2 *Number of full pages of advertisements devoted to each category*

Category	N	%
Clothing	227	28.38
Make-up/Skincare	146	18.25
Fragrance	113	14.13
Jewellery	46	5.75
Cars	33	4.13
Hair	32	4.00
Watches	29	3.63
Shoes	24	3.00
Remaining 24 categories	150	18.75
Total	800	100.02

principal categories used by the magazine itself in its own textual organization (the table of contents entries in each issue) and the frequencies of each.

Half (49.8 per cent) of the 500 individual entries are concerned with fashion and the body, almost 80 per cent of the fashion entries being linked to clothing. This would seem to confirm the sample as a relatively rich source of data about such matters – hardly a surprise.

Feature articles and advertorials form only part of the content of the magazine, of course, and advertisements make up a large part of all magazines of this type. Table 4.2 shows the number of full pages devoted to the categories of consumer goods recognized in the sample. Full pages only were considered on the grounds that these would reveal the goods most forcefully promoted amongst the readership.

Only eight of the thirty-two categories discerned scored 3 per cent or more, and only three made more than 10 per cent. The top three alone form over 60 per cent of the total number of pages, suggesting yet again that the sample is an appropriate source of data on clothing and body matters.

Not very much seems to have changed since 1993: a comparison with the August 2006 issue showed clothing (41 per cent), makeup/skincare (32 per cent) and jewellery (9 per cent) as the top three categories. If anything, clothing and makeup/skincare are even more prominent in the magazine than before. We examine the feature articles and advertorials in detail in the next section, and follow that with an exploration of the advertisements. As all issues of the magazine date from 1993, the referencing convention Month: page is used. References to pages that are part of supplementary material inserted between the normal magazine pages are of the form Month: >x<y, where x and y represent the normal page numbers. Thus February: >68<72 indicates that the reference lies between pages 68 and 72, and also that it is not possible to distinguish unambiguously between the actual pages 69, 70 and 71 and the supplementary material.

*Vogue*ing the body I: feature articles and advertorials

Clothing advertorials differ to straightforward advertisements in that they contain editorial-style comments (often very brief) while, in the current sample, each image usually presents a model or models wearing a variety of items from different designers or manufacturers rather than single-designer outfits. This may also be considered editorial because it tells the reader how different looks might be put together through a combination of elements from disparate (if all rather upmarket, in the case of *Vogue*) sources. Advertisements proper are dealt with in a subsequent section. The feature articles and advertorials were examined for the presence of passages that contained body-related terms, these passages were then transcribed and the frequency of each term calculated. Similar terms were subsequently brought together under more general concepts (for example, 'comfort', 'comfy', 'ease', 'easy', 'loose' and 'relaxed' were placed under the general concept 'comfort'). Only the top three will be considered here: body (fifty occurrences), shape/line (forty nine) and comfort (forty six).

The analysis that follows is much more targeted to specific concepts, then, than Barthes' pioneering study of fashion magazines (1983 [1967]). His attempt to describe a structure exhaustively led him to the position that 'a rare feature of Fashion is as important as a common one' (1983 [1967]: 11), but the search for sociological significance rather than semiotic structure leads me to accept the importance of frequency and repetition. He also excludes advertisements and makeup (1983 [1967]: 11), but these are included here. The present analysis is also much broader than Borrelli's (1997) account of thirty one issues of American *Vogue* from 1968 to 1993, which considered only the 'Vogue's Point of View' section in each of these issues. Like Barthes and Borrelli, however, I concentrate for purposes of analytical simplicity on what he calls written–described clothing rather than on image-clothing (Barthes, 1983 [1967]: 8).

Writing on dress in fashion magazines like *Vogue Australia* is rarely of the argumentative style, with propositions carefully grounded and weighed and the relationships between them unfolding in a logical manner. Instead, we find a large number of descriptive–declarative clauses and sentences such as 'A timeless, double-breasted jacket that skims the body' (March: 212) or 'Simple, flowing lines are embellished with armfuls of bracelets' (January: 108–9). This is hardly a surprise, of course, as part of the function of these magazines is to act as arbiters of fashion for their readers. One turns to a fashion magazine in order to discover what is in fashion (unless one has other means of determining what is modish): one expects to be told in an authoritative manner so that one can be sure. The prose reflects this expectation. This poses both a disadvantage and an advantage for analysis. The disadvantage consists in the fact that one cannot probe for the reasoning behind the declarations (an arbiter *must not* give reasons, for then their judgements could be inspected and questioned). The advantage is really the same: instead of trying to find what is 'behind' declarations, as in an interview, interrogation or inquisition, we are free to look at the much more general ways in which the statements may be classified and related to each other.

The body disciplined

As we have seen, the Victorian dress reformers understood two opposed ways in which clothing and the body may be related: the former may have the disciplinary job of modelling the latter into an acceptably social shape (simple and efficient for projecting a status that was much more social and general than individual and peculiar) or, as was their preference, of revealing the lines of the body. The disciplinary role of dress has not been forgotten in the present sample, but is rare: 'Marilyn Said-Taffs, of Covers, stresses the importance of using "mouldable fabrics," such as crepe, acetate and faille, that hug the body without revealing too much. "Jersey is for seventeen-year-olds," she says. "For women over thirty, these fabrics give a better body shape"' (January: 69). Discipline serves the purpose of a general social category, as with the Victorians, only now it is not class but aged (female) embodiment and its acceptable forms (including acceptable forms of body revelation).

The body revealed

The reformers would no doubt be pleased, at least at first, that in this time of the 'new bareness' (June: 126) the idea of revealing the body was more common across the texts than the moulding role of fabrics:

'Bodysuits are high-collared, but shaped from wool/lycra blends that leave a tantalising minimum to the imagination' (February: 139); 'The cardigan has a renewed significance with the debut of the skinny silhouette...The sinuous cardigan, long and body-hugging, is one of the most welcome additions to anyone's wardrobe this season' (March: 54); 'Skin-tight...Body-wrapped, individual, intriguing' (March: 56); 'The finest knits have become the new wardrobe essentials. The basis: close-fitting cardigans, sweaters and bodysuits' (April: 109); 'The appearance of so much lace, crochet, net and loose, cobwebby knits continues the body-revealing theme' (June: 127); 'Filmy see-through fabrics and exposed flesh ruled on the spring runways' (September: 56). (Excerpts from *Vogue Australia*)

The words 'skinny silhouette' suggest that it is not necessarily a simple case of any body being revealed, however, but only those that possess the silhouette of the season: *this* is who the 'body-wrapped, individual, intriguing' person actually is, and the generalized wardrobes evoked in these extracts are more likely the particular wardrobes of the appropriately silhouetted. The seasonality of the silhouette becomes even clearer in some of the other passages where the term 'silhouette' is found:

'Strong new season silhouettes in imported European fashion' (February: 70–1); 'Winter. In the world of fashion, these are significant times. With a whole new play on proportion, silhouette and length' (February: 101); 'The longer silhouette. The flattering, long-line look is making news this season' (February: 116); 'Long, lean and sexy is the new silhouette' (June: 107); 'On runways throughout the world, a long-awaited new silhouette is revealed' (December: 44). (Excerpts from *Vogue Australia*)

Seasonally inappropriate bodies are thus left with a number of options: body modification to achieve the silhouette that signifies nowness, waiting until their unfashionable shapes in turn become seasonally appropriate, or not accepting the legitimacy of such attempts to restrict the sense of significant existence in the time of the season only to specific body types. The first provides a space for the body modification industries, and no doubt continual shifts in the characteristics of the in-season body across the years would encourage ongoing body modification on the part of those who always require the silhouette of the moment. Instead of clothing 'de-naturing' the 'natural' body in the name of social significance (the central reformer concern in the nineteenth century), we have the gym, the diet, the surgeon's knife and the liposuction pump to make the body socially appropriate. Valerie Steele (1999: 473) has remarked that the corset became internalized through diet and exercise, but we can also see that the knife and the pump are the transformed external manifestations of that item of (usually) underwear, presumably for those unwilling or unable to adopt the rigours of the more internal route. The second hopes that all body types get their turn at being fashionably now, but there is no guarantee that fashion cycles will seize on all body types within the compass of a single lifespan. The third opens a space for attempts to assert the claims of unseasonal bodies to social significance through criticisms of the socially exclusionary nature of the time of fashion, such as editor Cyndi Tebbel putting a size 16 model on the cover of the April 1997 issue of *New Woman* (Higson, 2000).

The body skimmed

Discipline and revelation, however, are not the only qualities of the clothing/body relationship in the sample. The notion of *skimming* is introduced:

'A timeless, double-breasted jacket that skims the body' (March: 212); 'Ease into the weekend in loose, pastel layers, fine knits and flowing pants that skim the body' (June: 128–9); 'Fabrics touch the body differently. Once used as armour to protect women from the outside world, clothes now aren't afraid to face reality, to skim, caress (and maybe even reveal) the body' (August: 97); 'Ice-cool layers of jersey that skim the body' (August: 106); 'Sheerness skims the body, surrounding it in gossamer layers' (September: 138); 'Soft, floaty dressing that skims the body with Bloomsbury-inspired romanticism' (November: 170). (Excerpts from *Vogue Australia*)

Skimming suggests a less intimate relationship between fabric and flesh than do discipline and revelation. Instead of a unification of dress and body through closely fitting garments or through offering some parts of the body to the gaze and concealing others, skimming implies a separation into entities that barely touch each other. Body and clothing are like two unrelated items, opening up the possibility of following independent logics and histories. We have already seen in the chapter on time that different parts of a dress may have their own periodicities not necessarily connected to the rhythms of other parts of the dress, so the notion of clothing as a complex changing object in its own right is not so strange. The body, as noted earlier in this chapter, also has a history – 'skimming' admits this separation, and so body and clothing come to meet each other in an in-principle unmotivated way. This understanding permits a new analytical conception of fashion as the ways in which the logico-historical complexes of body and dress happen to touch – skim – each other at particular points in time. One or the other of these two great evolving structures could conceivably stop moving for some reason: clothing might continue to evolve but the history of the body come to an end, or the body could continue to change and clothing remain static. Both could stop, as in science–fictional scenarios where standardized bodies draped in standardized apparel live in a sort of uniclone universe. They could cease skimming each other, which would presumably lead to the end of dress and the beginning of the reign of the body (which at that stage would no doubt be modified in order to provide some of the social cues at present neatly afforded by clothing). It is rather unlikely that *Vogue Australia* intended this sort of argument, but it does seem implicit in the notion of skimming.

The body pure and simple

The concepts of simplicity and purity frequently recurred when shape and line were invoked:

'For hot days and nights, dressing can be a simple pleasure. Pristine white – in liberating, simple shapes and fluid fabrics' (January: 97); 'Simple, flowing lines are embellished with armfuls of bracelets' (January: 108–9); 'The entire effect is uncomplicated and very, very lean, vastly different to the feeling of the short skirt' (February: 101); 'Designer tailoring adopts post-war severity, most apparent in the unadorned line of a long, lean skirt' (February: 105); 'Alongside this, we show the simplified lines of winter: spare, soft knit dressing, at home and at ease' (April: 85); 'Simple shapes, jewel colours, romantic nights' (April: 94); 'light and luxurious knitwear provides the best solution to simple winter dressing, in every shape from sleek dresses to oversized sweaters' (April: 108); '[Wendy Heather's] line remains uncluttered, simple and lean' (April: 117); 'basic shapes...will run throughout each season' (June: 32); 'The best resort dressing steers clear of excess: think strong, clean and graphic lines, with few (or no) accessories' (June: 69); 'Spare, streamlined dressing heats up the night, with cut-outs, thigh-high splits and bare midriffs' (June: 106); 'Enter beautifully simple pieces in flowing French and Italian fabrics, shaped to outdistance passing fashion' (August: 42); 'Pure lines, free of excess: the cardigan (with matching leggings) has never looked so modern' (August: 101); 'When designers' simple summer shapes are played up by accessories and fabrics with a primitive spirit' (August: 112); '[Richard Tyler's] crisply structured jackets are more formal than the European lounge jacket, with clean straight lines, firm shoulders and sharp creases' (August: 129); 'In keeping with this philosophy are our clean, precise lines of black and white fashion in its purest form. Free of excess, these pieces speak for themselves' (September: 148); 'Washes of psychedelic colour illuminate simple shapes' (November: 122). (Excerpts from *Vogue Australia*)

Simplicity and purity are 'airy' concepts that lift us above the messy realities of the complex and contaminated lives most of us (along with our bodies) lead. The promise is that simple and pure dress will also sign our bodies as equally simple and pure, granting us access to a life based on the intellectually attractive and precise shapes of classical geometry rather than the less certain virtues of untrustworthy (any maybe not so classically ordered) flesh. A part of fashion may indeed be a capacity to offer particular forms of simplicity at given points, as this makes it easier to convince ourselves that we are living in a particular socio-personal historical time (a bounded 'nowness') that we can 'see' thanks precisely to the simplicity of the fashion concepts of the era. We may laugh at our clothes in old photographs, but they show that our personal biographies have intersected with the greater social world in historically identifiable ways: fashion helps us prove that we have indeed *existed* in our times, and our bodies 'borrow' this quality. Fashion may not be capable of embracing the multitude of orders and disorders that mark our lives, but it is just this incapacity that can free us from the complexities and contaminations of our minds and bodies.

What of the more specific promises of line and shape in the above passages? First, line and shape articulate with notions of time: spare, streamlined dressing heats up the night, shapes will run throughout each season, simple shapes will outdistance passing fashion and lines that grant the cardigan (no less) modernity. The range spreads from the almost punctual time of the night to the uncertain and distant bounds of modernity, passing through seasonal time and the fugacity of fashion itself. We get excitement, an insight into what makes a series of seasons, economy across time, the transcendence of ever-shifting fashion, and, thanks to our cardigans, visible citizenship of our own era. Shape and line hold us together across various temporal modes. Second, shape is all-inclusive, from sleek dresses to oversized sweaters: any shape we like is permitted. There are simple shapes that liberate and clean straight lines to give more formality. This in itself leads to a third point, namely the capacity of fashion to hold contradictions together: simple lines are embellished, yet the line is unadorned. Both Simmel (1957 [1904]) and Davis (1989; 1992) saw fashion as the resultant of a series of oppositions (see Corrigan, 1997: 167–71 for a discussion), but this, illuminating as it is in the case of the fashion process generally, is perhaps too rationalist in the sense that it assumes the tension between oppositions to be in an always-activated state. In these passages, it is more a case of oppositions indifferently coexisting within an overall fashion discourse. If simplicity and purity offered us freedom from complexity and contamination, we are now relieved of the further burden of the necessity to live the tension between oppositions.

The body loose

If fashion leaves some oppositions to exist without activating their contradictory pulls, there are others it can activate when difference needs to be invoked. Clothing of the nineties is constructed by the magazines in opposition to the clothing of the eighties: where the latter is 'hard-and-mean' (March: 54) with a 'highly structured silhouette' (September: 58) characterized by tight dress and padded shoulders, the former is all softness, fluidity, relaxation, looseness and lacking in structure: 'softly tailored suits, knits, vests and shirts' (June: 32); 'Loosen up: the new move is fluid, feminine' (June: 130–1); 'Fashion's new thinking is relaxed and fluid' (August: 102); 'Flowing fabrics, relaxed lines: it's the deconstructed version of the eighties power suit' (August: 157); 'a general softening, a new fluidity' (September: 138). Eighties dress has been 'replaced by a loose, flowing, totally unstructured range of styles that carries clear echoes of seventies hippiedom' (September: 58). At its simplest, we are presented with the following imperative: 'let loose' (December: 178). The nineties reaction against the eighties seems like an echo of the dress reformers' reaction against the apparent constrictions of the late nineteenth century and, implicitly, of the eighties reaction against the 'hippiedom' of the seventies: each partakes of an oppositional logic which, as Davis (1989; 1992) in particular has suggested, is inherent to the movement of fashion.

If the era is one of fluidity, relaxation and looseness, then it will not be a surprise to find that the more directly body-centred terms of comfort and ease are other important concepts in the sample:

'Girls caught on quickly to the relaxed, easy fit of their guy's Stussy gear' (January: 33); 'Function is the main priority, with T-shirts, tanks, shorts, sweats and fleece pants specifically designed with comfort, coverage and freedom of movement in mind' (June: 42); 'The smoothest tailoring around cuts softened shapes in supple fabrics for looks that are easy on the body' (July: 122–3); 'I felt extraordinarily comfortable, loose and unbuttoned and unfettered' (September: 64). (Excerpts from *Vogue Australia*)

The standard-bearer of comfort is the cardigan, which is given a history to show its comfort-essence: stripped by Chanel of its military past, it was made from 'fluid fabric' and teamed with a 'languid' skirt to become 'a comfortable ensemble that has never lost its popularity with the suburban sherry set'. Eighties designers are criticized for making 'a travesty of the friendly cardigan by stitching in shoulder pads'. Its proper place is as 'the dear old knitted cardie...the comfy and sloppy thing we throw on when there's a chill in the air...an old friend, comfy and practical'. The diminutives 'cardie' and 'comfy' remove any formality the cardigan might have left as a garment, but it still manages to be infused with fashionability by the text: it is 'the nicest thing – apart from her partner's arms – that a girl can drape around her shoulders this year' (March: 54). In other words: comfort itself is simply a term of fashion ('this year'), rather than any absolute value in the context of body–clothing relations.

*Vogue*ing the body II: advertisements

Despite the number of advertising pages devoted to clothing, many are rather poor in terms of quantities of accompanying text and almost half of them (105 of 227) consist simply of a photograph of a modelled outfit with the name of the designer or manufacturer and, sometimes, the stockists. Writing of the relationship between photographs and words, John Berger has remarked that the 'photograph, irrefutable as evidence but weak in meaning, is given a meaning by the words' (Berger and Mohr, 1982: 92). If the name is famous enough, it will straight away conjure up a whole world of values and in this sense is directive: nothing more needs to be said, because we all 'know' what Chanel or Gucci or Hermès stand for. The clothing in the photo is suffused with these values and, at the same time, 'reaninates' Chanel or Gucci or Hermès in our minds through the presentation of a concrete instance. For a famous design house to use more directing text than the simple name would be to undermine its prestige by indicating that something other than the name was required to persuade the reader of its value. Indeed, the top five advertisers in the sample who elected what we might call the prestige model are generally very well known either internationally or, among the well-heeled, on the local Australian market: Chanel (eleven pages of clothing advertisements in the sample), Robert Burton (nine pages), Trent Nathan (eight) and Christian Dior and Ralph Lauren with five pages each. If the name is not known to the reader, the reverse process takes place: here, the photo of the dress directs us how to interpret the name and leaves a lot more space for the influence of our spontaneous and unanalytically 'felt' apprehension of the image. This is a risk for those who borrow the form of the prestige model of presentation from their better-known industry colleagues, because their name is relatively 'empty' and may be filled by the image in ways they cannot entirely predict. In such cases then, contra Berger, the words are weak and are given meaning by the image.

The prestige mode of presentation leaves the body–clothing relation textually unarticulated. The models themselves, however, are young and slim (as they are in the other clothing advertisements) so there is still an implicit claim about the appropriateness of body type to fashionable dress.

The body touches

More than half of the clothing ads had more elaborate accompanying text, but only about 15 per cent of the total related textually to the body in any clear way. Feeling and touching material, particularly wool, were the major concepts. Touch is used to convince us of the veracity of certain claims ('Wool is the most beautiful fibre in the world. You only have to hold it, touch it, feel it, to know that this is true' [March: 57]) or as a value in itself that may not be questioned ('There's nothing like the feel of wool in autumn' [March: 46]). Here, a bodily sense is invited to confirm a version of the world drawn up by advertisers. This can work because our sense of touch possesses a relatively underdeveloped analytical vocabulary (e.g., rough or smooth, soft or hard, wet or dry, hot or cold, etc.) and can therefore more easily be persuaded by pre-supplied terms that what it is sensing is indeed what it is being told it is sensing. There are few things more sensuously 'real' than touch, and if we are told that we can touch an abstract category such as 'beauty' this both increases the realm of what we can use touch for and turns the claimed beauty of whatever is being advertised into something possessing a solid sense of existence that touch only confirms. Amongst these, only those categories that more usually associate with touch, coolness, softness and warmth of material or item have prevailed. Comfort was evoked in the case of the materials Lycra and wool, but was in general not articulated as an important concept in clothing advertisements. The body in clothing ads, then, is present in the unspoken form of the youth and slimness of models and in the sense of touch as a way to reach certain concepts and experiences.

The body odoured

One of the most intense ways a body can be present to other bodies is through the sense of smell. Before the development of the mass hygiene society and its accompanying daily ablutions, manufactured fragrance may have been used to mask the malodorous body and its often unwelcome sense of presence. But now most bodies in public space are relatively olfactorily inert because of widespread frequent washing and the use of anti-perspirants, and are thus no longer present to others in the ways they once were. Fragrance now can work on a nearly neutral background and is not really competing with body smells. This opens up the possibility of making one's body emphatically present to others in a very deliberate and controlled way through choosing a particular fragrance. But what is the nature of this presence? This question will be answered in the context of the fragrance advertisements in our sample of *Vogue Australia*.

A sentence in an advertisement for JOOP! points to a key characteristic of smells that are not obviously 'of' something specific (the smell of coffee or burnt toast, for example): 'A message in the mystic language of fragrances, sensual and intangible' (March: inside cover). Although we may undoubtedly sense a fragrance, and Classen *et al.* (1994: 109) claim that we can distinguish thousands of different odours, it can be very difficult indeed for those not working in the perfume industry to put what this sensual experience might mean into words. Sometimes smells may remind us of times, places, people or events from our own life experiences, but here the meaning of the smell is provided by something outside of itself. Furthermore, this means that any given aroma can give rise to widely varying meanings across individuals. This is hardly an ideal situation for advertisers, who need to control as much of the meaning of what they are selling as possible. This is accomplished in three different ways in the sample.

First, we again discover what was described as the 'prestige mode' in the discussion on clothing advertisements: here, we get the name of the perfume and the manufacturer (and sometimes their location) and a photograph of the bottle and sometimes a model. There is no other directing text. Forty per cent of the fragrance pages consist of this type of advertisement. Examples of the prestige model are 'Paris. Yves Saint Laurent' (January: 15) or 'Insensé Givenchy' (October: 75). The meaning of the fragrance is here all the prestige already attached to the famous names that use this mode and to their location where identified. 'Paris' occurs on no less than thirty one occasions in the advertisements as a whole, followed far behind by 'Firenze', 'Tuscany' and 'Beverly Hills' with four each. No other locations are mentioned (apart from Byzance, which refers to an ancient and sophisticated city culture and is here the name of a perfume, not a manufacturing location).

Second, the name of the perfume, where different to that of the manufacturer, also works to steer meaning in particular directions. Twenty nine separate fragrances of this type were located (including Miss Dior, as the 'Miss' differentiated it from the simple manufacturer's name, and COCO, which uses Chanel's byname but which I considered sufficiently differentiated from the maker itself).

Table 4.3 summarizes the concepts associated with fragrance names, several of which are linked to more than one concept. Eleven resonate with Frenchness, ten evoke states or types of the person (Cabochard is a stubborn person and Cabotine means a woman who shows off by adopting affected manners), eight relate to the natural world (Shalimar is assumed to have something to do with the famous gardens of that name in Lahore and Ysatis is presumably a reference to isatis, the plant from which indigo comes), five seem to indicate a general Eastern exoticism, three are names of attractive places and two are linked with the classic modernity period of the twentieth century, the 1920s (both jazz and Chanel's No. 5 are associated with this time). Escada and Red remain as residual categories. The fragrances allow us easy access to these fascinating and appealing sites of existence, some of

Table 4.3   Concepts associated with fragrance names

Frenchness	State or type of person	Natural world	Exoticism	Places	Classic modernity	Residual
Arpège	Beautiful	Cool Water	Byzance	Byzance	Jazz	Escada
Byzance	Cabochard	Dune	Dune	Paris	No. 5	Red
Cabochard	Cabotine	Jardins de bagatelle	Opium	Tuscany		
Cabotine	Insensé	Shalimar	Samsara			
COCO	L'égoïste	White Diamonds	Shalimar			
Insensé	Miss Dior	Wings				
Jardins de bagatelle	Narcisse	Youth–Dew				
L'égoïste	Obsession	Ysatis				
Narcisse	Unforgettable					
Paris	Youth–Dew					
Volupté						

which promise guiltless indulgence in the self in ways which are not necessarily socially admired (Cabochard, Cabotine, L'égoïste, Narcisse, Obsession, etc.). We can thus simultaneously be very self-centred yet establish a low-level and rather one-way type of relationship with others through the insistent presence of the fragrance. We may be able to ignore them, but they cannot ignore us. The fragrance helps the wearer claim a world as *theirs*, as they are the one silently imposing a presence on others.

Third, more directive texts than simple names try to shape the meaning of the fragrance. Here, only those that relate to the body will be discussed.

Sensuality (including 'senses' and 'sensual') was easily the most common concept, with twelve instances across five different advertisers. Indeed, in some instances the fragrance appears to be promoted as providing free and unqualified access to the very essence of sensuality: Yves Saint Laurent's Opium promises 'Sheer sensuality' (March: 27) and nothing else, Oscar de la Renta's Volupté, specially for us, liberates the sensual world of all constraints with its 'Trust your senses' (April: 43). JOOP! sees its fragrance as expressing sensuality accompanied by mystery, allure and the intangible, while Chloé and Davidoff qualify it slightly: the 'quiet sensuality' of the former's Narcisse (April: 1) and the 'sensuality tamed by a sense of civility' of the latter's Cool Water (September: >16<17). Untrammelled or civilized, sensuality as general value is made available by the products. The generalism and accompanying low level of specification allows us a large space to interpret what sensuality might mean with respect to our own bodily practices. The important thing is that we can now access the general concept in principle through the perfume bottle.

The only other concept of importance was quite the opposite to sensuality: COCO is 'L'esprit de Chanel' (March: 45), Cool Water, as well as possessing a civilized sensuality, is 'the spirit of the wind' (September: >16<17), Wings by Giorgio Beverly Hills will 'Set your spirit free' (October: >48<49) and White Diamonds is the 'fragrance dreams are made of' (September: 63). Fragrance, then, can lead us to the world of spirits and dreams as well as the senses: we can be Caliban on Saturday and Ariel on Sunday, as parfumeur Prospero takes the marketing penny.

The body surfaces

But it is not in advertisements for clothing or fragrance that the body is most present. It finds its starring role in the publicity for skincare and makeup. Here, the body is not something 'thick' that may be modified in the manner of the garments that horrified the dress reformers, it is not something substantial to go under the knife or lift weights, nor is it an entity that worries about comfort. Instead, the body is a surface to be treated. Table 4.4 lists the top ten terms in the texts of the seventy six separate relevant advertisements in the sample. Some terms have been amalgamated into more general concepts: for example, temporality includes words such as lasting, age and youth, moistness includes water and (de)hydration, colour includes tone and shade, protection includes care, and so forth.

The body timed

Terms associated with time appeared in almost three-quarters of the advertisements.

The notion of newness cropped up in twenty-three of the fifty-five advertisements in this group, suggesting a relatively high level of importance for the corpus as a whole. Generally, stress is laid upon the newness of the product itself or, in the case of already-existing products, the newness of a range of colours. What does newness accomplish? At its most abstract and fundamental, it offers to split the history of the ad reader's body into two parts: an old time of the body and a new time of the body, the split being made possible through obtaining the new cosmetic product. The new is also the most heightened form of the now because the now experienced specifically through the new is a now that is distinctly different to the now

Table 4.4 *Top ten concepts in skincare and makeup advertisements*

Concept	Overall frequency of occurrence	Adverts (N)	% of all skincare and makeup ads in which concept appears
Temporality	287	55	72.4
Skin	280	47	61.8
Moistness	111	32	42.1
Colour	96	31	40.8
Lips	80	19	25.0
Beauty	63	27	35.5
Care and protection	60	32	42.1
Appearance and look	49	29	38.2
Cleansing	40	7	9.2
Natural	36	25	32.9

that may be seen as a continuation of the past. Our new now is ahead of the past-burdened nows of those who do not have the product (and of the now we would have had had we not obtained it). Our answer to the question 'Are you using yesterday's makeup for today's face?' (March: 9) is, happily, in the negative. The product promises us the social superiority of being one of those who is the living representative of the now: we *are* the now, because others existing now count only as embodiments of a (pre-product) past. On a biographical level, it promises our body a new life and offers the opportunity of a break with our past body and that which is associated with it. Unlikely as it may seem, a new shade of lipstick can rupture social and personal history on the bio-symbolic level: we are no longer the embodiment of what was, but are now a different entity.

Ten advertisements locate the product as part of the routine recurring practices of the body, with references to 'daily face protector' (January: 11), 'the individual daily care necessary' (February: 99), '1 time a day for 60 days' (March: 108), 'Used day and night' (April: 75) and so forth. It is clearly in the interests of the manufacturers to maximize use of their product, and here they accomplish this aim through colonizing the rhythms of our relevant body practices. Our routine everydayness becomes inseparable from the product: if it were suddenly to go missing, the nature of the routine and the everyday would become an open question again. If routine everydayness is the bedrock of the mundane levels of existence, removing the product would threaten its stability. Through temporal colonization of a particular type, then, the product holds our mundane everyday existence in place.

If we have products to keep our mundane existence safe from uncertainty, twelve advertisements propose products that promise magical transformations of the body. The relationship here is simple: product + body + specific time duration → magic transformation. 'Body' might be replaced with 'skin' in this very specific context, because all products here claim to transform its quality. The durations range from the instant ('immediate hydrating boost' [July: 1], 'instant treats for the skin' [October: 17], 'instant and intense moisturisation' [October: 51]) to hours ('Use it tonight, see progress tomorrow' [March: 5], 'The 2-Hour Tan' [September: 134]) to days ('as little as 7 days!' [June: 27]) to weeks ('in just a matter of weeks' [August: 90]). This is a rather different temporal strategy to routine everydayness, recognizing that one of the problems of the latter is the very safeness of mundanity: it is boring. It is closer to the new, but uses more specific durations and the gains are more concretely related to actual body transformations than the somewhat abstract gains of the new and the now. The product here colonizes our desire to access a time of positive transformation rather than a time of repetition or the time of the negative transformation of the body towards decay and death.

Fifteen advertisements extol the lasting qualities of the product, lipstick in particular being singled out here: 'Twenty lasting lip colours' (January: 45) is a typical claim. The time of the product that attaches to the body is of longer duration than rival products, thus appealing more perhaps to the sense of the economical than the sense of the magical. The product time is consumer money.

The macro time of the body, usually known as the ageing process, is a focus of thirteen advertisements. Without exception, the body here is treated entirely in its surface appearance as skin and the target of the products is time as encapsulated in this surface appearance through the likes of lines, wrinkles or spots. Slowing or even reversing this time are among the claims made for the products: 'skin ages much more slowly' (March: 108), 'resist the time-clock' (November: 19) and 'Promotes healthier, younger-looking skin' (January: 17) are typical examples. Looking younger is not so much a value in itself but takes its meaning from the fact that it covers visible evidence of the body's increasing proximity to the terminal state of the dead and the rotting (assuming an average life span). The ultimate promise of the products, then, is that we have more time to live because that is what our (product-modified) surface appearance tells us. The products stretch that fuzzily-bounded part of our body macro time where we do not think very much about the termination point of our material existence because hints of the latter are not obviously inscribed upon us.

The argument of this section may be put most fundamentally as follows: the product seizes the body in order to latch onto and modify aspects of temporality in directions desirable for manufacturer and (rather less certainly) consumer.

The body skinned

Emily Martin (1987: 42, 47) has shown how medical textbooks have applied negative evaluative terms to descriptions of the processes of menopause and menstruation, discursively constructing the female body as on the side of the weak and the degenerating. This makes control of the body by a third party appear natural and legitimate. Twenty two advertisements in the sample construct the skin in a very similar way, establishing its negative qualities in order to supply grounds for the intervention of the product. The products deepen the legitimacy of their intervention by explaining how the skin got to be in an unfortunate state in the first place, with seven adverts evoking causes: environmental stress, the physical and mental strains of everyday life, sun damage and pollution. The skin is cast as vulnerable, and in need of the aid and protection of the product. Table 4.5 lists the negative qualities of skin on the left and the qualities brought to it by the product on the right. Numbers in brackets indicate the total number of occurrences of a term across the twenty two ads, where greater than one.

To use the most frequent descriptions, skin is oily or dry, tired, lined, wrinkled and marked by acne, while the products bring smoothness, beauty, health and improved texture. We are promised not simply better skin, but also the more abstract qualities of what might be called, with apologies to

Table 4.5 *Skin and product qualities*

Characteristics of the skin	What the product gives
acne (3)	anti-ageing (2)
age spots	attractiveness
blemishes	beauty (5)
breaks out	brightness (2)
broken capillaries	clarity (3)
coarseness	firmness (2)
dead	flawlessness (2)
discoloured	freshness (3)
dry (8)	grace
flawed	health (5)
fragile	improved appearance (3)
lined (4)	improved texture (5)
muddy	improved tone (2)
oily (8)	poreless look
open-pored	radiance (3)
pigmented (2)	relaxation
pimpled (2)	smoothness (7)
puffy	softness (3)
rash	vitality
red	youthfulness (3)
sallow	
sensitive (2)	
signs of ageing	
sluggish cellular activity	
taut	
tired (4)	
weakened	
worn-out	
wrinkled (3)	

Note: Number within parentheses in columns indicates number of occurrences.

Bourdieu, beauty capital. The attractive qualities listed in the right-hand column help us obtain whatever such capital may get on those markets where it is exchangeable.

The body wet

Moistness, in the form of moisturizing, is sometimes presented as a value in itself without need of justification, suggesting that its value is beyond question: phrases such as 'Longlasting, moisturising, rich, matte colours for lips' (April: 81) or 'Sixteen superb fashion colours in a moist, long-lasting lipstick' (November: 93) do not indicate why moisture might be important. This lack of connection with any concrete function allows full space for the reader's imagination to read desired values into the moist, such as contrasting various positive ideas and states evoked by wetness against various negative ideas and states evoked by dryness. Thirteen advertisements, however, spell matters out. More than anything else (nine occurrences), moistness functions to protect the skin and lips: against pollution, the sun, the atmosphere, dryness or age. It is also constructed as conditioning, nourishing, perfecting, smoothing and softening the skin. Overall, there emerges a negative image of a vulnerable 'dry' body and a positive image of a protected 'wet' body, a transition from the former to the latter being made available by the product. Again, the body is constructed as lacking the essentials to preserve itself against the dangers of the world, the moisturizing film promising to make it invulnerable.

The body coloured

Although colour was occasionally presented as a value in itself or linked to personal colour matching, it appears to have one overwhelming role in the sample: to offer choice to the consumer. Seventeen advertisements bear witness to this, with the choice ranging from the simplest duo 'Tinted or untinted' (January: 17) up to '31 fabulous shades' (October: 43) via less precise terms such as collection, range, pallette and 'rich tapestry of shades' (December: 155). The body is again surface, but this time to be decorated rather than protected.

The body parted

Second only to skin as the most frequently mentioned part of the body, lips are clearly a privileged target of the cosmetics industry. Perhaps this is because they are the most obvious site where protection and decoration/transformation come together through lipstick, itself the subject of all nineteen advertisements in this section. All but one mention the range of colours available for the decorative/transformative aspect, six evoke protection against dryness through indicating the moisturizing capabilities of the product and five claim to protect against the effects of the sun. Lipstick, then, allows the reconciliation in the one product of two desirable concepts that do not necessarily always tug in the same direction. The lips themselves act as the bodily support and evidence of this happy meeting of concepts.

The body beautiful

Despite the number of times that beauty is invoked, it is not possible to use the sample to answer the question 'what is beauty?' in any philosophical sense as beauty is not subject to that sort of treatment here. Because it remains analytically undefined, beauty becomes a fuzzy but desirable concept open to be invested with whatever the reader might imagine or the advertiser might propose. It is nevertheless concretized in terms of answers to the question 'what is beautiful?' This is a more practical matter than a disquisition on the nature of beauty, permitting us to recognize beauty in certain places and allowing advertisers to propose certain products as pathways towards it. Skin, nails, lips and the face are these sites in the sample, accompanied by the appropriate lipsticks, nail polishes and skin treatments. Examples are 'thirty superb international fashion shades for nails that look beautiful for longer' (January: 45) and, even more strikingly for the present argument, 'The classic and timeless shades of Nuances Marine, enable you to realise your full beauty potential' (March: 149). In sum, beauty remains the desirable, if intangible, concept, but the beautiful provides a practical bodily means of accessing it.

The key aspects of care and protection have already been covered under skin and lips, and so will not be discussed further. Appearance also is generally associated with concepts already discussed, especially temporality and skin, and thus will not be discussed in any detail here. Nine advertisements propose the product as a way of avoiding the negative temporality of lines, wrinkles and signs of ageing and four speak of attaining a younger look. Four ads evoke beauty as appearance, and the only major new concept is the natural look (six advertisements). The latter is discussed in its own right below. It would be misleading to claim that appearance is a concept present only explicitly in the sample; however, as it could be argued that the transformation of appearance is implicitly present in almost all of the advertisements in the collection.

The body cleansed

Cleansing occurs in less than 10 per cent of the advertisements in the sample, and more than half of the forty mentions are concentrated in one single ad. That is not really enough to provide material for more general statements, except to say that it seems to indicate that the principle of cleansing has now been broadly acquired (even if that took centuries of the civilizing process dear to Elias [1994 {1939}]) and readers are not in need of much reminding. Having been acquired as a fundamental value, it may be assumed both that cleansing takes place anyway and that it is not much more than a relatively neutral base for the existence of the more lively concepts of protection and decoration linked to other products.

The body natural

Sometimes the best way of understanding what a term accomplishes is to replace it with its opposite and see what difference this makes. This old semiotic technique is especially useful where the value of a term in the context under investigation is not explicitly established against its opposite. Here, the term simply appears to have an intrinsic positive or negative value of its own: we take it in but do not analyse it, because the context provides us with no grounds for questioning why or how we 'know' what the term means. We simply 'know'. This makes it easy for an advertiser to put a particular spin on a product through the use of such terms without having to demonstrate their well-foundedness through the risky strategy of an argument – risky, because an argument provides an opportunity to examine the grounds of a reasoning.

'Natural' has two possible opposite terms, 'unnatural' and 'artificial'. These have quite different values: 'unnatural' evokes something that should not, according to the laws of the natural world, exist, and has a distinctly negative and even threatening edge to it while 'artificial' refers to human fabrications as opposed to natural ones and has no intrinsic negative value. The continual rise since the 1960s of the natural as positive value has, however, tended to cast anything that might be opposed to it in a negative light, so both of the terms opposed to 'natural' come to be seen as 'bad'. Artifice being the very business of the cosmetics industry, it is not surprising that it has chosen to take on the mantle of the natural in almost one-third of all advertisements in the sample. Even where artifice in the form of science is deliberately invoked, it tends to be linked closely to nature, thus reducing, or even cancelling, any negative reverberations: 'Nature has always represented an immense reservoir of resources for feminine beauty. Today, modern cosmetology has not forgotten nature; quite the contrary, it has learnt how to make scientific use of the best ancient knowledge by means of the state-of-the-art instrumentation and technology' (February: >68<72); 'Containing the finest ingredients from nature and science...' (June: 33). Even the alpha hydroxy acid ('science's latest weapon against visible wrinkles') that is used in a particular product is 'naturally occurring... in sugar cane' (August: 90). The first of these citations suggests that scientific techniques are not at all in opposition to nature but simply the best way to reach it, while the second proposes that they are complementary rather than oppositional. The third suggests that science's latest weapon could hardly be more natural or less artificial. Even consumer choice of colour in makeup, which might strike one as definitely lying on the side of artifice, is a choice among that provided by nature: 'Drawing from nature's palette of subtle tones, Thalgo presents... "The shades of the ocean"' (March: 149), 'we created a rich tapestry of shades chosen from nature and translated into lipsticks and nail enamels' (December: 155).

In terms of the body, the natural generally refers to a type of look. Inserting 'artificial' and 'unnatural' instead of 'natural' gives us the examples depicted in Table 4.6 (the asterisks indicate that the phrase is partly made up).

Table 4.6 *The natural and its opposites*

Natural	Artificial	Unnatural
A naturally glowing and vital looking skin (February: >68<72)	*An artificially glowing and vital looking skin	*An unnaturally glowing and vital looking skin
An exclusive formula that protects the natural beauty of your lips (March: 33)	*An exclusive formula that protects the artificial beauty of your lips	*An exclusive formula that protects the unnatural beauty of your lips
Skin looks naturally flawless (March: 96)	*Skin looks artificially flawless	*Skin looks unnaturally flawless
Natural looking tan (September: 134)	*Artificial looking tan	*Unnatural looking tan

From the point of view of a historical era where 'the natural' has become a highly positive value, the centre column will read as something to be avoided through appropriate products and the right hand column will read as disturbing, with hints that something is wrong. In those periods where bodily artifice is exalted (among eighteenth-century aristocrats, possibly among future cyborgian populations), the left-hand column will read as gauche and unsophisticated as the central column does to the naturalists of the present day and the right-hand column as, perhaps, a state to aspire to beyond the artificial: a sort of organic artificiality that would see the natural and the artificial as earlier stages (thinkable for cyborgs, if not for the aristocrats of the past). A description of the world from the point of view of the right-hand column I leave to the science fiction writers.

In the naturalist era, artifice is not so much a visible human way of transforming the world but a way of confirming the dominance of the natural.

The body advertised

Having discussed each concept, it is now time to consider briefly how they relate to each other. Table 4.7 shows the number of advertisements in which each concept is co-present with the others.

Temporality and skin are the terms which are co-present with others more frequently than any other concept and cleansing and lips are the least frequently co-present with the rest. This would appear to confirm the importance of temporality and the notion of the body as surface, as well as the suggestion made earlier that cleansing is not something that people need persuading of any more. Lips are relatively rarely co-present with other terms presumably because they are a very specific part of the body and thus not likely to be as broadly linked as the more general concepts.

Conclusion

Table 4.8 attempts to summarize some of the key characteristics of the body as explored in this chapter, with the addition of a column on possible future directions. The analysis has shown that matters are more complex and subtle than depicted in the Table, but it is deliberately simplified in order to bring out broad tendencies. The first row proposes answers to the question 'Whose body is it?' and the second to the question 'What body is it?'. The answers to the first suggest strong connections with the broader social concerns of the era contemporary with the writings: the struggle of eighteenth-century science to understand the living body through the dead, the health concerns of a nineteenth century marked by the huge and rapid

Table 4.7 *Co-presence in advertisements of top 10 concepts with respect to each other*

Concepts	Temporality	Skin	Moisture	Colour	Lips	Beauty	Protection	Appearance	Cleansing	Nature
Temporality	–	39	25	24	14	21	26	27	4	21
Skin	39	–	24	17	3	18	26	24	6	22
Moisture	25	24	–	14	9	11	20	15	5	12
Colour	24	17	14	–	14	14	14	15	2	14
Lips	14	3	9	14	–	7	8	4	0	4
Beauty	21	18	11	14	7	–	18	12	2	13
Protection	26	26	20	14	8	18	–	15	4	18
Appearance	27	24	15	15	4	12	15	–	3	18
Cleansing	4	6	5	2	0	2	4	3	–	3
Nature	21	22	12	14	4	13	18	18	3	–

Table 4.8   *Key steps in the history of the aesthetic body*

	18th century anatomy	19th century dress reform	1920s Constructivists	1990s Fashion magazines	21st century daily life?
Whose body is it?	Body of skeleton	Body of health	Body of producer	Body of consumer	Body of cyborg
What body is it?	Bony body	Visceral body	Active body	Surface body	Programmable body
What rules the body?	Aesthetics and science	Aesthetics and idealized natural body	Aesthetics and work	Aesthetics and protection	Aesthetics and flesho-machinality

growth and crowded and unsanitary conditions of the cities of the industrial revolution, the building of a new society according to a productivist philosophy of the species-being applied to bring about a transition from a peasant to an industrial economy, the marketing of the fruits of advanced production through widespread consumerism, and the possible rise of a new information economy requiring a direct plug-and-play connection with its human components.

The answers to the second question refer to how the body itself appears in each of these eras. There seems to be a tendency towards a shift outwards from bony interiority to the internal organs clustering around the foundational skeleton to the skin as surface: this is body as object of science, medicine and cosmetics, the first two presumably having already largely solved their internal body knowledge problems thus today leaving the outer level open to the potentially limitless play of cosmetics. In the remaining eras, the body is no longer thinkable as a thing in itself (the skeleton, organs and surface of a self-contained body) but is linked to machinery. The active body of the producer, as we know from Marx, will be caught up in the machine-centred logic of the production process (even, perhaps especially, in the bright new industry-awed Soviet Union of the 1920s), and the cyborg body may deepen this phenomenon through its own potential programmability: instead of body and machine as separate, we have an intimate link between the two. Such programmability could, of course, be applied in the consumption process as well.

Despite these differences, the deeper history of the body in the present context turns out to be an aesthetic one, with beauty's privileged partner shifting from science to nature to work to protection and potentially onwards to flesho-machinality among cyborg populations. In the present sample, science and nature in particular are actually built upon original aesthetic foundations for reasons already explored, while the Constructivists saw aesthetics as an integral part of the clothing of the new worker's body. The happy coincidence of aesthetics and protection is a selling point for many skincare and makeup products. Given the historical insistence of concepts of beauty up to now, it is hard to imagine cyborgs of the future being able to do without an aesthetic dimension. If the past is anything to go by, they will most likely be organized at least partly according to aesthetic principles. That, however, is one peek into the future too far for the present work.

Note

1 This particular text would not have been available to the Constructivists, as the 1844 *Manuscripts* were not published until 1932 (Colletti, 1975: 7). Nevertheless, the positions of Marx and the Constructivists clearly converge here.

5

Gift, Circulation and Exchange I:
Clothing in the Family

Introduction

In Chapter 2, we touched briefly on the question of the circulation and exchange of clothing in utopian texts. Here we pick up again on this point, treating clothing as a material object to which things may happen rather than simply a canvas upon which various social meanings are displayed. This chapter, for reasons that are soon to become apparent, consists principally of an empirical study of the circulation of clothing within a particular sample of families. The classic literature on the gift relationship is then considered in the light of our findings. First, however, we look very briefly at some earlier studies of exchange within families.

Distribution within the family

Work on intra-familial circulatory patterns grew out of criticism of economic theory's relative neglect of the family (Pahl, 1980; 1983; Sen, 1984). Jan Pahl (1983: 238) shows that intra-familial – or, more accurately, intra-*couple* – money allocation is not equal sharing but gender-sensitive, a finding confirmed by Gail Wilson (1987). British, French and Indian studies indicate that similar remarks hold for food (Charles and Kerr, 1987; Delphy, 1984 [1975]; Sen, 1984). The spending of money also runs along gendered lines: Gullestad (1984: 268–70) and Brannen and Moss (1987: 87) show that 'men's money' is considered to be spent on essentials and 'women's money' on extras in both Norway and Britain. Resources can be distributed in a gendered manner even after death, as Gotman (1988: 164–5) shows in her study of French inheritance patterns.

This chapter differs from the above writers in that attention is directed neither to money flows nor food distribution but to flows of one particular good into which money is converted: clothing. There are some parallels between these spheres, but differences too. Both food and clothing are traditionally female areas of responsibility (Edgell, 1980: 58), and there are some analogies between, say, a refrigerator and a wardrobe. Most people in a family can claim to have their 'own' wardrobe (a term that will be discussed later), but few would claim to have their 'own' refrigerator. Furthermore, food tends to be consumed fairly quickly, whereas an item of clothing can be active in a family over a number of years. We will find, however, that age/gender differences mentioned by Sen (1984: 347) in the case of food also prove important in the case of clothing.

Clothing circulation

My interest in family clothing circulation grew from the results of an investigation into wardrobe contents. I noticed that between a quarter and a third of all items present had not been self-purchased on the market by their owners, but obtained from other sources. These other sources turned out overwhelmingly to be family members. For example, items of clothing might take the form of a gift from mother to daughter. However, a gift is clearly just one sub-category of the more general category of circulation. Consequently, it was decided to examine all forms of circulation in a sample of six Dublin families selected through snowball sampling: which sorts out items (such as shirts, sweaters) circulated in what sorts of ways between which categories of relationships between persons (such as sister–brother, mother–daughter). Quite definite gender-based patterns emerge. With the exception of the middle-class Robinsons, all of the families were 'respectable' working class. Data were collected through interviews, talk about family photographs and wardrobe 'tours', so both present and past versions of family clothing practices and beliefs were accessed.

At first sight, it might appear obvious that every individual has their 'own' wardrobe (by 'wardrobe' I mean a collection of clothes that any given individual in the family considers to 'belong' to them. 'Belong' is placed in inverted commas because, as we see below, this concept turns out to be ambiguous). Indeed, we frequently encounter the popular idea that clothing is (or ought to be) an 'expression' of 'individuality'. We might expect, then, to find a number of exclusive wardrobes corresponding with given persons. While each family member considers that they do indeed have a wardrobe of their own, clothes belonging to several members might share the same physical space – in the 'wardrobe' understood as an item of furniture – in one member's bedroom. The potential for confusion here is generally recognized and overcome by dividing space such that, for example, A's clothes are all on the left hand side and B's on the right. As we will see below, however, these neat distinctions remain anything but inviolate. Nevertheless, it will be convenient to start out from the initial idea of given individuals corresponding with given wardrobes and see how this connection is upheld, modified or undermined through actual dress practices. The following are the individual-to-individual relations possible in the families researched, and we consider each of them in the light of their associated clothing practices: (1) husband–wife; (2) father–son; (3) father–daughter; (4) mother–son; (5) mother–daughter; (6) sister–sister; (7) brother–brother; (8) sister–brother; (9) family members–others.

The following forms of circulation were discovered. It is possible that other samples may provide different forms. It is unlikely, however, that many other basic forms of circulation could be found in contemporary Western societies.

- *Market gifts:* These gifts originate on the market and are subsequently presented to the recipient. This category includes purchases made on special occasions (overwhelmingly birthdays and Christmas in the sample) as well as more mundane buys, such as mothers regularly bringing home items of clothing for their younger children.
- *Family-made gifts:* This form includes any item of clothing made by any family member that has been given to another family member.
- *Family-made commodities:* This quite rare category includes such cases as the paid ordering of items from family members who have clothes-making skills.
- *Cast-offs:* These comprise items of clothing originally, but no longer, worn by the donor. The term 'hand-me-downs' also refers to this and indeed is used by several of the families, but as it connotes older-giving-to-younger (not always the pattern in practice) I have preferred the more neutral term.
- *Borrowing:* (that is, taking an item for wearing on particular occasions with the permission of the 'owner').
- *Stealing:* (that is, taking an item *without* first obtaining the permission of the 'owner'. This does not imply permanent possession, but 'stealing' will be retained as it is the term the interviewees themselves use to describe the practice).
- *Self-purchased:* As a rule, it has been assumed that all items not described by their 'owners' as having been obtained by the modes listed above have been self-purchased. The transition to self-purchasing turns out to be one of the pivotal moments of mother–daughter clothing-mediated relations, and this is discussed in detail below.

From Table 5.1, which maps clothing types onto mode of circulation and uses the clothing terms employed by the interviewees themselves, we can see that more types of items circulate as market gifts than in any other mode (21/30, or 70 per cent), followed by stealing (12/30, or 40 per cent); cast-offs (10/30, or 33 per cent); borrowing (7/30, or 23 per cent) and family-made gifts (6/30, or 20 per cent). There is a single occurrence of a family-made commodity. Although these figures should be interpreted as merely a guide to tendencies, we can already see the centrality of the gift relationship in the circulation of clothing within the family: both market gifts and stealing – which can, of course, be seen as a negative gift – have the highest penetration rates among actual items of clothing. Blouses, jumpers (sweaters, in North American English), scarves, shirts and ties are the most purchased gift objects. Jumpers/sweaters, indeed, appear to be the most universal objects of circulation: they partake of all modes, being particularly frequent as market gifts and stolen items. As we see below, they partake of all the possible family relationships already listed, with the exception of sons giving to fathers. The jumper, in sum, seems to be the basic unit of circulation in the family clothing economy. Although there is no clear evidence from the sample, this may be because such apparel is both less gender-marked than most other items of clothing and will cover a greater range of body sizes than almost any other garment. Almost 'anyone' could wear a given jumper.

Table 5.1 *Clothing types mapped onto mode of clothing circulation*

Clothing item	Market gifts	Family-made gifts	Family-made commodities	Cast-offs	Borrowing	Stealing
Anoraks						+
Aprons	+					
Blouses	++			+	+	
Cardigans	+	+		+	+	+
Coats	+			+	+	+
Dresses		+				
Football gear	+					
Gloves	+					
Jackets	+	+		+	+	+
Jumpers/Sweaters	+++	+	+	+	+	++
Knickers	+					
Pants	+					
Ponchos		+				
Pyjamas	+					
Raincoats						+
Scarves	++					+
Shirts	+++			+	+	+
Skirts	+			+		
Smocks				+		
Socks	+					
Suits	+					
Sweatshirts						+
T-shirts	+					+
Tanktops	+					
Ties	++			+	+	
Tops						+
Tracksuits				+		
Trousers		+				
Underwear	+					
Vests	+					+

KEY: + 1–4 occurrences. ++ 5–9 occurrences. +++ ≥10 occurrences.

If we exclude the very rare family-made commodity, cardigans and jackets assume an equivalent role to jumpers, but they still fail to reach the same intensity levels. The family-made commodity, indeed, is quite anomalous. All other clothing-mediated relations within the family are characterized by some variant on the gift relationship – even stealing, as has been remarked already, can be reformulated as a negative gift. Commodity relations appear to be so rare precisely because they do not quite fit into family clothing relations.

Let us now look at how Table 5.1 maps on to the separate family relationships. We begin with the spouses.

Husband–wife

The most remarkable thing about husband–wife clothing relations in the sample is the fact that they take place exclusively via market gifts, with wife giving husband a much greater variety of clothing than the reverse. Even when sharing the same physical closet space, there seemed to be no cases of one wearing an item belonging to the other. In other words, the wardrobes of husband and wife appear to be the most closed off from each other of all the wardrobes in the family. During the marriage, wife sometimes bought husband clothing on an everyday – in the sense of not a special occasion – basis as well as on definite occasions such as birthdays and Christmas, while husband bought wife gifts of clothing only on the latter two days. So while the woman's giving is at least sometimes a mundane event, the man's takes place only on special occasions. This may be linked to the fact that all the married women in the sample were housewives and all the married men employed outside the home, thus mapping domestic (including clothing matters) and non-domestic spheres onto women and men respectively. We might expect to find different patterns in other family types.

The mundane/special distinction may also be related to the fact that husband and wife dress different parts of each other's bodies. The ceremonially based giving of the husband is restricted to covering just one part of his wife's body with three types of items which are very similar to each other, viz. cardigans, jumpers and sweaters. Wives, however, dress all parts of their husband's bodies in quite a variety of garments. To put this another way: husbands can be totally dressed by gifts from their wives, but wives here can only be dressed very partially by husbands and only on one specific area of the body. It should be said, however, that I was never likely to be given information on any erotics of intimate garments operating in the sample.

As will become evident below, mundane gifts are more typical of the mother–child relationships found in the sample (although this is linked to age–gender variables), and engaging in this sort of relationship with a husband might not always be appreciated. So relations between spouses have a tendency to remain at the ceremonial level.

Father–son

There was very little incidence of direct purchase of clothes by fathers for sons. The cast-off is seemingly the closest to a 'typical' father-to-son relation (cardigans and jumpers).

Son's gifts to fathers consisted of shirts and ties and tended only to happen in collaboration with the latter's sisters (i.e., *joint* gifts) and then only on birthdays or at Christmas: lone male gift-giving was quite rare in the sample, and usually met with resistance, as we shall later discover. Compared to the relations discussed below, there was very little mutual borrowing or swapping of clothes between fathers and sons, whether their clothes tended to follow similar styles or not.

Father–daughter

There is also very little interaction between fathers and daughters in the area of clothing. Contemporary cases of fathers giving market gifts were extremely rare. Money tends to be provided, but this implies a different type of relationship. In the mother–daughter relation, there is a tendency for mothers to cease giving clothes and begin giving money, while fathers only ever give money.

Relations in the daughter-to-father direction were confined to market gifts (shirts, socks, ties) and stealing (cardigans, sweaters) but were not common in the sample.

Mother–son

Just two modes are involved in this, the single non-symmetrical relationship in the sample totally devoid of any form of reciprocity. To put it bluntly, mothers give and sons receive. Family-made gifts are more typical of mothers past making for children aged under 12, rarer for teenage boys or young men.

Where mothers cease to make direct purchases of clothing items for their daughters after a certain age (see below), most continue to do so in the case of their sons. Describing the items in his wardrobe, Jonas Robinson (22) frequently said that 'the ma gave me that' or 'that's a present from the ma', while his brother stated about his shirts that 'my mother probably bought them, I really don't know'. The rule to be followed seems to be: when in doubt about the origin of an item, assume it came from the mother.

In general, the evidence is that children of both genders receive clothes from the mother in the early years of life but it is only with sons that this initial relation is continued beyond the age of about 12 or 13.

Mother–daughter

Flows of clothing from daughter to mother are generally quite restricted. Market gift relations take place only on birthdays and at Christmas and are frequently joint presents from two sisters. It may be noted that daughters tend to give accessories rather than clothing to their mothers, scarves and gloves being particularly good examples of this.

Broadly speaking, there are two phases in the mother-to-daughter relation: an earlier one where the mother, her direct family or friends act as more or less exclusive sources of clothes, and a later one (after about 13) where daughters refuse clothes bought or made by the mother, sometimes begin to take clothes the mother acquired for herself, and almost invariably begin to swap clothes with non-familial girlfriends of their own age.

In all cases, a point came where the daughters would no longer accept clothes from the mother: 'They change completely after the confirmation' [which takes place at about 13 or 14 in Ireland]; 'now after the confirmation, then I had no hand or part'; 'after 13 or 14 they change completely' was how Sophie Kennedy (43) put it on several occasions, while Patricia Robinson (58) also stated that confirmation marked the last occasion she dressed her daughters. For most of the mothers in the sample, this transition point was the source of some problems. As this transition seems to be one of the central dress-related events in family life, it merits further illustration. The following example from Patricia is the most elaborated story, and may be taken as typical of the sample:

PC: What sorts of clothes do you give to your kids now as gifts, or would you at all?

PR: Well I'll be honest and say that I am afraid to buy a handkerchief, for any of the girls, and I really mean that now because if you bought as much as a handkerchief you'd find that the hem would be too narrow, or, there was a blue dot in it and they really would have preferred a red dot, and. I hate not being able to buy them, like for Christmas now I like to go into town, buy the present, have it as a surprise for Christmas, but there's no way I'd do that, because I wouldn't run the risk of them not liking it, and it's amazing what they don't like, little, what you think is lovely they can just, you know *by* them that they don't like it yih know. I remember buying a nightdress for Kerstin...just about two years ago now, and it was a grandfather style which she had said she would like, and I bought this in Clery's and I thought it was very nice, and it was expensive for a nightdress. And I gave it to her and I knew by her that, she wasn't so keen on it so I said to her well now if you don't like it, bring it back and you can get something instead of it. And eh, she went in to Clery's, and she didn't see anything she liked now even though Clery's is a big department store there was nothing in it, so I said to her well then *I'll* keep it and give it to somebody else and I'll give you the money and you can buy it for yourself. And she went off to town and she arrived home, full of enthusiasm, just got exactly what I wanted, and she opened the bag, what she took out was a shirt, a white shirt yih know with a sort of vaguely stiff in the front, which I think was second hand, that men used to wear them as dress shirts. And that's what she bought like, I'd say if I had got it for nothing I wouldn't've thought of buying it for her. So I never buy anything for the girls now, literally.

The stories illustrate the problems mothers face in coming to terms with the emergence of an independent understanding of the dressed world on the part of their daughters. This independent understanding comes about around the age of 13 in these families, and the mothers found it difficult to understand and accept. It was as if they were faced with a new conception of the world the logic of which they could not quite grasp.

Patricia's inability to give her daughters appropriate – as they would see it – gifts is dramatized by the supposed rejection of a handkerchief because of some small details that were 'wrong'. The implication would seem to be that if fault could be found with even such a tiny gift then there would be no point in even attempting a larger one. The example establishes different mother–daughter understandings of the meanings of dress in terms of disagreements over the appropriateness of small details such as narrow hems or blue dots: sophisticated analyses are made on both sides. Patricia clearly has difficulty in understanding the conceptual clashes between mother and daughters: 'it's amazing what they don't like'. She then illustrates this with a detailed example.

The story about Kerstin's nightdress begins with apparent coincidence of mother–daughter understandings: 'which she had said she would like'. The eventual gift is not appreciated, and Patricia suggests an exchange. This was unsuccessful, however. Not only was the gift of the mother rejected, but nothing suitable was found *anywhere* in the store the mother chose to visit to buy her that gift. Here, there is a typical daughterly rejection not only of the original gift, but also of all possible gifts that could be obtained from the site, which the mother thought of as an appropriate repository of possible gifts. In the end, Patricia is forced to offer money. Kerstin's subsequent purchase – that into which she transformed the money-gift of the mother – was 'exactly what I [Kerstin] wanted'. Patricia's reaction to this indicates complete lack of understanding of her daughter's version of the dressed world: 'I'd say if I had got it for nothing I wouldn't've thought of buying it for her'. This episode appears to mark the end of the mother's buying: 'so I never buy anything for the girls now, literally'.

Patricia has clearly been prevented by her daughter from making clothing purchases for the latter, and, although clearly hurt and a little puzzled, accepts the situation. It would seem that the independent attainment of daughterly understandings lies through the refusal of motherly gifts of clothing and the acceptance by the latter of their daughters' ways.

The shift to giving money rather than clothes seems to be a major component of the transition period, and the significance of this is discussed below.

The mothers' difficulties in accepting that their daughters have quite different accounts of the meanings of dress seem to be exacerbated by claims that their clothing-mediated relations with their *own* mothers were quite unproblematic. Patricia Robinson (58) maintained that there was 'no bone of contention' over apparel and that 'shopping [for clothes] with my mother was a pleasant experience'; while Sophie Kennedy (43) claimed that: 'anything that I ever wore *when* I was young I loved it yih know, even though maybe I hadn't got the choice of saying, em, I like this colour and I like that colour, the colour that was chosen for me I really loved it'. Claire Sheehan (31), whose own daughter (aged 10) has not yet reached the 'critical age', also said that she 'can't remember any disagreement with my mother over clothes'. There is a shift, then, from mother–daughter consensus to mother–daughter conflict. When the mothers interviewed were younger, mother–daughter understandings of dress were shared (more accurately, the mother's understanding was the only one in play). Now, mothers and daughters have different conceptualizations of the 'same' world. Although no conclusive evidence is available from the sample, I suspect that these difficulties are linked to the different implications for family relations implicit in the different technological states of clothing production and consumption at the time of the interviews as compared with the time the mothers interviewed were themselves teenage girls. When the mothers were that age, a much greater proportion of clothing, at least in Ireland, originated in family-based production, and where clothing was not family-made each family generally had their own dressmaker or tailor. Clothing, then, was much more under family control and mother/daughter disputes over the matter seemed rare. The much greater penetration of mass-produced items several decades later, however, means that a shift has taken place away from family-orientated clothing and towards clothing orientated to more abstract ideas of 'society'. Teenage girls now dress much more for society than for the family, and this is what caused most distress to the mothers.

What of the daughters' accounts of the above problems? Although considerably less expansive or articulate about the matter (from which one might deduce that the said matter caused few problems for them now), almost all confirmed that they did indeed now refuse to wear anything bought for them by their mothers. For example, Helena Cash (19) said that she 'never wanted to wear what her mother wanted to put her in' while Kerstin Robinson (20) said quite simply that 'my mother wouldn't buy clothes for me now because I wouldn't like them.' The refusal appears to have little or nothing to do with any concrete characteristic of the actual item that might be bought, so it would be reasonable to infer that the refusal is tied rather to the fact that the item of clothing was given by the mother. That is, the source of the gift and the subsequent relation between mother and daughter mediated by this gift – and not the gift itself as particular type of concretely existing object – lies at the base of the reason for refusal. This should be particularly clear after the analysis of Patricia's attempted nightdress-gift to Kerstin. Refusal of the motherly gift would certainly seem to mark the assertion of separate conceptualizations of the clothed world on the part of daughters.

Sister–sister

Sisterly clothing circulation patterns in the sample were found to fall into two quite distinct modes, each corresponding to a generational difference. Market gift relationships predominated among sisters who were themselves mothers, while teenage/young adult sisters – the daughters of these mothers – partook to a remarkably intense degree of the stealing mode of relating. Furthermore, market gift items were given only on birthdays or at Christmas (blouses, jumpers, scarves), while stealing (jackets, jumpers, scarves, shirts of various kinds), as we shall see, characterizes the everyday (quite literally everyday, in most cases) relations of the younger generation of sisters.

The degree of stealing from each other's wardrobes was considerably higher among sisters than in any other relationship, and appeared to take place quite regularly: at least weekly, with Kerstin Robinson (20) saying that 'we steal each other's clothes an awful lot' and Isabelle Kennedy (17) claiming that 'every single day I wear something belonging to my sister'. Indeed, the Cash, Kennedy and Robinson sisters were all wearing something (usually a jumper or blouse) belonging to the other a minimum of once during my series of interview sessions. Borrowing was quite rare in the sample, and sisters seemed almost never to ask each other's permission before taking an item of clothing. Stealing was in no case one-way, but always mutual: a negative reciprocal gift relationship. This was both balanced, with definite periods between theft and retaliation, and violent in its own way. In reply to my question about whether she ever failed to ask for her sister Niamh's (15) permission before taking one of her garments, Helena Cash (19) said:

HC: Yeh, and there's always war at the end of it, yih know.
PC: And would she do the same thing to you?
HC: Yeh just to get her own back. Like if I took this [a top of Niamh's she happened to be wearing at the time of the interview] without asking her she'd give out to me, I could always say don't forget last week or something you took something belonging to me, so it's kind of.

Not asking permission led to 'fights with Helena' (Niamh Cash); 'causes most fights in this house' (Isabelle Kennedy); while Anita Robinson (18) said that 'The worst rows in this house are over clothes'. Anita added that items were frequently taken 'in revenge', but her most elaborated story is the following:

PC: When was the last time you wore any of your sister's clothes?
AR: Today actually heh...
PC: ...what was it?
AR: It was just a jumper.
PC: Did she remark on it?
AR: She doesn't know...I take it when she goes out and I put it back before she comes back.
PC: Why is that?
AR: Because she'd kill me
PC: It sounds a bit extreme.
AR: I know, no she *would* go mad.
PC: Really?
AR: ...we always have *arguments* over it...
PC: Did you *often* take her clothes?
AR: Not that often, no, no...
PC: What about the time last time you *didn't* ask her permission and she saw you?

AR: She goes mad ... Well what she always does then is she picks something out of *mine* ... something that she knows ... that I don't really like giving her and she'd say, can I have that? And if I'd say no then she says well you took that, yih know ...

PC: This would be sometime later would it?

AR: Yeh, or. It could be a few weeks later, she'd always remember heh ...

Brother–brother

Compared to other clothing-mediated relationships, this one is not very intense, consisting only of cast-offs and borrowing. It is a rare example of the non-occurrence of market gifts. I have much less data on fraternal clothing relations because of the peculiarity of the sample, and none of it in elaborated form. Nevertheless, all indications are that they are not as intense as the sisterly relations described above. Boys, indeed, do not appear ever to serve as the source of clothing gifts, except in alliance with sisters when buying for parents on birthdays or at Christmas, and their wardrobes are more closed to each other: where sisters are continually stealing one another's clothes, brothers seem only to touch clothes the other no longer wears or, at most, ask permission to borrow for special occasions. Far from sisterly confusion, special efforts are sometimes made to uphold separation. So we have a strong contrast between individual male isolation and the passionate collectivity of the sisters.

Sister–brother

In general, there was very little active flow from brother to sister, while sisters gave (single or joint) gifts of clothes (jumpers, shirts) to brothers on the special occasions that are birthdays and Christmas.

Family members–outsiders

Although my research design was very family-centred and little attempt was made to go outside family boundaries, all evidence from the data indicates that clothing remains very much a 'family affair'. A form of reverse proof can be found in the two cases (Cashes, Robinsons) where a non-kin friend of the mother made clothes for the children: in each instance, she was called 'aunt' by the latter. Such a bestowal of fictive kinship would seem to be a way of overcoming the threat to the family implicit in a gift of clothing coming from the 'outside'. It is threatening precisely because, as we have seen, clothing circulation appears to take place almost exclusively within the family. This being so, an item from outside would imply that the giver was making some sort of claim to be part of the family – a claim that might or might not be acceptable, depending on the claimant. Generally speaking, fictive kinship can be seen as a way of solving the problems that arise when the relationship between A and B is characterized by practices that are seen as appropriate to a relationship between the two that is different to the 'officially' existing one. The officially existing relationship is re-defined:

> we may describe as fictive kinship the instances where persons who are related genealogically in one way adopt the forms of address and behaviour prescribed for a different relationship. This is commonly the case where their roles in a household have constrained the members to mutate their kin ties to conform with their mutual behaviour. (Pitt-Rivers, 1968: 409)

So in the case of the 'aunt' in our sample, she is so addressed because her dress-mediated behaviour is appropriate to that of a mother's sister. The use of fictive kinship to overcome potentially threatening situations is mentioned by Mintz and Wolf (1971 [1950]), while Esther Goody (1971: 344) sees it as a way of linking adults (the mothers and their friends in the present case) and generations (the Robinson/Cash daughters and their 'aunts').

Apart from this, only daughters seem to have definite dress relations with non-kin. They may shop for clothes with their girlfriends and borrow items from their respective wardrobes, but we do not normally find the negative reciprocity we came across in the case of sisters. Such dress-based alliances can disrupt the family clothing economy we have identified by breaking its exclusivity.

General model

In sum, the family clothing economy is organized along very clear gender lines. Women and girls are highly active (even though mother–daughter relations change over time), and men and boys highly passive: the latter, indeed, barely participate at all. The former are also highly active with respect to each other, and we can see very clearly that stealing is *the* typical sisterly mode. It is now time to consider our findings within a more general framework.

The gift relationship

In the case of apparel, as we have just seen, the flow of resources in the family turns out to be quite complex: family clothing circulation can be characterized in terms of six different modes, five of which can be classified as variant forms of the gift relationship. The exception, family-made commodity, occurred only very rarely. A review of the literature on the gift relationship is essential in order to understand the contribution our findings make to this specific field. Many of them are in accord with the literature, but question the accepted status of negative reciprocity. We begin, however, with a discussion of commodity relations, and then consider the implications of the buying and making of gifts, gifts of money, the balance of indebtedness and negative reciprocity.

Commodity relations

The rarity of commodity relations between kin has been remarked upon in the anthropological literature. Paul Bohannan and Laura Bohannan (1968: 147), for example, note that: 'Tiv agree with the almost universal dictum that people do not "sell" to kinsmen. Gift-giving relationships and exchange relationships are felt to be antithetical'; while Gregory Bateson (1958: 83) writes that 'like a father he [*wau*] avoids entering upon crudely commercial transactions with his *laua*'. The modern families in our sample appear to operate in a very similar manner. Chris Gregory (1982: 19) succinctly characterizes the gift/commodity distinction: 'commodity exchange establishes a relationship between the objects exchanged, whereas gift exchange establishes a relationship between the subjects'. Commodity exchange is object-dominated while gift-exchange is subject-dominated. The positions that can be taken up can be shown more clearly if we consider Gregory's further comment (1982: 43) that 'commodities are *alienable* objects transacted by aliens; gifts are *inalienable* objects transacted by non-aliens'. Clearly, any attempt by a family member to engage in commodity relations with another family member amounts to replacing family-based intersubjective relations with market-based objective ones. Of course, this can be interpreted as a way of escaping from the subjective relations of the family by treating other members in the same way as any non-kin exchange partner: thus may family ties be loosened.

Buying gifts/making gifts

In an early statement, Ralph Waldo Emerson distinguishes between two types of gift in the following terms:

> The only gift is a portion of thyself. Thou must bleed for me. Therefore the poet brings his poem; the shepherd, his lamb; the farmer, corn; the miner, a gem; the sailor, coral and shells; the painter, his picture; the girl, a handkerchief of her own sewing. This is right and pleasing, for it restores society in so far to the primary basis, when a man's biography is conveyed in his gift, and every man's wealth is an index of his merit. But it is a cold, lifeless business when you go to the shops and buy me something, which does not represent your life and talent, but a goldsmith's. (Emerson, 1890 [1844]: 130)

This distinction is very similar to the difference between market gift and family-made gift forms of circulation, with the former referring to items obtained on the market and the latter to garments made by a family member. There is a difference, however. Emerson's categories of true gift givers refer to the professional activities of poets, shepherds, farmers, miners, sailors, painters and seamstresses (even if he refuses to grant 'girl' the dignity of a professional title). His gifts are portions of a 'self' that is defined by particular competencies. However, there is nothing about, for example, 'brotherness' or 'sisterness' that would indicate the nature of gifts appropriate to these statuses. Emerson's true gifts display *social* standing and a tight fit between person and activity, but family gifts refer precisely to *family* relations and are therefore free of the person/activity coincidence. One could argue that family gifts *should* avoid the person/activity coincidence: giving a professional gift to a family member could be read as treating them as non-family. This would hold particularly on those occasions when the family: (a) celebrates itself as 'the Family' (Christmas), and (b) celebrates the anniversary of individual members' arrival in the family (birthdays). David Cheal (1988: 148) maintains that 'Christmas and birthdays are uniquely opportune times for staging the cult of the individual', but his analysis misses the familial dimension of these occasions. The same thing, however, does not hold for the case of mundane gifts, as these could be seen as part of the everyday professional activity of, say, the mother. This tends to be confirmed by the sample evidence: family-made gifts were quite rare at the time of the interviews, but were far more frequent when the children were young. Then, Patricia Robinson (58) and Sophie Kennedy (43) both knitted for their children on an everyday basis.

Emerson implies that gifts which do not form part of the self in his very specific understanding of the term are not 'true gifts'. Looked at abstractly, there is no reason for a coincidence between person and thing given to take the particular form indicated in the above citation. Once A gives B something, then a gift-mediated relationship is set up between the two. What matters from the point of view of establishing a relationship between the two parties is not the fact that one gives an object of one's own manufacture, but the fact that something is *given*. We have already seen this at work in our sample, when daughters refused gifts from the mother simply because they were given by her. Marcel Mauss (1969 [1925]: 18) mentions the 'confusion of personalities and things', and writes that 'in Maori custom this bond created by things is in fact a bond between persons, since the thing itself is a person or pertains to a person. Hence it follows that to give something is to give part of oneself' (Mauss, 1969 [1925]: 10). A thing can 'be a person' or pertain to a person without necessarily having been manufactured by that person. A gift is part of the self because one gives it, not because one has made it. Of course, certain items such as jumpers/sweaters or armshells (Malinowski, 1922) can become privileged objects in gift circulation, but that does not mean that they have to be manufactured by the giver.

From the above, it is clear that a gift that has been obtained on the market is no less a gift for all that. The transition of an object from being a commodity purchased on the market to being an object circulated as a gift within the family (market gifts – the most frequent in our sample) is by no means unusual or odd. Helen Codere (1968: 239–40) points out that 'for reciprocal gift giving to take place in industrial society, it is necessary for the donors to go into the market for the gifts they will exchange; even the crudest *Kindergarten Handarbeit* will have required for its manufacture some tool or material obtained in the market'; while Cheal (1987: 157) writes: 'In a society whose economic system is founded upon wage labour, the use of commodities as gifts is an economical practice that most people take for granted as the rational way of doing things.' One would gather from the above that market gift relations were peculiar to advanced industrial societies, but this is certainly not the case. It holds also for much simpler societies, as Maurice Godelier points out:

> when *entering or leaving* these societies, precious objects provisionally took the form of bartered commodities at fixed, or barely fluctuating prices. *Within* each society they usually ceased to circulate as commodities, and became objects to *give or distribute* in the social process of social life, kinship relations, relations of production and power, etc. (Godelier, 1977 [1973]: 128)

Gifts of money

We have seen that where gifts circulate *within* primitive societies (Godelier) or families (our sample), money comes into operation at *boundaries*: those between societies (Godelier) and between the family and the commodity economy (the sample). But money itself can become a gift, and indeed, according to Mary Douglas and Baron Isherwood (1978: 59), acts as a gift in our modern societies only within the family. There are dangers inherent in giving money, however:

> Only transactions for money have that character of a purely momentary relationship which leaves no traces, as is the case with prostitution. With the giving of money, one completely withdraws from the relationship; one has settled matters more completely than by giving an object, which, by its contents, its selection, and its use maintains a wisp of the personality of the giver. (Simmel, 1971 [1907]: 121)

In this sense, it resembles the dangers to the family inherent in family-made commodity relations.

If the giving of money sails uncomfortably close to the commodification of family relations, there is yet another factor at work. Barry Schwartz writes:

> the concrete Christmas present, especially chosen in terms of the personality of giver and receiver, is more specifically reflective of and incorporable into their respective life systems. To this extent, the giver of the Hannukah *gelt* inevitably surrenders to the recipient a measure of control because money, unlike a particular commodity, does not presume a certain life system: it may be used in any way and thus becomes a more flexible instrument of the possessor's volition. (Schwartz, 1967: 5)

It is precisely this aspect of money-as-gift that daughters, in particular, turned to their advantage in the sample. By their refusal to accept gifts of clothing from the mother after the age of 13, they forced the mother to give money instead, thereby gaining autonomy in terms of their own choices.

In other words, the peculiarity of money – the general equivalent of the commodity economy – as gift permits daughters to control their own clothing through making their own self-purchases on the market. But what is so undesirable about gifts of things other than the general equivalent? This question brings us to one of the major preoccupations of writers on the gift relationship.

The balance of indebtedness

Suppose that A gives B a gift. What are B's options? B can refuse the gift or accept the gift. If accepted, B can then make no return gift at all, return a similar gift, return an inferior gift or return a superior gift. The social implications of these choices are clearly indicated by George Homans:

> Should Other spurn the gift, he admits himself an enemy. Should he take it and make a fair return, he becomes a friend. But what if he takes it and fails to make a return? Since the man that makes a fair return is by that fact the giver's social equal – he has demonstrated his ability to provide equally rare and valuable rewards – the man that fails to do so confesses himself neither the giver's enemy nor his friend but his inferior. He loses status relative to the giver. What is more, he may, in becoming an inferior, become also a subordinate: the only way he can repay his debt may be to accept the orders of the giver. (Homans, 1961: 319)

Let us begin with refusals to accept a gift. For Homans, this amounts to making oneself an enemy, a position shared by Mauss (1969 [1925]: 11): 'To refuse to give, or to fail to invite, is – like refusing to accept – the equivalent of a declaration of war; it is a refusal of friendship and intercourse'.

In the sample of families investigated, refusals to accept gifts of clothing were very typical of daughters' relations with mothers and very rare in all the other cases. On this interpretation, daughters 'declare war' on the mother as giver of clothing – quite successfully, as we have seen.

There are also risks involved in accepting a gift. Once accepted, a gift creates a relation of indebtedness between the giver and the receiver so long as no gift is returned. Alvin Gouldner (1960: 174) puts it thus: 'between the time of Ego's provision of a gratification and the time of Alter's repayment, falls the shadow of indebtedness'. Before considering the problems inherent in this relationship of indebtedness, let us look at a problem *absence* of indebtedness poses.

If B immediately returns A's gift with one exactly equivalent then the 'shadow of indebtedness' has no time to fall. However, 'If neither side is "owing" then the bond between them is comparatively fragile. But if accounts are not squared, then the relationship is maintained by virtue of "the shadow of indebtedness," and there will have to be further occasions of association, perhaps as occasions for further payment' (Sahlins, 1974: 222). Schwartz refers to

> the rule which prohibits an equal-return 'payment' in gift exchange. This suggests that every gift-exchanging dyad (or larger group) is characterized by a certain

'balance of debt' which must never be brought into equilibrium... The continuing balance of debt – now in favor of one member, now in favor of the other – insures that the relationship between the two continue, for gratitude will always constitute a part of the bond linking them. (Schwartz, 1967: 8)

Absence of indebtedness has similar effects to commodity relations (family-made commodity in the sample) and the giving of money: it leads to the weakening of subjective relations between the actors involved. Just like commodities and money, then, it is basically an *economic* rather than a *social* relationship: 'a perfect level of distributive justice is typical of the economic rather than the social exchange relationship' (Schwartz, 1967: 8). Some sort of 'balance of debt' is needed to uphold social relations between actors. There are nevertheless dangers and risks in this too, as we shall now see.

The 'balance of debt' referred to by Schwartz can easily reach exaggerated forms and eventually become unilateral. This is most clearly seen in the case of potlatch, which is a form of competitive giving. The first gift is a challenge that can only be overcome by the return of a greater gift (obviously, such a challenge cannot be met by the return of an inferior gift):

Whole cases of candle-fish or whale oil, houses, and blankets by the thousand are burnt; the most valuable coppers are broken and thrown into the sea to level and crush a rival; The only way to demonstrate his [the chief's] fortune is by expending it to the humiliation of others, by putting them 'in the shadow of his name'. (Mauss, 1969 [1925]: 35; 37–8)

But what happens if a person cannot answer a potlatch challenge? Mauss (1969 [1925]: 41): 'The person who cannot return a loan or potlatch loses his rank and even his status of a free man.' But this holds for all cases where a return gift is impossible:

'Gifts make slaves', the Eskimos say, 'as whips make dogs'... generosity is a manifest imposition of debt, putting the recipient in a circumspect and responsive relation to the donor during all that period the gift is unrequited. The economic relation of giver-receiver is the political relation of leader-follower. (Sahlins, 1974: 133)

In general, then, the gift relationship is one in which power struggles are inherent – not just the extreme case of potlatch, but *all* gift relations. Yet much of the anthropological literature maintains that power aspects of the gift have no place in *family* relations, an assertion that must be questioned: 'Intra-clan gift giving is governed by altogether different principles. The principle that the giver is superior does not operate here' (Gregory, 1982: 52). Marshall Sahlins (1974: 193) refers to this as 'generalized reciprocity', and finds its ideal type in what Bronislav Malinowski called 'pure' or 'free' gifts: 'an act, in which an individual gives an object or renders a service without expecting or getting any return... The most important type of free gift are the presents characteristic of relations between husband and wife, and parents and children' (Malinowski, 1922: 177). But even if it is true that the person giving has no expectation of return, this does not rule out the power dimension: dominance is all the greater where no return can come. The latter certainly seems to play a part for the teenage daughters of the present sample: why else would they refuse gifts of clothing from the mother, if not to put an end to the motherly dominance of the clothing economy? The potlatch response – returning a greater gift – does not seem to be operative, as it implies an acceptance of the mutual relations implied in gift exchange. The teenage girls set up their *own* dress economies through the overthrow of the mother as source of clothing gifts and with the help of money.

Far from the family being free of the power struggle implied in the gift relationship, we can see the unilateral clothes gifts of the mother as one of its elementary forms. Sahlins (1974: 205) rather hesitantly seems to admit something like this: 'Often, in fact, high rank is only secured or sustained by o'ercrowning generosity: the material advantage is on the subordinate's side. Perhaps it is too much to see the relation of parent and child as the elemental form of kinship ranking and its economic ethic'. As this chapter has shown, it is by no means 'too much'.

Negative gifts

So far, we have treated the gift as positive. But gifts in negative form are also possible: Sahlins refers to this as 'negative reciprocity', and we can recognize it as the stealing we frequently met among the sisters in the sample. He discusses this form in detail:

> 'Negative reciprocity' is the attempt to get something for nothing with impunity...The span of social distance between those who exchange conditions the mode of exchange. Kinship distance...is especially relevant to the form of reciprocity. Reciprocity is inclined toward the generalized pole by close kinship, towards the negative extreme in proportion to kinship distance.

> The reasoning is nearly syllogistic. The several reciprocities from freely bestowed gift to chicanery amount to a spectrum of sociability, from sacrifice in favor of another to self-interested gain at the expense of another...close kin tend to share, to enter into generalized exchanges, and distant or nonkin to deal in equivalents or in guile. (Sahlins, 1974: 195, 196)

However, the 'nearly syllogistic' reasoning does not seem to be operative in the case of the family: stealing does *not* correspond to increasing kinship distance. Indeed, it is hard to imagine a closer kinship relation than sister–sister, a relation characterized more than any of the others precisely by stealing practices. Stealing among sisters, as we have seen, is not unilateral but reciprocal and thereby the exact negative image of the exchange of gifts familiar to anthropology. Where the latter is a means of binding persons (usually strangers to each other) but upholding their difference, the former is a means of binding persons (already kin-related, at least in the present case) through *abolishing* difference. It is not that kin steal from one another as a matter of course (brothers, for example, were found never to do so), but rather that reciprocal stealing among kin constructs their relationship in a particular way. To put this more generally: rather than looking upon family relations as determining particular forms of clothing gifts and circulation, we can look upon the latter as continually establishing and re-establishing intra-familial relations in different ways, depending on the mode and persons involved at any given time. The ceremonial market gifts of Christmas can now be seen as a way of binding family members *as if* they were strangers needing to be related through positive gifts. Ceremonial gifts bestowed on birthdays are somewhat different: they take the form of unilateral gifts from various family members to the one celebrating her or his birthday. 'The Family' here reminds one member that *it* is the dominant one.

Conclusion

The parallels between simpler societies and the contemporary family appear to be quite striking in their frequency, and we can see that the family can usefully be considered in terms more usually associated with 'primitive' exchange. At first sight, it might seem surprising that such an economy should be thriving in the midst of a contemporary capitalist society, but the more the public world is seen as the arena in which production is accomplished and the more the private family world is treated as the area in which consumption takes place, the more likely the development of two distinct economic forms. Once a commodity crosses the border from the outside world to the family, it is susceptible to insertion into a gift-based economy. But why a gift-based economy? Why not, for example, a family economy based on individual consumption? Perhaps the answer can be found in Gregory's remark that 'the concept commodity, which presupposes reciprocal independence and alienability, is a mirror image of the concept gift, which presupposes reciprocal dependence and inalienability' (Gregory, 1982: 24). If we divide our world into private and public parts, then it is not so surprising that the economic forms of these worlds should be 'mirror images' of each other.

It would appear that the familial gift economy is also a women's economy, a point noted by Cheal (1987; 1988) and many of the papers in the Brannen and Wilson (1987) collection. Indeed, male passivity is striking. The only 'successful' male gifts were those given in alliance with sisters, a pattern that appears to be valid both cross-culturally and for items other than clothing: in Winnipeg, 'The usual pattern of male giving consists of collaboration with a close female relative who does most of the gift work' (Cheal, 1988: 29). But there would appear to be a difference between the circulation of food and the circulation of clothing: Delphy (1984 [1975]), Sen (1984) and Charles and Kerr (1987) all show how women tend to lose out in food distribution, but indications are that it is men who lose out in the clothing economy. It may be that this is linked to traditional notions of men as substance (food) and women as appearance (clothing). Nevertheless, it seems as if there might be a number of economies at work in the contemporary household, each benefiting specific genders and ages in different ways. Recognition by men that the family clothing economy is an overwhelmingly female area may explain mothers' continued, and generally uncontested, giving to sons. Recognition by women that this is so may account both for mother–daughter conflict and for the less obviously explicable mutual sisterly stealing. If this economy is feminine, then each woman would seem to need to attain her own independent control over it: hence mother–daughter conflict. But where teenage and young adult sisters attempt to differ from their mothers, it would seem as if they lay claim to the same understandings as each other: hence, the other's clothing cannot be seen as entirely independent and stealing seems a perfectly 'natural' thing to do. That this is interpreted by sisters in conflictual terms may be due to the violations of notions of the individual wardrobe that this entails.

This chapter has considered the clothing–family relation from the point of view of clothing as a circulating object. We have seen how clothing circulation 'constructs' family relations, and that particularly crucial clothing-mediated relations are those between mother and daughter.

But the circulation of clothing and related goods is not necessarily restricted to the family. What happens when a group of people interested in fashion and dress find each other through the Internet? The next chapter explores this question.

6

Gift, Circulation and Exchange II: Clothing and Fashion in Cyberspace

We have just seen how clothing as object marks, upholds and undermines relations within the intimate domain of the family. What of appearances in the new realm of strangers that has come into being in the virtual world of the Internet? The same notions of gift, circulation and exchange structure relations in this world, too. The bulk of this chapter presents an analysis – a cyberethnography, if you will – of an Internet newsgroup called alt.fashion, but first we address the bigger picture of clothing-related newsgroups in general.

Although there are many newsgroups where clothing might be an issue in terms of content, such as (at the moment of writing this sentence) the 5 devoted to the posting of pictures of cheerleaders or any of the 432 with the word 'erotica' in their names, restricting the sample to those with a specific link in their titles to some aspect of dress promised a tighter focus on the topic. Newsgroups primarily devoted to the posting of images were excluded, as were fetish groups and those dedicated to the craft aspects of dress. The idea was to search for general rather than specialized talk on the subject as this was considered to be more likely to lead to the discovery of groups with broad internal differentiations. These are, of course, more likely to lend themselves to a greater variety of social processes and are thus more interesting for the sociologist or anthropologist looking for the elementary structures of online life. A search of all English-language groups carried out on 23 October 1999 showed 15 that, by their titles and by the criteria already mentioned, showed a concern with dress. The newsgroups were revisited on 11 April 2000 and 5 July 2006 to obtain updated statistics on the number of posts mailed to each group, and Table 6.1 details in descending order of the 2000 data the numbers that appeared in a period of approximately two weeks up to and including those dates (they are not normally kept on the server for longer periods). Groups that did not show a minimum of ten posts in each of the sampling periods were excluded. The total number of posts across all relevant groups was 11,474 in 2000 and 8,169 in 2006. Only alt.fashion and alt.gothic.fashion show a substantial number of posts, and alt.fashion is far ahead of alt.gothic.fashion: 2.6 times as many posts in 2000 and over six times as many in 2006. Alt.fashion – produced similar numbers of posts in both sampling periods: 6,819 in 2000 and 6,161 in 2006.

Table 6.1 *Messages posted in clothing-related newsgroups sampled April 2000 and July 2006*

Newsgroup	2000 (N)	2006 (N)	2000 (%)	2006 (%)
alt.fashion	6,819	6,161	59.4	75.4
alt.gothic fashion	2,604	972	22.7	11.9
alt.society.underwear	641	98	5.6	1.2
alt.support.crossdressing	532	395	4.6	4.8
alt.fashion.crossdressing	322	189	2.8	2.3
alt.lycra	248	101	2.2	1.2
alt.clothing.lingerie	58	30	0.5	0.4
ncu.bbs.fashion	54	26	0.5	0.3
alt.supermodels	53	18	0.5	0.2
alt.clothing	32	33	0.3	0.4
alt.clothes.designer	30	15	0.3	0.2
alt.clothing.sneakers	26	51	0.2	0.6
alt.fashion.corsetry	23	10	0.2	0.1
alt.culture.underwear	17	12	0.1	0.1
alt.fashion.men	15	58	0.1	0.7
Total	11,474	8,169	100.0	100.0

The alt.fashion newsgroup

Alt.fashion was founded on 26 May 1992 by Steve Frampton, whose final post on 13 May 1994 contained the words 'This group is deteriorating from its intended purpose. 'Nuff said'. The original charter was posted by Steve on 4 October 1992 and stated:

> This group will be used for the discussion of the art and business of fashion, including design, illustration, marketing, tailoring, consulting, manufacturing, as well as many other fields.

> This group will deal with diverse topics such as design illustration, textiles and fabrics, pattern making, alterations, history of costume, target markets, colour story [themes], famous designers and their collections, fashion magazines, celebrity designs, and manufacturing techniques & equipment (including new CAD/CAM methods), fashion modeling, as well as any fashion-related topic that is of interest.

> People are encouraged to participate if they have any interest in the fashion world, whether they be fashion professionals, celebrities, students, or hobbyists. (http://groups.google.com/group/alt.fashion/browse_thread/thread/9da8bf7b 18e82d7c/eaf7021ab5794a02?hl=en#eaf7021ab5794a02)

As we shall see, the group took on a life of its own that has relatively little to do with the industry slant of the charter and much more to do with people creating community, relating through descriptions of what they are wearing and exchanging gifts.

Table 6.2 charts the number of threads posted between 1992 and 2005 based on an analysis of data produced by the Google Groups search facility. Note that these figures refer to threads, not posts: there are many more

Table 6.2 *Threads posted in alt.fashion 1992–2005*

Year	1992	1993	1994	1995	1996	1997	1998	1999	2000	2001	2002	2003	2004	2005
Threads (N)	153	400	1,610	1,510	31,900	48,100	51,100	60,900	88,800	126,000	171,000	215,000	79,000	36,800

posts than threads. Up to 31 December 2005 the group had produced 912,273 threads and many millions of individual posts.

All messages found on this group between 12 and 27 October 1999; a total of 7,355 posts, posted from 626 different participants, were downloaded. This is an immense amount of data in the context of the qualitative approaches generally preferred by the author, and so a number of principles were drawn upon to make the analytical task more feasible. The very off-topic *word association football test* thread, cross-posted across many groups, was removed, and all threads with fewer than ten posts and three participants were discounted. This increased the chances of discovering the central concerns of the group as a whole as well as reducing the numbers to more manageable proportions. A total of 585 posters and 4,286 messages remained. The 585 posters represent over 93 per cent of the original 626, so they may reasonably be considered as the core of the newsgroup. These posters and messages provide the data for the following analysis.

At no stage did I post to the group or contact its members. The following is, then, an observational study of, rather than a participative study in, what is a public space (anybody with a computer and Internet connection can look here). But just as those who are observed in public spaces are often quite anonymous, it seems appropriate to anonymize the identities of the newsgroup members. In a sense, the posters are anonymous already as only a bare 20 per cent used the form 'given name plus surname', and there is no guarantee that even these bore any necessary correspondence to the 'real life' names of the posters. As Richard MacKinnon (1997: 207) points out, 'Life online is lived through the personae of the users of technology, not the users themselves.' But each persona tends to take on a life of its own and become what Tim Jordan (1999: 59) calls a 'stable online personality'. Poster names are not anonymous in the context of cyberspace, then, but are more 'real' here than any conventionally 'real' name because this is their proper space. 'Real' names and poster names belong to different realms of existence, but both may continue over time and thus accurately designate ongoing identities in their respective dimensions (see Harley, 2000, for an extensive discussion of what she terms 'polynymity'). I follow Susan Zickmund's (1997) example and use the convention User 1, User 2, etc., instead of actual poster names. Unfortunately, this means that the wit, elegance, invention and humour of many poster names are lost behind rather prosaic designations.

Demographic details of participants

Before analysing the contents of the newsgroup, it may be useful to consider the question of the sorts of people involved in this virtual social space. In other words: to whom does this social space belong? Demographic details are less reliable than one might wish, as it is easily possible to present oneself virtually as an identity that may bear little or no relationship to one's non-virtual self. Location needs to be treated as apparent and gender and age as presented.

Apparent location

Location was determined through the national domain of the e-mail address (e.g., addresses of the type *.sg are located in Singapore) or, in its absence, by clues internal to the messages. This still left an initial 362 unknown locations representing almost 62 per cent of the total. Messages hosted by the two major providers, namely aol.com (America on Line) and my-deja.com, were examined more closely. It was discovered that of the 220 aol.com posters 166 were of unknown location, 54 were found in the USA and none in any other country; while in the case of the 60 my-deja.com e-mailers 48 were unknown, 10 were in the USA and 2 in other countries. These proportions were extended to the unknowns in each case, such that all aol.com posters and 83.3 per cent of the 48 unknowns at my-deja.com were now assumed to be located in the USA. A similar logic was applied to the number of posts. This reduced the number of unknown locations to 156. These had no country identifier, which makes it very likely, although not certain, that the great majority were also located in the USA since that country does not use a specific national domain (any more than does the UK in the case of postage stamps: in both instances, the country which first used a new form of communications technology saw no need to indulge in the irrelevancy of particularist namings of itself. The side-effect of this, however, is that countries that follow the technology next and wish to work on the international level are indeed obliged to name themselves, becoming marked terms with respect to the originators. The unmarked appears as universal, which is presumably why some Australian and British enterprises with global aspirations try to ensure that they are registered as simple *.com rather than *.com.au or *.co.uk companies. A similar logic seems to hold for some e-mail providers, hence the impossibility of simply claiming that *all* *.com addresses are located in the USA).

Table 6.3 shows the distribution of posters and posts according to location. Clearly, participants in this newsgroup are to be found located in the USA in considerably greater numbers than anywhere else, and they also post more messages (77.8 per cent of the total) than their proportion of all posters (64.4 per cent) would suggest. A general study of the national domains of posters to the net made by Marc Smith (1999: 197) also showed that the USA housed by far the greatest proportion of posters (40.69 per cent of all users), with Taiwan in second place (5.65 per cent) and Germany third (2.21 per cent). All posts to the present group were in English, however, which should shift the figures a little towards Anglophone lands. Even so, the combined totals of the other major English-speaking countries of Australia, Canada and the UK are very similar in this newsgroup and on the net as a whole: 5 and 4.53 per cent of posters respectively. Varying levels of Internet accessibility across different territories no doubt play a part in

Table 6.3   *Apparent location of posters and apparent origin of posts*

Location	Posters (N)	Posters (%)	Posts (N)	Posts (%)
USA	377	64.4	3,336	77.8
Unknown	156	26.7	658	15.4
Canada	11	1.9	68	1.6
UK	10	1.7	38	0.9
Australia	8	1.4	47	1.1
Singapore	5	0.9	30	0.7
Germany	4	0.7	6	0.1
Norway	3	0.5	11	0.3
Indonesia	2	0.3	29	0.7
Korea	2	0.3	13	0.3
Sweden	2	0.3	22	0.5
Europe	1	0.2	9	0.2
Greece	1	0.2	1	0.0
Ireland	1	0.2	1	0.0
New Zealand	1	0.2	12	0.3
Spain	1	0.2	5	0.1
Total	585	100.0	4,286	100.0

Table 6.4   *Presented gender*

Presented gender	Posters (N)	Posters (%)	Posts (N)	Posts (%)
Presents as F	451	77.1	3,676	85.8
Unknown	95	16.2	271	6.3
Presents as M	39	6.7	339	7.9
Total	585	100.0	4,286	100.0

shaping these figures, as may more cultural questions about the appropriate place of virtual communities in different socio-interactional formations (i.e., 'societies' understood as interactional entities).

Presented gender

The presented gender of each poster was determined either through first names where available (read entirely conventionally) or through clues internal to the messages. It was not assumed that descriptions of cosmetics such as lipsticks or nail varnish being worn that day were sufficient for gender allocation, but it was assumed that references such as 'my husband' indicated a female poster. Table 6.4 shows the distribution of presented gender. Overwhelmingly, this newsgroup presents as a feminine space.

Presented age

There were considerably fewer data on presented age to be found during the sampling period, and it was possible to determine this only in the cases

Table 6.5 *Presented age*

Presented age	% May–July 1998 (N = 133)	% October 1999 (N = 42)	% March–April 2001 (N = 72)
12–19	22.6	21.4	9.7
20–29	36.8	45.2	33.3
30–39	24.1	14.3	18.1
40–49	12.8	11.9	25.0
50–59	3.0	7.1	11.1
60–69	0.8	0.0	1.4
70–79	0.0	0.0	0.0
80–89	0.0	0.0	1.4
Total	100.0	100.0	100.0

of 42 posters. Poster age was presented in the body of many messages in the threads *Fragrance and age* and *Ignoring the young*, but was otherwise not a routine declaration. It was therefore decided to search outside the sampling period for further information. The threads <*{(Age Check)}*>, which ran from 21 May to 11 July 1998, and *How old are you?*, which ran from 28 March to 7 April 2001, provided respectively 133 and 72 informative responses. Table 6.5 compares the results from 1998, 1999 and 2001. In all cases, the single biggest group consists of the 20–29 age range. The 1999 figures are likely to be 'younger' than the others given that it is likely that more younger than older members would participate in the *Ignoring the young* thread, but there is no reason for such a bias in the other data. The group seems to be getting older on average, with 39 per cent over 40 in 2001 compared to less than half that earlier. No doubt this is due partly to the ageing of the core members, but also the ever-expanding access to a medium once associated more with college age people than anyone else. Nevertheless, the group is still clearly more young than old. It is certainly adult, though.

Overall, then, the figures suggest a newsgroup composed primarily of young(ish) adult women located in the USA. But what do the posters post?

Analysis of message contents

Where possible, each thread was assigned to the general concept that seemed best to match the particular topic under discussion. Table 6.6 indicates the results of this exercise, listing each concept in descending order of frequency of posts. Only those concepts that could be linked to a minimum of 100 posts are listed, as this increases the chances of discovering the core newsgroup concepts. Two threads comprising 285 posts have been counted in both Todayness and Economy as they seemed equally relevant to each. Even after adjusting the figures for this, the relatively small number of key concepts still account for almost exactly half of all posts in the final sample. The remaining 114 threads represent two thirds of threads but only about half of the posts.

Perhaps the most striking aspect of Table 6.6 is that it reveals a large number of concepts that we have already met in quite different places in

Table 6.6 *Key concepts in threads*

Concept	Threads (N)	Posts (N)
Todayness	9	745
Economy/exchange	9	452
Favourites	13	386
Poll/survey	15	288
Body size	2	220
Community	5	186
Necessity	2	108
Total	55	2,385

this book: community shares utopias' interests in what makes a society, todayness is obviously a form of temporality, economy and exchange were last looked at in the context of the family, and the body is again prominent. This newsgroup, then, seems to confirm the aliveness of the concepts discussed in earlier chapters to a virtual fashion community today.

Community

Howard Rheingold (1993: Introduction) has described 'computer-mediated social groups' as 'virtual communities', and that term, as we shall see, fits alt.fashion very well. All of the posts can be considered as contributing to the construction of a community in one way or another through the generalized exchange of messages. Posters are more or less prominent in the community: there are regular posters, occasional posters and an unknown number of 'lurkers' who read the messages but do not post (until their moment of 'delurking', if it ever comes). It should be noted, however, that the community will not necessarily appear the same to all posters: the killfile option available in some newsreaders allows one to make the community appear to be composed only of those one wishes to let in through the screening-out of messages from posters one has come to consider undesirable. To some degree, then, one can now customize community membership according to one's desires. Perhaps the path to the ideal (virtual) society is paved with killfile decisions. The posts considered here have not been filtered through killfiles and represent what those not using this option have received.

Table 6.7 lists the participation levels per poster in the group as a whole, and shows that they may roughly be broken up into four groups. Over one third posted a single message, almost 45 per cent posted between two and nine, there is a smaller third group of almost one sixth who posted between ten and twenty nine, and a very much smaller fourth group (4.44 per cent) who posted over thirty each, one of the latter posting 162 messages in total during the 16 days under consideration. This tiny group was responsible for 34 per cent of all postings in the sample. In terms of sheer volume of

Table 6.7   *Participation levels per poster*

Messages per poster	Posters (N)	Posters (%)
1	201	34.4
2–9	263	45.0
10–19	69	11.8
20–29	26	4.4
30–39	8	1.4
40–49	7	1.2
50–59	5	0.9
60–69	2	0.3
70–79	1	0.2
80–89	1	0.2
90–99	0	0.0
> 100	2	0.3
Total	585	100.0

Table 6.8   *Community threads*

Thread	Posts (N)
Blah mood fixes??	67
give me strength	49
This newsgroup and its posters…	44
Curious… what's a troll?	14
AF ALERT: Proof 'User 534' is a TROLL	12
Total	186

messages, then, there certainly appears to be a marked stratification from the postings-rich to the postings-poor.

That, however, is not really the aspect of community that interests us here. For the purposes of this section, only those posts that explicitly reflect upon the nature of and/or actively construct the group as a community will be considered. Instead of an external description of the community as provided above, the aim here is to explore how the participants themselves see their peculiar form of groupness. Table 6.8 lists the threads relevant to this concept. The thread names are furnished here and in subsequent sections in order to allow interested readers to check the contents for themselves through searches on archiving sites.

One way of looking at the community-creating side of a newsgroup is to see if there are any off-topic threads that are silently deemed appropriate to the group through the absence of any comment on the inappropriateness of the thread (such as accusing the poster of trolling – see below for a discussion). Such a thread can provide us with a group-approved answer to the question 'what sort of group are we, aside from our shared interest in fashion?' The large *Blah mood fixes??* thread was provoked by 'Is there anything that helps you get out of a really dull dreary mood?' (User 481), the replies having little to do with fashion but much to do with medication, light, domestic pets, being with others, types of food and watching comedy films. The group proposes itself as prepared to help lift the depressed mood of one of its members – and, indeed, of all of its members with the same problem, as the suggestions are posted to everyone. The group, then, cares for the state of its members, even though they may never have met.

The generally positive construction of the group is continued in the thread *This newsgroup and its posters...*, and was initiated by the message

> Just wanted to say that this group, and the people who lurk and post here, are AWESOME. This is THE BEST source of info for makeup and fashion. Every time I post a question, I get many helpful answers. Thanks, alt.fashion. :-)
>
> [firstname] (hoping that didn't sound cheesy) (User 128)

Six replies enthusiastically agree, while most of the rest 'do' community by picking up not on the praise but on the 'cheesy' comment and swapping stories about fondue sets. Again, there is the use of evidently off-topic material for social solidaristic purposes, material apparently acceptable to the group (there was only one very gentle suggestion that it might be off-topic, but even here the poster amusingly attempted to relate cheese to fashion). The group constructs itself here as a very polite society indeed, with praise accepted in an understated way through the humorous deflection of the discussion onto the original poster's slightly uncertain appreciation of his/her own post.

But not all is sweet harmony in the alt.fashion garden, for this group is alert to the threatening existence of the typical newsgroup enemy: the troll. The thread *Curious...what's a troll?* produced this definition: 'A troll is someone who says something controversial to stir up trouble. Frequently they don't believe what they say; they're just trying to get the greatest response' (User 208).

There is an understanding, then, that on the one hand there are good-faith authentic posters who are 'true' members of the group and on the other there are bad-faith inauthentic posters whose aim is to cause trouble among the 'true' members. There is a problem in identifying trolls, however, as not everyone is troll-sensitized: 'unsuspecting souls get sucked in and respond to Trollish drivel as if it were normal language. This is why some of us sometimes jump in and point out "This is a troll. The post is bogus. Do Not Feed The Troll"' (User 169).

User 169 proposes a tripartite division in the newsgroup community: trolls, 'unsuspecting souls' who do not recognize trolls, and 'some of us' who recognize and warn about them. But there appears to be no clearly unambiguous way of distinguishing 'Trollish drivel' from 'normal language' except through some sort of unspecified expertise or experience and one always runs the risk of 'mak[ing] a mistake and call[ing] an innocent person a troll' (User 135).

It should be pointed out that the troll-as-enemy is not a universal among newsgroups. Michele Tepper's (1997) study of alt.folklore.urban shows how trolling is used deliberately by group members to distinguish between those who are really 'in' the group and those who are not: the latter will innocently 'bite' on the trollish bait which is laid down by the insiders and clearly visible to them as such. In Tepper's words, trolling 'works both as a game and a method of subcultural boundary demarcation' (1997: 40). But alt.fashion's line on trolling defines it as an inclusive and welcoming group of non-trollers who do not try to humiliate or exclude others. This does not, however, prevent insiders from distinguishing themselves in coded ways. A simple way to demonstrate long-term membership is for the group to institutionalize the use of deliberate misspellings that may originally have been simple typos. To take Tepper's examples from alt.folklore.urban, ' "veracity" is spelled "voracity", and "co-worker" has become "cow orker" ' (1997: 46). For alt.fashion, 'panty' is spelled 'pnaty' (as in 'pnatyhose') – apparently an ironic reference to earlier trolling attempts by those with only one hand available for QWERTY keyboard duties. The generally anti-troll tone of alt.fashion is neatly demonstrated again, with trolls being turned into figures of ridicule (while at the same time posters demonstrate membership by displaying insider knowledge).

The sample provides a case study of the problems in deciding whether a post(er) is a troll or not in the thread *give me strength*. The thread began with a post from User 374 that is too long to reproduce here (see http://groups. google.com/group/alt.fashion/browse_thread/thread/e6a23e9e369255c3/a a1405054a30b61a?hl=en#aa1405054a30b61a if interested), but was rather insulting about the customers who came into his clothing shop. It provoked discussions about two fundamental characteristics of virtual community life: first, whether there is a structure of privilege such that a post by a (labelled rather than self-proclaimed) member of a particular category variously referred to as the 'oldbies', a 'clique', a 'select few' or an 'elite' is evaluated for trollishness differently than a post from someone who does not consider him/herself a member of such a class, and, second, whether trollishness resides in the post or the poster.

The first highly negative reaction to the post set the tone for much of what followed:

> what a bunch of hypocrites the alt.fashion oldbies are! if anyone other than one of the clique had written User 374's post, you would be flaming their preparation-h a** right now. and accusing him of being a troll, too! how about a little consistency people!!! (User 84)

The implicit argument here is that length of time ('oldbies') gives rise to a sense of groupness and that this groupness grants certain rights over those who have not done their time (even if the length of time it takes to become an 'oldbie' is by no means obvious). Although the link between time served and special privileges is denied by some ('There is no "clique" on a.f. There are simply people who have participated for a longer or a shorter length of time' [User 169]), there can hardly be a doubt that time served together in almost any context will lead to the emergence of sense of belonging to a recognizable social cell. The time may range from a brief service interaction between strangers to many years working in the same institution, and the group may be harmonious, riven with internal divisions, loosely structured, highly structured, strongly internally differentiated, weakly internally differentiated, or any mixture of these – it does not matter. Time furthermore allows for the accrual of privileges to some, even if only by virtue of experience and demonstrated commitment. If the group is as democratic of access as an unmoderated newsgroup (anyone anywhere with a computer, and Internet connection can post), then length of time in the group becomes one of the relatively few ways in which privilege may be obtained. Newsgroups are *not* like those MUDs studied by Elizabeth Reid (1999: 110) that are characterized by their clearly distinguished grades of membership and accompanying privileges ranging from God to Guest by way of Wizard, Privileged User, Basic User (social) and Basic User (adventure). In alt.fashion, experience and long-term commitment to the group mark the oldbies off from the newbies, and the fact that time has been served *together* greatly increases the likelihood that the oldbies will indeed treat each other differently than they will the newbies: they 'know' each other. Indeed, exactly this argument has been used to defend the original post:

'anyone who's read a.f. for a while knows User 374's opinions on this subject and can remember long and thoughtful discussions of this he has posted' (User 13); 'I can't imagine why anyone would think that User 374 is a troll <snip> All you had to do was do a Deja search under User 374's name to see that he posts here all the time, and has for a long time' (User 363)

User 363 seems to suggest that it is actually a *duty* of newbies to do an archive search in order to check a poster's oldbie status, and therefore presumably 'respect' it. The oldbie/newbie difference is obviously not peculiar to alt.fashion, and Judith Donath (1999: 44) has noted the special treatment given to high status participants elsewhere in cyberspace.

The double standards pointed out by User 84 in her complaint about a lack of consistency are echoed by others who do not accept that anyone deserves special treatment, the most pithy version coming from User 443: 'God forbid you or I would have said something that crass-we'd be crispy critters in no time!'. For the oldbies, the central question is the poster: 'Since he's User 374, I'll cut him some slack' (User 363). For those who do not consider they belong to this group, the central question is the post, and they do not understand why User 374 (or anyone else) should be cut some slack: 'this is the part that confuses me' was User 221's reaction to that suggestion. Newbies by definition lack a history in the group, and therefore see the contents of a post as the primary phenomenon towards which one orientates: poster names would not have any particular temporally accrued resonances at this stage. Oldbies have a sense of the history of the group and 'know' the posters, therefore seeing the identity of the poster as the primary orientational phenomenon. Putting this more simply, the newbies want to know what is written and the oldbies want to know who writes. User 363's suggestion to do an archive search indicates that an orientation to the 'who writes?' question is a sign of 'proper' group membership. The different temporal statuses of different posters, then, lead to quite different ways of orientating to the newsgroup, such statuses, as we have seen, having definite implications for forms of interaction and senses of power differentials in the alt.fashion community.

Todayness

The socio-temporal distinction between newbies and oldbies evolves across the history of the newsgroup, but there is a shorter temporal dimension that also helps constitute the group as a community on a daily basis: the exchange of messages about what is being worn or was received on any particular day. Table 6.9 lists the todayness threads in the sample. The orientation to todayness is, rather appropriately, a daily obsession for most threads: six saw posts every day during the sample period, one missed only one day, and one made it on eleven out of the sixteen days. There is, then, a very persistent sense of todayness in the group, even if not everybody posts to these threads. Table 6.10 shows the number of posters that do contribute to them. Almost one third (32.82 per cent) have posted to at least one of the todayness threads, and two members of the group have contributed to all seven of them.

Two of the threads (*What are *you* wearing today?* and *What *makeup* are you wearing today?*) are concerned with overall looks, and the posts are strikingly similar in form across both. The vast majority are describable in terms of a combination of a list of items worn, the make or retail source of at least one of those items, and a comment.

What are *you* wearing today? was interpreted by participants as referring to clothing, and the comments alluded to the contexts in which

Table 6.9 *Todayness threads*

Thread	Posts (N)	Days thread posted
what I *bought* today + what did you *buy* today? (14)	166	16/16
What Fragrance Did You Wear Today + today's fragrance (16) + what scent did you wear today??? (14)	136	16/16
What I got in the *mail* today + What I received in the mail today (16) + What I got *from* the MALE today! (9)	119	15/16
What are *you* wearing today?	104	16/16
What *lipstick* are you wearing today?	84	16/16
What *makeup* are you wearing today	83	16/16
What nailpolish are you wearing today? + Your *nailpolish* du jour (25)	50	11/16
Total	742	

Table 6.10 *Poster participation in todayness threads*

Threads/7 (N)	Posters (N)	Posters (%)
7	2	0.3
6	3	0.5
5	5	0.9
4	6	1.0
3	24	4.1
2	40	6.8
1	112	19.1
0	393	67.2
Total	585	100.0

the outfit was worn (the weather, a work or school setting, a social occasion, or a combination of these). Comments in the makeup thread referred to the characteristics of the product, the 'look', the context, or a combination. Given the simple and broadly shared structure of form, it is easy to provide typical examples from each thread:

Example 1:
Its Friday, and aside from chasing the end-o'-week-paperwork, we're lunching with a client today, and in the afternoon, scoping out specs for a new upcoming project. In the evening, taking a good girlfriend out to dinner for her birthday.

Sunny skies, highs in the low 60s.

- White cotton v-neck blouse;
- Off-white cotton twill trousers (LLBean);
- Multi-color floral silk jacquard vest (tunic length);
- Off-white Hanes SR knee-highs;
- White kidskin pumps (2" heels) from Easy Spirit;
- Brown leather carcoat (North Beach Leather). (User 321)

Example 2:
stila face concealer g
px vibrant for eyes
stila eye concealer in warm
guerlain powder twin set in bronze
versace brow pencil
versace v2052 eyeshadow trio
yellow all over
pink on lid
plum mixed with paula dorff transformer to line upper lashline
sephora black mascara
versace glam touch blush
vincent longo current lip lux (User 444)

Although one might be tempted to argue that the provision of designer or retailer names allows one to read off the amounts of cultural and economic capital available to each poster, there is no evidence from the posts in the sample that the newsgroup members actually attend to the posts in this way – at least, not in this public forum. But designer names are not an essential requirement of the more fundamental display of knowledge that shows what might be put together with what. There is little doubt that this sort of skill is being displayed in the lists, manifesting thereby what could be called, with apologies to Bourdieu, craft capital. This is closer to cultural than economic capital, as it refers to levels of skill and modes of knowing how to do in a craft context. The at least quasi-independence of craft capital from economic capital in the fashion context is neatly captured in the phrase 'more dash than cash', which is not to exclude dash getting on very well indeed with cash – or indeed the existence of those with more credit than merit.

It is also clear that there is a generalized daily exchange of descriptions of the appearing self. The descriptions rarely request specific comments from others, instead simply stating: this is how I appear today (in today's context, where mentioned). These two threads also suggest what combinations of clothing or makeup items might be possible, often in detail sufficient enough to allow both for an image of the poster to be imagined and for possible replication or modification by others. These are perhaps the main reasons for providing designer or retailer information. But these postings also permit an almost physical presence to exist in virtual space, and the fact that these presences are shared on a daily basis serves to construct the group in a gemeinschaftlich way: it is not so much that everyone knows everyone else and keeps running into them, but everyone knows the contents of the wardrobes and makeup cabinets of everyone who posts here, and what they are doing with them on the days in which they virtually bump into them. The co-temporal and co-present face-to-face meetings of the Gemeinschaft are translated into their virtual equivalents: asynchronous and space-independent face-to-screen meetings. The daily nature of the todayness posts also works to create a sense of a group existing across time: daily experiences of similar type are shared day after day resulting in a sort of accumulation of dailiness and a consequent sense of living with others through time in quite a stable and mundane manner. This is not the everyday life of the interacting strangers of the Gesellschaft frequented by a sociology that thinks in terms of the alienating space of the physical city, but the everyday life of the exchanging familiars of virtuality.

The nailpolish, lipstick and fragrance threads are structurally similar, but lists are fewer and shorter as entire looks are not being described here. Thirty-eight per cent of the posts in the nailpolish thread, almost seventy per cent of those in the lipstick thread, and over half of the fragrance posts simply mentioned what was being worn with no comments of any sort. This reinforces the picture sketched above of the importance to posters of providing the newsgroup members with simple self-descriptions on a daily basis: just like people in the street, we 'see' them and make up our own minds on what their appearances might mean, but in the newsgroup we can also put names to the imagers and therefore participate in a more intimate space. Where there are comments, they are overwhelmingly about an evaluation of the product and/or a description of how it looks on the poster, thereby channelling the interpretation in particular directions. Typical examples are: 'UD Plague with a coat of UD Litter over it. Oooo pretty even on my short, short nails' (User 297); 'Sonia Kashuk Luxury Lipcolor in Mulberry. Very nice shade! No nasty flavor, good texture, well-pigmented, perhaps a tiny bit on the dry side, which is easily remedied' (User 149); 'Sephora Romarin..ahhhhh!' (User 268). No matter where we look in these posts, then, we find an exchange of similars among familiars. A daily mass egalitarianism amongst these posters is built up through the continual exchange of the same formal constructions, an egalitarianism nuanced through content by hints about craft capital and economic capital.

Although a sense of enduring presence over time may be created through the accumulation of daily descriptions, there is a shorter way of discovering–displaying continuities in the fashion-identified aspects of the posters: listings one's favourites. The most long-term aspect of continuity was manifested in the thread *if you couuld (sic) have just ONE fragrance for the rest of your life!!!* (22 posts). This is a way of discovering–displaying what one most fundamentally is through the consumption of a single product over the longest imaginable duration for a body. Further aspects of identity may be filled in by posting about one's five favourite lipsticks (67 posts), five favourite lipglosses (62), favourites of the moment (41), favourite powder foundation (32), favourite skin care products (30) or by answering polls about whether one wears skirts, dresses or pants the most (30) or on what clothing one finds most seductive (26). There are also threads describing what posters consider absolutely necessary to their cosmeticked lives (37) and (displaying what they are not as much as what they are) what they consider the most unnecessary cosmetic item (71). Here, alt.fashion identities may be more familiar to the group than some of the people they meet everyday in the 'real world', because in this quadrant of cyberspace we are informed in some detail about how the identities are actually put together. Instead of the instant, and hence relatively unreflective, apprehensions of appearances familiar from the worlds of the street, the train, the airport, the nightclub or the restaurant, we are presented with lists of the key elements that go into making up identity in this group. The construction of identity becomes explicit in ways not possible in the 'real world'.

Economy

Table 6.11 lists the relevant threads. We have already seen how lists of items operate in the construction of todayness. Lists in the threads *items you covet? :-)*, *Christmas Wish List.....* and *November Wish List* orientate not to today but to the (near) future. Rather than the everyday mundanity of how one appears now with what one already possesses, the aspirational self is described through a description of the aimed-for items that, if attained, will represent the next step in the poster's consuming life. There are almost no unlikely fantasies listed, and even these are embedded in straightforward lists such as those already met and therefore clearly meant unseriously. Remarks made above about the display of various sorts of capital through lists could be repeated here, with the addition that future-orientated lists offer the opportunity of displaying that one's store of relevant capitals might be changing for the better (or the worse – or stagnating). The time-restricted nature (16 days) of the present sample, however, makes it impossible to pursue individual posting histories. Table 6.12 lists the objects of desire found in these threads. Over half the 'other' items are to be found in the Christmas list, and stray away from the usual topics of the newsgroup.

Some of the todayness threads reappear here as they also relate to notions of economy, and as these have been partially analysed already I shall limit the present discussion to the contents and origins of what was received in the *What I got in the *mail* today!* thread. Table 6.13 lists the contents.

Table 6.11 *Economy threads*

Thread	Posts (N)
what I *bought* today + what did you *buy* today? (14)	166
What I got in the *mail* today + What I got *from* the MALE today! (9)	119
Secret Santa...Update...Upping the limit? + AF Secret Santa 1999! (12) + Clinique soap/Santa (1)	59
items you covet? :-)	36
Christmas Wish List...	24
Swaplifted!!!! =(	14
November Wish List	12
Another Chanel Ripoff...IMO!	11
Do you wonder where some of these swap items come from?	11
Total	452

Table 6.12 *Objects of desire*

Item	Items (N)	Items (%)
Cosmetics	142	49.0
Clothing	62	21.4
Other	86	29.7
Total	290	100.0

Table 6.13 *Contents received in mail*

Item	Posts (N)	Posts (%)
Cosmetics	71	62.8
Clothing	4	3.5
Other	27	23.9
Unspecified	11	9.7
Total	113	100.0

Not all posts were on topic, and some mentioned more than one category, hence the post total here is not equal to the total number of posts in the thread. The category 'other' generally refers to catalogues and magazines and 'unspecified' to phrases of the form 'my order from X'.

User 447 once remarked that 'You could call this [newsgroup] alt.cosmetics, and nobody would know the difference', an observation lent weight by the figures in Table 6.13. Cosmetics outdistanced clothing by 17.75:1, presumably partly because dress usually demands actual fitting to a physical body and obtaining clothing through the mail thus runs a higher risk of disappointment than cosmetics. Where clothing is difficult to swap with another if unsuitable, the same is not true of many cosmetics, and this provides a second reason for the high traffic in makeup: it provides an easy way of relating poster to poster through the exchange of specific physical real-world objects through conventional snail mail. The importance of this traffic can be gauged from Table 6.14, which indicates the sources of the items received.

Almost exactly half of the retail mentions refer unambiguously to online retailers, and some of the remainder may be online as well. Although this indicates high levels of electronic commerce among the posters, of more interest from the point of view of the sociology of the group is the fact that over a third of relevant traffic refers to exchanges among the members of the alt.fashion community itself. There appear to be high levels of reciprocity involved, with half indicating explicitly that what was received in the mail was part of a swap between individual members of the group. Virtual relations are now supplemented by real object relations, the combination of virtual and real promising to reinforce community solidarity. As we shall now see, real object-mediated relations turn out to be of considerable importance to the life of alt.fashion posters.

Crimes against the gift

The swap is, of course, a form of the gift relationship that we have already considered at length in a different context in Chapter 5. The sample discusses gift exchange in the cases of both poster–retailer and poster–poster relations and provides a model of what the relationship ought properly to mean.

The reader will doubtless recall that gift exchange, unlike commodity exchange, institutes a relationship of personal obligation between giver and

Table 6.14 *Sources of mailed items*

Source of item	Mailed items (N)	%
Retailer	62	58.5
Member of alt.fashion community	37	34.9
Other	7	6.6
Total	106	100.0

receiver of gift, a relationship that continues until the gift has been returned in some way. There can of course be a long series of unequal gifts exchanged such that something always remains 'owing' in the relationship, a situation that ensures that the relationship continues over time. The concepts of honour and trust are embedded in the gift relationship: one trusts that a recipient will honour the symbolic debt in some way and the recipient feels obligated to do the honourable thing and return it in whatever form is appropriate in the circumstances. Where the commodity relationship is impersonal and is tied to a regulatory legal system, the gift relationship is personal and is tied to a system of symbolic obligation.

The posters to the *Another Chanel Ripoff...IMO!* thread were concerned that the (for them) properly gift-based relationship between the retailer and store makeovers' recipient was being transformed into a commodity-based relationship through the forced payment of an upfront fee (redeemable for goods). The retailer was thus constructing them as dishonourable consumers who could not be trusted to honour a symbolic obligation. The posters' idea of themselves as honourable payers of symbolic debts comes across quite clearly in several mailings, with User 385 writing that 'When I got my MAC makeover in TO, it was understood that I was obligating myself to purchase at least $40 in products (yeah, like that's tough for me!), but I did not have to pay any money up front. <snip> User 385, who nearly always ends up buying *something* at a makeover but would never pay $ in advance' and User 214 commenting that 'I've had so many free makeovers and have never left a makeover without purchasing many items, but I don't want to be coerced into doing it'. The honourable members that compose the group are contrasted against those without honour: 'Most people who post to alt.fashion would buy, but we are not the only people who go to cosmetics counters. There are others out there that just waste time and never buy anything' (User 45). So the honourable consumers (alt.fashion's members) are bound by the classic logic of the gift, the dishonourable ones are not, and the retailers are beginning to treat the former as the latter: as responding only to commodity logic in all its symbolic poverty.

Irrespective of the drift towards commodification just discussed, there is still a legitimate relationship between the retailer and the means required to put together a makeover: it is hard to imagine that the products used in store makeovers might not legitimately belong to the retailer. The posters to the thread *Do you wonder where some of these swap items come from?* raise the possibility that there may not be a legitimate relation between possessor and object through voicing suspicions that some goods being offered for sale or swap on certain online sites might in fact be stolen. This is a more serious threat to a gift-based than a commodity-based relationship, given the impersonal nature of the latter. A stolen object is not appropriately linkable to the person who possesses it, as it still legitimately belongs to someone else. A gift-based relationship here cannot be authentic because it is impossible to determine where the object 'really' comes from (and who comes 'attached' to it) if one suspects illegitimate possession on the part of the purported owner. One can hardly be obligated to someone with no legitimate rights over the object in the first place. Here, then, is a second threat to the gift-based relationship.

A third threat concerns the fact that reciprocation may not take place at all. Here, the non-returner spurns the honourable logic of obligation relating exchangers and effectively 'steals' the object destined to be part of a swap. As User 288 described one instance of non-return, 'She ran a swap & got all the goodies'. This 'crime' is known as swaplifting. Posters to the *Swaplifted!!!! =(* thread bemoaned some instances and discussed ways of trying to find a swaplifter who had apparently disappeared. Any measures that could be taken by the 'swap police' in such instances were unclear from the thread (presumably they keep consultable lists of those who have been reported to them), but one online facilitator of swaps puts a Negative Swap Token against the name of anyone who has been complained about (Makeupalley, 2007). Gift exchange has at least some institutional protection in this case.

Alt.fashion has its own form of institutionalized exchange in the form of the Secret Santa, which was about to enter its third year during the period the newsgroup was sampled and which has continued to run every year to 2005 (the latest period for which information was available). This was the first time I had come across the term, but the institution seems quite popular to judge by the 648,000 hits produced by Google when 'secret santa' was entered as an exact phrase search term. See Jandreau (2002) for an analysis of the Secret Santa in the context of an office Christmas party. Here, the Secret Santa coordinator (User 247) randomly matches a Santa (who gives a gift 'at least vaguely related to the subject of this newsgroup' up to a US$20 limit) to a Santee (who receives the gift). The latter is also a Santa to a different member of the group. In other words, A gives a gift to B, B gives a (different) gift to C, C gives something to D, and so forth. A gift is also received by A, and so a *ring chain* that may involve hundreds of participants is formed (see Figure 6.1).

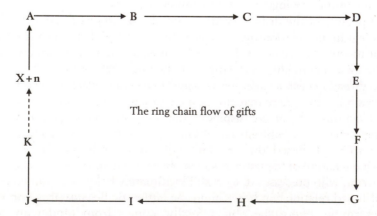

Figure 6.1 *The ring chain of the secret Santa*

I employ the term 'ring chain' rather than 'chain ring' because gifts symbolically 'chain' givers and receivers together and thus the notion of chaining is primary. The ring is one particular form that chaining can take. Santas know who their Santees are, but the Santee does not know who their Santa is until the gift is actually received sometime in December (hence *Secret* Santa). The cash limit ensures that any commodity aspect is ruled out because all gifts involved in the ring chain are, at least in principle, more or less equal on that level. Differentiation lies elsewhere in the choices made by the Santas within the limit set, and so the gifts here have all the personal qualities that remain foreign to the commodity-based relationship. As in Malinowski's (1922) account of the Kula ring, the institution relates individual strangers to each other and at the same time establishes solidarity at the higher level of the group. It does this because it is *not* a question of A and B exchanging among themselves. That would establish solidarity simply at the level of the dyad with no implications for anyone else. The fact that it is a ring chain means that *every* participant is involved in its creation in the same way and thus this ring chain solidarity is a form of mechanical solidarity in Durkheim's sense, with the addition of individual differentiation lying at the level of the choices that went into the gift. Where an individual link in the chain threatens to break down through the non-transmission of a gift and thus imperil the integrity of solidarity, institutionalized measures are available to combat the danger: 'In previous years, "Angels" have volunteered to send a "consolation" gift to the burned Santee. If you are interested in being an Angel, please let me know that when you sign up' (User 247).

Although angelic intervention may stave off such a menace to solidarity, there are other ways of troubling the Secret Santa's role in creating the group in the preferred way. The first of these would have led to the splitting of the group into two based around the amount of money spent (the present US$20 group and a new US$50 group, as suggested by User 171). Creating 'poor' and 'rich' ring chains clearly does nothing for the solidarity of the group that is to emerge through the operation of the original Secret Santa protocols, and the suggestion was received negatively. A second subversion can be found in attempts by the receiver to influence the choice of their unknown giver even though a 'surprise' element is integral to the Secret Santa ('the whole point' as User 83 remarked). These 'buy me this' posts, as User 12 described them, attempt to remove the giver choice that permits an individual to join the group-level ring chain while retaining individuality: 'I prefer to look for the unique or unusual gifts and hope the recipient will be happy with my selection'. Such posts attempt to transform the gift relationship into something resembling a commodity relationship. A third problem concerns gifts that are contaminated by histories external to the ring chain, for these perturb the 'pure' quality of the relationship being newly set up. Such gifts are explicitly excluded by the rules: 'It should be a NEW gift, purchased explicitly for this event. Gift-with-purchase items, swap items, or used things are NOT considered appropriate for this event' (User 247). It is the very impersonal quality of the commodity that allows

Table 6.15 *Crimes against the gift*

Relationship	Crime	Form	Sanction
Retailer–consumer	Dishonouring and distrusting the consumer	Commodification through upfront fees for store makeovers	Boycott
Possessor–object	Illegitimate possession	Stolen goods	Unclear
Swapper–swapper	Swaplifting	Non-reciprocity	Reported to swap police, removal from swap board
Santa–Santee	Disruption of ring chain solidarity	Non-transmission of gift	Exclusion from future Secret Santas
Santa–Santee	Pollution of 'pure' relationship	Contamination of gift by histories external to ring chain	Unclear
Santee–Santa	Subversion of Santa choice	Commodification through 'buy me this' lists	Ignored
All ring chain members	Dividing the group	Monetary stratification	Rejection of proposal

it to be uncontaminated by prior attachments and thus suited to establishing a new relationship in its gift form.

Table 6.15 summarizes the various dangers posed to the essentially gift-based relationships enjoyed in the sample.

It is clear that gift-based relations are central to the sort of community being built up in the newsgroup, and despite the fact that many posts throughout the threads list commodities acquired or desired or evaluated it is evident that commodity logic is not appropriate to the way members think of their relationships to each other (or even to retailers who stray from the commodity to the gift relation in the case of free makeovers: they have shifted onto the terrain of the alt.fashion newsgroup and are expected to behave appropriately). Commodities are taken out of the market, decommodified, transformed into gifts and go on to create solidarity (see Kopytoff, 1986, for a general discussion of the processes of commodification and decommodification). Those who wish to retain the commodity form of relationship through 'buy me this' lists are generally ignored.

The body: standardization and diversity

Although there were over 200 posts explicitly on the body in the *Complaints about Thin Models* and spinoff threads, there was really only one insistent theme here: body standardization. The standard-making instances of the media, advertising, 'these insane actresses who are now thinner than the models' (User 363), clothing manufacturers and weight charts were all considered to have negative and exclusionary effects on those who did not fit the standard. The negative effects included the health risks involved in trying to reshape recalcitrant bodies to the standard and the emotional damage to younger women who feared that their non-standard bodies would lead to an unsuccessful life. Excluded were all those whose body types were not represented in the media, ('I think it's spooky when, with rare exception, the entire female tv and movie population starts looking the same' [User 208]), those whose bodies differed from the Euro–American norms of weight charts ('A chart that applies to both a petite Bangladeshi woman and, say, a robust Samoan, is probably not worth much' [User 380]) and those with bodies that did not match the ideal-standard dress-sizing policies of manufacturers. The latter point was put most poignantly by User 214, who wrote that 'I don't believe that the "people" who constantly throw models in our face as the perfect figure have ever had to deal with an 11 year old girl crying in a department store because all the "in" clothes are too small for her'.

The generally anti-standard tone of the posts casts the members of the group as diverse themselves (several posters provided details of their own non-standard dimensions and characteristics) and as valuing diversity in representation as a corrective to some of the negative effects already mentioned. The group, then, constructs itself as inclusionary here both in terms of its own members and in terms of considering a larger- than- 'standard' range of people in the world as counting for something in the fashion, beauty and health contexts. This solidarity in diversity is a little different to Durkheim's organic solidarity: where the latter saw complementary differ-entiation and a coordinated division of labour as the keys to the success of complex social 'organisms', the former sees diversity as a value that is not marked by organico–functional notions of complementarity or coordination and their consequent inequalities but as an in-itself that springs from a world of independently diverse (i.e., *not* differentiated members of a whole) equals that happen to exist. The new principle of social unity lies in the shared appreciation of differences that are not necessarily either motivated, complementary or coordinated by any instances. This diversity solidarity may be rather hard to sustain in a 'real world' where differences are easily capable of including some and excluding others in almost any imaginable context, but it may be particularly suited to cyberspace newsgroups and their in-principle instant citizenships of anyone in the world with the right equipment. Benedict Anderson (1991: 6) remarks that the way in which a community may be imagined marks the type of community it is, and we may suggest that particular media foster particular types of imaginings. For Anderson, print was the medium that permitted the members of the bourgeoisie to imagine themselves as connected to other members of the same class whom they may never have met and therefore indeed to 'become' the bourgeoisie through solidarity 'on an essentially imagined basis' (1991: 77). For us, the Internet is the medium that permits the emergence of diversity–solidarity as an ideology that permits the imagining of a community of globe-scattered unknowns who may never be physically, or even temporally, co-present. As we have already seen in earlier parts of this analysis, however, it does nothing to prevent the subsequent emergence of certain types of status difference among posters (e.g., 'newbies' versus 'oldbies'). Just as organic solidarity can be read as a functional fantasy about how industrialized societies 'ought' to be, ideally, so diversity–solidarity can be read as a functional fantasy about how cyberized societies 'ought' to be, ideally.

The body odoured

It was proposed in Chapter 4 that the meaning of a smell is often provided by something outside of itself, and the ways in which advertisers and manufacturers construed and constrained fragrance meanings were explored. The thread *Fragrance and age* (54 posts) provides some examples of advertiser-independent meanings alongside lists of the type by now familiar. In fourteen cases, fragrances were associated with personal histories and memories of others. Two posts noted how constant their preferred fragrances had been over their lives ('A White Shoulder lady, 30 years' [User 571]), while seven divided their lives into periods associated with particular scents. Given the general bias towards youth evident from the demographic details sketched earlier, one would assume that many members of the newsgroup simply do not have a sufficient number of years in their histories for complex fragrance-based periodizations to emerge. An older group would likely provide much more material of this sort. Three posters said that they liked specific scents because they reminded them of their fathers and one because it brought her mother back to her. Another rather enigmatically referred to a scent bringing back 'some oooooold memories.....bittersweet and tucked away' (User 582). Fragrance, then, can be used as a temporal marker in autobiographical accounts and as a way of making newly present those who may be long gone. Smell in the latter case is associated with memories of the presence of particular bodies rather than with any meanings fancied by advertisers.

Conclusion

Although we have considered a number of different concepts in this chapter, one overwhelming impression comes across: the group's interest in creating and sustaining itself as a community. This is achieved through several different forms of solidarity:

- *Epistolary solidarity* is the most general form, and refers to the exchange of messages in the newsgroup. There are two types of this: *direct* epistolary solidarity refers to the relationship between those who post to a particular thread (they engage with each other, even if they completely disagree) and *indirect* epistolary solidarity to those who read the thread but do not post to it. Any post can be understood as a potential engagement with the group as a whole, as anyone could read and respond to it. Epistolary solidarity, then, is the most basic form available to anyone who might open their newsreader. The indirect form includes lurkers, as they at least read the messages – and if they do this on a regular basis, then a sense of belonging will inevitably arise. For the alt.fashion group in particular, epistolary solidarity can have two further inflections: the presumed 'good faith' of the majority of post(er)s and the 'bad faith' of trollish post(er)s designed to provoke reactions. The group's preference is clearly for the former.

- *Temporal solidarity* also has two forms. *Quotidian* temporal solidarity refers to the effects of the sheer dailiness of the posts: the original 7,355 messages in 16 days in the sample works out at a daily average of almost 460, so the group can be seen as very actively constituting itself as an everyday reality. In alt.fashion, the daily quality is deepened even further by the regular occurrence of the 'what are you wearing today?' types of posts. *Stratified* temporal solidarity refers to the time-based motives available for dividing the group into sub-groups. The newbie/oldbie distinction is the obvious example from the sample.

- *Craft solidarity* refers to the exchange of tips and techniques in the general area of the newsgroup topic. Here it is the concrete theme of fashion that creates senses of belonging, rather than the more general behavioural aspects of the newsgroup.

- *Dyadic solidarity* indicates ways of relating any A and B. In the present newsgroup, it refers to the off-line 'real-world' swapping of mostly cosmetic items among members.

- *Ring chain solidarity* refers to the Kula-like institution of the Secret Santa, and manages to combine the sameness of a Durkheimian mechanical solidarity with individuation through Santa choice. This makes it a very powerful way of simultaneously linking individual with individual and individual with group, as well as a mode of integrating a virtual community with the 'real world'.

- *Diversity solidarity* refers to the way the group sees itself as composed of the communion of independently existing differences through the newsgroup topic area. This form, as suggested above, seems most suited as the ideology of an equal-access globalized cybersociety.

A number of the above forms are based on variations of the gift relationship, which makes it impossible to read alt.fashion as a simple space for the extolling of commodities. Instead, the group uses the products of commodity society as a means to accomplish social solidaristic ends that commodification might otherwise have been assumed to undermine.

Update

The newsgroup was revisited in October 2005, and 8,594 posts were found from 15 May to 4 October. Alt.fashion continues to be a very lively community. The top threads will be familiar ones: *what are *you* wearing today* remains, with 443 posts, or over 5 per cent of all posts; *what I bought* *today* is still there with 196 messages (2.25%), fragrance of the day threads made 148 posts (1.7%), and *what came in the mail today* and its variants are also still present (95 posts, or 1.09%). Indeed, there have been posts under the '*what are *you* wearing today*' rubric every year since 1996, when 3,453 messages appeared on the matter: there was a total of 6,196 posts on the topic in the calendar year 1999 (an average of almost 17 per day) and 4,842 in 2005 as a whole (13 per day). *What I bought* today also began in 1996 with 934 posts: there were 6,441 messages on the theme in our sample year of 1999 and 820 in 2005. *What came in the mail today* also began in 1996 and has been present every year since to 2005 at least. The basic form and structure of the community appears to be unchanged. Twenty five of the posters from the 1999 sample were still there in 2005, but whereas in 1999 they represented 15 per cent of all posts in 2005 they accounted for 26 per cent. There is clearly a continuing core population, and its members have become more quantitatively dominant in terms of newsgroups postings. The basic picture, though, is one of continuity and stability over a 10-year period.

7

Conclusion: A Hermeneutics of Dress

Dress appears to have two major dimensions: it can be understood as an appearing surface that lends itself to interpretation (a phenomenon) and it can be also be considered as an object in the world to which things may happen (a substance). The first of these relates more to the structural aspect of the social world (e.g., it may signal social class) and the second more to the relational side of individuals and groups. In the second, the adventures of the object turn out to reveal the structuring of the relations in the social domain(s) to which the object belongs (such as families or Internet groups, to take examples that were analysed extensively earlier).

Dress as appearance

Although each of the senses allows us to apprehend clothing in its own way and even though they can all work together to permit a multi-sensorial experience, it seems clear that seeing is the sense that matters most in this context. Compared to sight, the other senses are here relatively limited in scope: they do not tell us as much about the phenomenon and they do not provide as much room for wide ranges of meanings as appearance does.

Appearance has a poor reputation in philosophical, scientific and moral worlds: it is often contrasted with 'reality', it is something that we need to get beyond or behind, it is superficial. The contemplation of 'mere appearance' is beneath our dignity as serious persons. But we meet it every day: together with other sensory phenomena, it is how the world presents itself to us. Do we take the time to make deep analytical investigations of every appearance we come across? Of course not: mostly, we take appearances and what they tell us about the world for granted because we do not have the time to doubt them. Looked at like this, we can see that appearance is a crucial way in which the meanings of the world into which we find ourselves thrown are made manifest. Appearances are so important precisely because we do *not* have the time to get beyond them while plunged into the busyness (and business) of our everyday lives. But what, then, does clothed appearance tell us?

The utopians understood the relationship between dress and the world very well indeed. If we apprehend the world through appearance, then appearance should be a true manifestation of the structure of the social world. There should be no gap between what appears and what is. All the social categories that are important to a given society should be clear from appearances. Here, dress is the authentic materialization of more abstract economic, philosophical, political and social arrangements and relationships. Most importantly, it says that this *is* the way the world is: there is no way it can be doubted.

The societies designed by the utopians tended to be relatively simple and had relatively few categories, but dress nevertheless allowed for subtle and complex information to be communicated. If we ourselves were to take a utopian approach and design a world, what would be the role of dress? If it is to make the social structure clear, then we would have to be able to say what the significant social differentiations in the society were and how they related to each other. Let us take some examples. If gender is a significant differentiation, then we would have distinct forms of dress for males and females; but if it is not a significant differentiation then whatever distinction there was would have nothing to do with gender. Imagine that significance is attached to age classes rather than sex: here, dress would be differentiated according to age and men and women of the same age group would not differ from each other in clothing, but they would be dressed differently from men and women in another age category. Significant visual differentiation would be related to age rather than sex. If age is of no importance, then there should be no differentiation between the clothing of different age groups. It is easy to imagine social class or occupation as socially significant, and one would therefore have differentiation at this level.

Normally, there would be a series of significant social categories and differentiation would be needed among them all. Table 7.1 shows how a simple system based on two genders, three classes and six age groups rapidly leads to complexity. Differentiation in dress would need to be subtle and complex to capture even something as simple as this. If we add things like occasion, time of day or season to the mix, then matters become a little difficult to represent on a piece of paper of modest size. Add more divisions to classes, throw in marital or reproductive status, and dress becomes as epic as a Tolstoy novel, if rather more quickly read. Figures 7.1 and 7.2 try to capture this sense of complexity. There are separate boxes for male and female if these categories are imagined to be more primary than the others. Not all categories necessarily apply to both, and in this example I have made marital status a significant dimension for men but not for women, while occupation is significant for women but not for men. Furthermore, the dimensions are of varying importance: for example, class and time of day are more important for men than the other dimensions while age and class are the most important dimensions for women. The figures aim to help the reader conceptualize dress in a certain way: they do not purport to be actual descriptions of specific societies.

We can turn the utopian insights into a way of understanding the state of significant differences in society at any given moment. It is easier to do this if we take one dimension at a time. Say that we wanted to know about the significance of age differences. If there is clearly a matching of specific age

Table 7.1 *Simple example of the complexity of social categories*

Male																	
Upper class						Middle class						Lower class					
0–15	16–30	31–45	46–60	61–75	≥76	0–15	16–30	31–45	46–60	61–75	≥76	0–15	16–30	31–45	46–60	61–75	≥76

Female																	
Upper class						Middle class						Lower class					
0–15	16–30	31–45	46–60	61–75	≥76	0–15	16–30	31–45	46–60	61–75	≥76	0–15	16–30	31–45	46–60	61–75	≥76

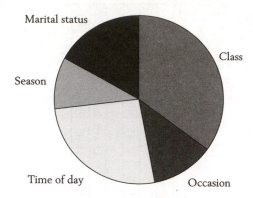

Figure 7.1   *Sample dimensions of dress in an imagined society: male*

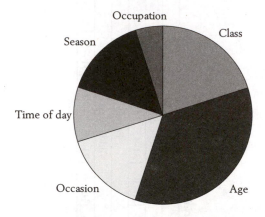

Figure 7.2   *Sample dimensions of dress in an imagined society: female*

and specific dress, then it is highly likely that age differences are important and that they map onto differential access to resources, power, privileges, responsibilities, prestige, activities, interests and so on. The size of the age range will tell us about the numbers of age classes: for example, there could be a division based on a decade or something as vague as young, middle aged, or old. There might be a lot of subdivisions up to the age of 20, and then a single category over that age – or the reverse, indeed. If each age group keeps its appearance throughout the life course but remains different from other groups, then we have a cohort that is primarily orientated to its own members. If dress changes as one moves from one age group to another, then the orientation is less to the group than to the social structure of society as a whole. If, over time, appearance shifts from clear age differentiation to a relative lack of differentiation, then that would suggest that age has lost differential significance for some reason and that other things are more important. If there are 'border disputes' about appropriately aged dress, then it means that age is still related to differential access to whatever is desirable in the context but that there is now a conflict over the appropriateness of the nature of the differences and their social consequences. The research question here would be 'what does it mean to dress one's age?', and the answers should tell us a lot about the meanings of age in the society in question – and a lot about the meanings of society for the age in question. Clearly, we could apply this sort of reasoning to other social divisions as well. Whatever the divisions, differentiation on the level of appearance will have consequences. We should be able to ask: 'what sort of society is this?' and get to some basic answers from appearance.

If dress is revelatory of socially significant differences, it is likely that measures may be necessary to ensure that appearance remains trustworthy. The risk is obvious: if who and what we are is visible to others through dress and therefore a change of clothing means a change of status in one or more dimensions, then we can give the impression that we are other than what we actually are by wearing clothing to which we are not actually entitled. This tends not to be an issue in utopian societies where everyone seems perfectly happy to echo the social structure all day long. Less utopian societies might need laws on the matter, as we saw in the cases of sumptuary dress: here, class and rank were to be preserved against pretenders. If you were a woman in the Paris of 1800 desiring to wear apparel conventionally marking a being as a man, then you could only legally do so on health grounds by applying to Police Headquarters armed with a certificate of health and documents signed by a mayor or police superintendent (ruling of the 16 brumaire an IX [7 November 1800]). Those caught without a licence were considered to be out to take advantage through their cross-dressing and would be arrested (Bard, 1999).

But most modern societies generally regulate at lower levels: the family, friends, work colleagues, class mates, the street, the peer group. All seem happiest with dress that is *comme il faut* in the context of the group and will exercise pressure to maintain it: dress in, or risk finding yourself out. Here, dress serves to both link people living in the same region of social space and to separate these people from those living elsewhere: clothing simultaneously unites and divides. This may seem to go against the contemporary belief in the importance of individualism, but in fact it gives us a clue as to how better to understand individualism in this context. If we take a leaf out of Bourdieu and look upon various consumer practices as part of a repertoire that is relatively limited by our position in social space, then we can see that how we actually deal with that repertoire can mark out our individual selves. For example, our position in social space may suggest that we have available to us a specific collection of clothing styles or a particular range of food: but we may have our own little twist on the clothing style or add something not in the recipe. We may all work with the same givens as those similar to us, but we do not necessarily perform them in quite the same ways. This is where personal style comes in. We can see here that consumer goods work at both social and individual levels: the contents of the repertoire link us to those who are socially like ourselves and separate us from those who are not; while the performance of the repertoire accomplishes those modulations of individuality that are important to others like us. This also explains why we tend to see other groups as groups and not as individuals: we may be able to recognize the repertoire as marking the position of the group in social space, but we do not know enough about it to be able to recognize the individual performances that may be important to that particular group.

The physical characteristics of clothing

Clothing is not simply a signalling light or a canvas to be interpreted: it is also an object with physical characteristics. It has weight, texture, size and strength; it can sit lightly on the body, mould it, shape it and constrain it. It can thus fit easily into a dialectic of bodily oppression/liberation or healthy/diseased and stand in metaphorically for the degrees of freedom a given society is seen to have. A starched collar or a whalebone corset could condemn a whole historical era for later more 'relaxed' generations, but present clothing that sits lightly on the body may be seen as an index of unfocused lives devoid of discipline by those who have not yet come into existence. Constraining dress may hold the body to a socially acceptable shape, lack of such dress may imply that the work will be done directly on the body by the plastic surgeon.

We know that, for Veblen (1975 [1899]), constraining dress functions to mark a body out as one not suited to physical labour and its accompanying low prestige: one's honour rises in proportion to one's clothing-induced physical incapacities. Even today, dress that is constraining in one way or another connotes the more prestigious mental type of labour: the tie versus the open collar, expensive delicate materials as against cheap robust cloth, shoes designed for grace and elegance rather than the health of the walking foot. Clothing is not entirely adapted to the demands of bodily comfort because that would set the body above the abstracting intelligence attracted by form, line and texture – the intelligence that sees itself as managing the world rather than as producing 'stuff' at the behest of others. Nevertheless, our analysis of the Dress Reformers suggested that health has become another factor in the design of clothing, and few would object to lighter, breathable, responsive fabrics: there is still plenty of space for the expression of an abstract elegance that raises us above the mundanities of comfort.

Dress may move as we do: it flaps, parts, rides up, flops over, reveals and hides and so forth. The potential for an ambulatory erotics here should be evident, and an analysis of the categories of persons whose clothing operates in such a way would tell us a great deal about patterns of eroticization in a given society.

Dress as circulating object

We have considered dress as an object to which things may happen in the context of the family and an Internet newsgroup. In these cases, dress-objects are caught up in a variety of forms of circulation that may establish, uphold and break particular sorts of relations between particular categories of persons. They are the objects that permit us to see the relational economies at work in particular contexts. We saw, for example, how sisters related to sisters through high levels of the mutual stealing of items of clothing or how alt.fashionistas established the daily nature of their relations through swapping descriptions of daily appearances. On a global level, Baden and Barber (2005: 4) suggest that trade in second-hand clothing has reached $1 billion annually and report that this may be undermining local industries in developing countries but also creates new jobs on the distribution and consumption side. Dress as circulating object, then, can shape worlds from the intimacy of the family to global economies.

Obviously, many different types of object may be caught up in the patterns of circulation that form the tissues of relationships between individuals and among groups. One could analyse the life of an individual by analysing the circulatory history of the objects they have handled, or understand how a group holds together by looking at what circulates between its members. We could find out something about the relations between groups by looking at the modes and directions of the flows of objects between them. For example, if objects flow only in one direction are they tributes paid to the greater power of protection or signs of the lack of power of those who can only receive? We may use simple appearance to tell us about the groups we do or do not belong to, but it is the flow of objects that concretely establishes relations beyond the 'imagined communities' of Anderson (1991).

As we saw in the analysis of alt.fashion, objects may be messages posted to the group as well as, say, a lipstick sent in the mail. As we communicate more and more through computers, the natures of the flows of object-messages are likely to become increasingly important in establishing relations and the natures thereof. We need to combine higher-level content analysis with attention to individual events: the former may tell us what the group is generally 'about' (e.g., fashion or football or philosophy or physics; revolution or reform or reaction or resistance), the latter tells us how the group exists as a peculiar tissue of relationships with an object-mediated structure.

Summing it up

Figure 7.3 attempts to sum up some of the contentions of this book by sketching the various dimensions at play in dress. The drawing shows both the sorts of things we need to take into account when analysing dress in

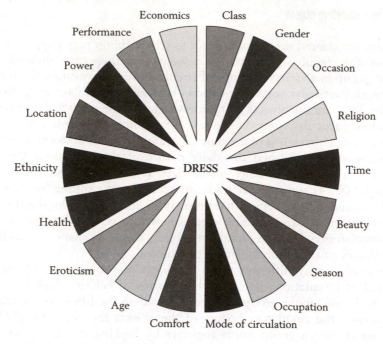

Figure 7.3 *Some dimensions of dress*

concrete contexts and also the dimensions of the world that dress can help shape in meaningful ways. The dimensions will not necessarily all be present in all contexts, and some will prove to be more important than others in given instances and at given times. The equal distributions in the figure are for illustrative purposes only, and would not be reflected in the actual world. Some dimensions may be so dominant that the others fit within them rather than operating autonomously. There may also be more dimensions than are mentioned here. Dress is an integral part of social structures, social relations, histories, politics and economics; it tells us who we and others are and is a key to the meanings of the world. Some of them, at least...

References

Abdallah, nd. *Le Foulard Islamique et la République Française: Mode d'emploi.* ftp://ftp2.al-muslimah.com/almuslimg/Foulard.pdf. Accessed 11 March 2005.

Adam, Barbara (1990) *Time and Social Theory*. Cambridge: Polity Press.

Afetinan, A. (1962) *The Emancipation of the Turkish Woman*. Paris: UNESCO.

Ahmed, Leila (1992) *Women and Gender in Islam. Historical Roots of a Modern Debate*. New Haven, CT and London: Yale University Press.

Al-Shouli, Catherine (2004) 'Lettre ouverte à Monsieur Jacques Chirac Président de la République'. *Ligue Française de la Femme Musulmane*. www.lffm.org/index. php?nav=communiques. Accessed 22 March 2005.

Althusser, Louis (1977 [1965]) *For Marx*. Translated by Ben Brewster. London: NLB.

Amin, Qassim (1976 [1899]) *Tahrir Al-Mar'a*, in *Al-a'mal al-kamila li Qassim Amin*. Beirut: Al-mu'assasa al-'arabiyya lil-dirasat wa'l-nashr. Quoted in Ahmed (1992), *q.v.*

Anderson, Benedict (1991) *Imagined Communities. Reflections on the Origin and Spread of Nationalism*. Revised edition. London: Verso.

Andreae, Johann Valentin (1916 [1619]) *Christianopolis. An Ideal State of the Seventeenth Century*. Translated from the Latin by Felix Emil Held. New York: Oxford University Press.

Anonymous (1715) *A Treatise upon the Modes; or a Farewell to French Kicks*. London: Printed for J. Roberts, at the Oxford Arms in Warwick Lane.

Anonymous (ca 1880) *How to be Strong and Beautiful. Hints on Dress for Girls by a Member of the National Health Society*. London: Allman and Son.

Anonymous (1882) 'Dress. An Article on a Paper by J.A. Gotch, read before the Architectural Association', *Hibernia*, I (July 1882): 98–101.

Anonymous (1919) 'Rabochii kostyum', *Zhizn iskusstva*, 142.

Anonymous (1983 [1981]) '*Hijab* Unveils a New Future', pp. 94–5 in *Issues in the Islamic Movement 1981–82 (1401–1402)*. Edited by Kalim Siddiqui. London: The Open Press Limited.

Anonymous (2003) 'Malentendu sur le sens du foulard'. *Al-Muslimah*. www. al-muslimah.com/articles/2003_07_28_malentendu_sur_le_sens_du_foulard.html. Accessed 4 September 2005.

Anonymous (2004) 'Tokyo Talks Tough on Sex, Lies and Used Underwear'. *Mainichi Interactive* January 15. www12.mainichi.co.jp/news/mdn/search-news/923112/ underwear-0-17.html. Accessed 7 February 2005.

Appleton, Jane Sophia (1984 [1848]) 'Sequel to "The Vision of Bangor in the Twentieth Century"', pp. 49–64 in Kessler (1984), *q.v.*

Ariès, Philippe (1962 [1960]) *Centuries of Childhood*. Translated by Robert Baldick. London: Jonathan Cape.

Arnold, Odile (1982) *La Vie corporelle dans les couvents de femmes en France au XIXe siècle*. Thèse de 3e cycle, EHESS.

Azari, Farah (1983) 'Islam's Appeal to Women in Iran. Illusions and Reality', pp. 1–71 in *Women of Iran. The Conflict with Fundamentalist Islam*. Edited by Farah Azari. London: Ithaca Press.

Bacon, Francis (1924 [1627]) *New Atlantis*. Edited, with an Introduction and Notes, by Alfred B. Gough, Oxford: Clarendon Press.

Baden, Sally and Barber, Catherine (2005) *The Impact of the Second-Hand Clothing Trade on Developing Countries*. Oxfam. www.maketradefair.com/en/assets/english/shc_0905.pdf. Accessed 23 July 2006.

Baldwin, Frances Elizabeth (1926) *Sumptuary Legislation and Personal Regulation in England*. Baltimore, MD: Johns Hopkins.

Ballin, Ada S. (1885) *The Science of Dress in Theory and Practice*. London: Sampson Low, Marston, Searle, and Rivington.

Barber, Bernard and Lyle S. Lobel (1952) 'Fashion in Women's Clothes and the American Social System', *Social Forces*, 31: 124–31.

Bard, Christine (1999) 'Le << DB58 >> aux Archives de la Préfecture de Police', *Clio*, 10. clio.revues.org/document258.html. Accessed 14 July 2006.

Barnes, Ruth (1992) 'Women as Headhunters. The Making and Meaning of Textiles in a Southeast Asian Context', pp. 29–43 in *Dress and Gender. Making and Meaning in Cultural Contexts*. Edited by Ruth Barnes and Joanne B. Eicher. New York and Oxford: Berg Publishers.

Barthes, Roland (1983 [1967]) *The Fashion System*. Translated by Matthew Ward and Richard Howard. New York: Hill and Wang.

Bateson, Gregory (1958) *Naven*. Second edition. Stanford, CA: Stanford University Press.

Bauman, Zygmunt (1982) *Memories of Class. The Pre-History and After-Life of Class*. London: Routledge and Kegan Paul.

Bauman, Zygmunt (1995) *Life in Fragments. Essays in Postmodern Morality*. Oxford: Blackwell.

Bayrou, François (1994) *Neutralité de l'enseignement public: port de signes ostentatoires dans les établissements scolaires*. www.assemblee-nationale.fr/12/dossiers/documents-laicite/document-3.pdf. Accessed 19 January 2005.

Bell, Quentin (1976) *On Human Finery*. New edition. London: The Hogarth Press.

Bellamy, Edward (1986 [1888]) *Looking Backward 2000–1887*. Edited with an Introduction by Cecelia Tichi. London: Penguin.

Bennett, Tony, Emmison, Michael and Frow, John (1999) *Accounting for Tastes. Australian Everyday Cultures*. Cambridge: Cambridge University Press.

Berger, John and Mohr, Jean (1982) *Another Way of Telling*. London: Writers and Readers.

Bergman, Eva (1938) *Nationella Dräkten. En studie kring Gustav III:s dräktreform 1778*. Stockholm: Nordiska Museets Handlingar: 8.

Bergson, Henri (1929 [1908]) *Matter and Memory*. Translated by Nancy Margaret Paul and W. Scott Palmer. London: George Allen & Unwin.

Blumer, Herbert G. (1968) 'Fashion', pp. 341–5 in *International Encyclopedia of the Social Sciences*. Volume 5. New York: Macmillan and The Free Press.

Boehn, Max von (1971 [1932]) *Modes and Manners*. Translated in two volumes by Joan Joshua. New York: Benjamin Blom.

Bogatyrev, Petr (1971 [1937]) *The Functions of Folk Costume in Moravian Slovakia*. Translated by Richard G. Crum. The Hague: Mouton.

Bohannan, Paul and Bohannan, Laura (1968) *Tiv Economy*. London: Longmans.

Borrelli, Laird O'Shea (1997) 'Dressing Up and Talking about it: Fashion Writing in *Vogue* from 1968 to 1993', *Fashion Theory*, 1 (3): 247–59.

Bourdieu, Pierre (1984 [1979]) *Distinction. A Social Critique of the Judgement of Taste*. Translated by Richard Nice. London: Routledge and Kegan Paul.

Bradley, Herbert Dennis (1922) *The Eternal Masquerade*. London: T. Werner Laurie Ltd.

Brannen, Julia and Moss, Peter (1987) 'Dual Earner Households: Women's Financial Contributions After the Birth of the First Child', pp. 75–95 in Julia Brannen and Gail Wilson (eds), *q.v.*

Brannen, Julia and Wilson, Gail (eds) (1987) *Give and Take in Families. Studies in Resource Distribution*. London: Allen and Unwin.

Braudel, Fernand (1958) 'La longue durée', *Annales*, 13: 725–53.

Breward, Christopher (1995) *The Culture of Fashion. A New History of Fashionable Dress*. Manchester: Manchester University Press.

Brooke, Iris (1949) *A History of English Costume*. London: Methuen.

Butler, Samuel (1932a [1872]) *Erewhon*, pp. 1–191 in *Erewhon. Erewhon Revisited*, London: J.M. Dent.

Butler, Samuel (1932b [1901]) *Erewhon Revisited*, pp. 193–390 in *Erewhon. Erewhon Revisited*, London: J.M. Dent.

Byrde, Penelope (1979) *The Male Image. Men's Fashions in Britain 1300–1700*. London: B.T. Batsford.

Cabet, Etienne (1848) *Voyage en Icarie*. 5ème. édition. Paris: Bureau du Populaire.

Calthrop, Dion Clayton (1934) *English Dress from Victoria to George V*. London: Chapman and Hall.

Campanella, Tommasso (1981 [1602]) *The City of the Sun. A Poetic Dialogue*. Translated by Daniel J. Donno. Berkeley: University of California Press.

Campbell, Colin (1983) 'Romanticism and The Consumer Ethic: Intimations of a Weber-style Thesis', *Sociological Analysis*, 44 (4): 279–96.

Campbell, Colin (1987) *The Romantic Ethic and the Spirit of Modern Consumerism*. Oxford: Basil Blackwell.

Caperdi Trading (2005) www.kingdoms.co.uk/acatalog/__400___Seductive_ Clothing_7.html. Accessed 6 February 2005.

Caplin, Roxey Ann (1857) *Health and Beauty; or, Corsets and Clothing Constructed in Accordance with the Physiological Laws of the Human Body*. London: Darton and Co.

Caplin, Roxey Ann (1860) *Woman and Her Wants. Lectures on the Female Body and its Clothing*. London: Darton and Co.

Carlyle, Thomas (1908 [1831]) *Sartor Resartus*. London: Dent.

Caroline, B. (2005) www.caroline-b.com/happy.html. Accessed 1 February 2005.

Cavendish, Margaret (1992 [1666]) The Description of a New World Called the Blazing World, pp. 119–25 in *The Description of a New World Called the Blazing World and Other Writings*. Edited by Kate Lilley. London: William Pickering.

Charles, Nicola and Kerr, Marion (1987) 'Just the Way It Is: Gender and Age Differences in Family Food Consumption', pp. 155–74 in Julia Brannen and Gail Wilson (eds), *q.v.*

Cheal, David (1987) ' "Showing Them You Love Them": Gift Giving and the Dialectic of Intimacy', *Sociological Review*, 35 (1): 150–69.

Cheal, David (1988) *The Gift Economy*. London: Routledge.

Circulaire du 12 décembre (1989) *Laïcité, port de signes religieux par les élèves et caractère obligatoire des enseignements*. www.assemblee-nationale.fr/12/dossiers/documents-laicite/document-2.pdf. Accessed 19 January 2005.

Clarke, Magnus (1982) *Nudism in Australia. A First Study*. Waurn Ponds: Deakin University Press.

Classen, Constance, Howes, David and Synnott, Anthony (1994) *Aroma. The Cultural History of Smell*. London: Routledge.

Codere, Helen (1968) 'Exchange and Display', pp. 239–45 in *International Encyclopaedia of the Social Sciences*. Volume 5. London: Macmillan and Co.

Colletti, Lucio (1975) 'Introduction', pp. 7–56 in Karl Marx, *Early Writings*. Translated by Rodney Livingstone and Gregor Benton. Harmondsworth: Penguin, in association with *New Left Review*.

Combe, Andrew (1852 [1834]) *The Principles of Physiology Applied to the Preservation of Health and to the Improvement of Physical and Mental Education*. Fourteenth edition. Edited by James Coxe. London. Quoted in Newton (1974), *q.v.*

Comité National Coordination des groupes de femmes Egalité (2003) *La réponse au problème soulevé par le << port du voile à l'école >> ne peut être que globale, de lutte et d'explication sur plusieurs fronts*. eleuthera.free.fr/html/182.htm. Accessed 19 January 2005.

Concannon, Eileen (1911) 'Our Dress Problem. A Proposed Solution', *Catholic Bulletin* 1 (February): 66–9.

Cooley, Winnifred Harper (1984 [1902]) 'A Dream of the Twenty-First Century', pp. 205–11 in Kessler (1984), *q.v.*

Corbett, Elizabeth T. (1984 [1869]) 'My Visit to Utopia' (1869), pp. 65–73 in Kessler (1984), *q.v.*

Corbin, Alain (1995 [1991]) *Time, Desire and Horror. Towards a History of the Senses*. Translated by Jean Birrell. Cambridge: Polity Press.

Corrigan, Peter (1988) 'Backstage Dressing. Clothing and the Urban Family, With Special Reference to Mother/Daughter Relations'. Unpublished PhD dissertation, Department of Sociology, Trinity College, Dublin.

Corrigan, Peter (1997) *The Sociology of Consumption. An Introduction*. London: Sage.

Crane, Diana (2000) *Fashion and Its Social Agendas. Class, Gender, and Identity in Clothing*. Chicago, IL: The University of Chicago Press.

Cridge, Annie Denton (1984 [1870]) 'Man's Rights; or, How Would You Like it?', pp. 74–94 in Kessler (1984), *q.v.*

Cunnington, C. Willett and Cunnington, Phillis (1952) *Handbook of English Medieval Costume*. London: Faber and Faber.

Cunnington, Phillis (1981) *Costume in Pictures*. Revised edition. London: The Herbert Press.

d'Allais, Denis Vairasse (1966 [1702]) *Histoire des Sévarambes*. Translated in Frank E. Manuel and Fritzie P. Manuel (eds), *French Utopias: An Anthology of Ideal Societies*. New York: Schocken Books.

Damasio, Antonio (1994) *Descartes' Error. Emotion, Reason, and the Human Brain*. London: Penguin.

Damasio, Antonio (1999) *The Feeling of What Happens. Body and Emotion in the Making of Consciousness*. San Diego, CA: Harcourt.

Davis, Fred (1992) *Fashion, Culture, and Identity*. Chicago, IL and London: The University of Chicago Press.

Debré, Jean-Louis (2003) *Rapport fait au nom de la mission d'information sur la question du port des signes religieux à l'école*. Tome I. Paris : Assemblée Nationale.

Dekker, Rudolf M. and van de Pol, Lotte C. (1989) *The Tradition of Female Transvestism in Early Modern Europe*. Basingstoke and London: Macmillan.

Delphy, Christine (1984 [1975]) 'Sharing the Same Table: Consumption and the Family', in *Close to Home. A Materialist Analysis of Women's Oppression*. Translated by Diana Leonard. London: Hutchinson.

Descartes, René (1984 [1641]) 'Meditations on First Philosophy', pp. 1–62 in *The Philosophical Writings of Descartes*. Volume II. Cambridge: Cambridge University Press.

Diderot, Denis (1966 [1796]) 'Supplément au voyage de Bougainville, ou dialogue entre A et B', pp. 411–78 in his *Le Neveu de Rameau*. Paris: Livre de Poche.

Dodderidge, Esmé (1988 [1979]) *The New Gulliver, or The Adventures of Lemuel Gulliver Jr in Capovolta*. London: The Women's Press.

Donath, Judith S. (1999) 'Identity and Deception in the Virtual Community', pp. 29–59 in Marc A. Smith and Peter Kollock (eds), *Communities in Cyberspace*. London: Routledge.

Douglas, Mary (1966) *Purity and danger. An Analysis of Concepts of Pollution and Taboo*. London: Routledge & Kegan Paul.

Douglas, Mary and Isherwood, Baron (1978) *The World of Goods. Towards an Anthropology of Consumption*. Harmondsworth: Penguin.

Durkheim, Emile (1915 [1912]) *The Elementary Forms of the Religious Life*. Translated by Joseph Ward Swain. London: George Allen and Unwin.

Edgell, Stephen (1980) *Middle Class Couples. A Study of Segregation, Domination and Inequality in Marriage*. London: George Allen and Unwin.

Elias, Norbert (1991) *The Symbol Theory*. Edited with an introduction by Richard Kilminster. London: Sage.

Elias, Norbert (1993 [1987]) *Time. An Essay*. Translated in part from the German version by Edmund Jephcott. Oxford: Blackwell.

Elias, Norbert (1994 [1939]) *The Civilizing Process*. Translated by Edmund Jephcott. Oxford: Blackwell.

Emerson, Ralph Waldo (1890 [1844]) 'Gifts', pp. 130–1 in *The Complete Prose Works of Ralph Waldo Emerson*. London: Ward, Lock and Co.

Eng, Paul (1999) 'Tiny Beads for Always-Fresh Clothes. Technology to Create Fragrant Fabrics for Clothing and Carpets'. *ABC News*, March 11. abcnews.go.com/Technology/FutureTech/story?id=97696&page=1. Accessed 9 February 2005.

Enninger, Werner (1984) 'Inferencing Social Structure and Social Processes from Nonverbal Behavior', *American Journal of Semiotics*, 3 (2): 77–96.

Evans-Pritchard, E.E. (1940) *The Nuer. A Description of the Modes of Livelihood and Political Institutions of a Nilotic People*. Oxford: Clarendon Press.

Evelyn, John (1951 [1661]) *Tyrannus; or, The Mode*. Edited by J.L. Nevison, Oxford: Blackwell.

Ewing, Elizabeth (1975) *Women in Uniform. Their Costume through the Centuries*. London: Batsford.

Exter, Alexandra (1989 [1923]) 'On the Structure of Dress', p. 171 in Strizhenova and Organizing Committee (1989), *q.v.*

Featherstone, Mike (1991 [1982]) 'The Body in Consumer Culture', pp. 170–96 in Mike Featherstone, Mike Hepworth and Bryan S. Turner (eds), *The Body. Social Process and Cultural Theory*. London: Sage.

Featherstone, Mike (1991) *Consumer Culture and Postmodernism*. London: Sage.

Fedorov-Davydov, A. (1989 [1928]) 'An Introduction to the First Soviet Exhibition of National Textiles, Moscow, 01928', pp. 181–3 in Strizhenova and Organizing Committee (1989), *q.v.*

Feher, Michel with Naddaff, Ramona and Tazi, Nadia (eds) (1989) *Fragments for a History of the Human Body*. Three volumes. New York: Urzone.

Fénelon, François de (1994 [1699]) *Telemachus, Son of Ulysses*. Edited and translated by Patrick Riley. Cambridge: Cambridge University Press.

Finkelstein, Joanne (1991) *The Fashioned Self*. Cambridge and Oxford: Polity Press in association with Basil Blackwell.

Fischer, Michael M.J. (1980) *Iran. From Religious Dispute to Revolution*. Cambridge, MA: Harvard University Press.

Flügel, John Carl (1930) *The Psychology of Clothes*. London: Hogarth Press.

Foigny, Gabriel de (1990 [1676]) *La Terre Australe Connue*. Edition établie, présentée et annotée par Pierre Ronzeaud. Paris: Société des Textes Français Modernes.

Forty, Adrian (1986) *Objects of Desire. Design and Society since 1750*. London: Thames and Hudson.

Foucault, Michel (1973 [1963]) *The Birth of the Clinic. An Archaeology of Medical Perception*. Translated from the French version by A.M. Sheridan Smith. New York: Pantheon Books.

Foucault, Michel (1977 [1975]) *Discipline and Punish. The Birth of the Prison*. Harmondsworth: Penguin.

Frank, Arthur W. (1991) 'For a Sociology of the Body: An Analytical Review', pp. 36–102 in Mike Featherstone, Mike Hepworth and Bryan S. Turner (eds), *The Body. Social Process and Cultural Theory*. London: Sage.

Gearhart, Sally Miller (1985 [1979]) *The Wanderground. Stories of the Hill Women*. London: The Women's Press.

Geirnaert, Danielle C. (1992) 'Purse-Proud. Of Betel and Areca Nut Bags in Laboya (West Sumba, Eastern Indonesia)', pp. 56–75 in *Dress and Gender. Making and Meaning in Cultural Contexts*. Edited by Ruth Barnes and Joanne B. Eicher. New York and Oxford: Berg Publishers.

Gernsheim, Alison (1963) *Fashion and Reality, 1840–1914*. London: Faber and Faber.

Giddens, Anthony (1987) 'Time and Social Organization', pp. 140–65 in his *Social Theory and Modern Sociology*. Oxford and Cambridge: Polity Press.

Gilman, Charlotte Perkins (1979 [1915]) *Herland*. London: The Women's Press.

Goblot, Edmond (1925) *La barrière et le niveau. Etude sociologique sur la bourgeoisie française moderne*. Paris: Félix Alcan.

Godelier, Maurice (1977 [1973]) *Perspectives in Marxist Anthropology*. Translated by Robert Brain. Cambridge: Cambridge University Press.

Goehring, Brian and Stager, John K. (1991) 'The Intrusion of Industrial Time and Space into the Inuit Lifeworld. Changing Perceptions and Behavior', *Environment and Behavior*, 23 (6): 666–79.

Goody, Esther N. (1971) 'Forms of Pro-Parenthood: The Sharing and Substitution of Parental Roles', pp. 331–45 in Jack Goody (ed.), *Kinship*. Harmondsworth: Penguin.

Gotman, Anne (1988) *Hériter*. Paris: Presses Universitaires de France.

Gott, Samuel (1902 [1648]) *Nova Solyma. The Ideal City; or Jerusalem Regained*. Two Volumes. With Introduction, Translation, Literary Essays and a Bibliography by The Rev. Walter Begley. London: John Murray.

Gouldner, Alvin (1960) 'The Norm of Reciprocity', *American Sociological Review*, 25: 161–78.

Gregory, Chris (1982) *Gifts and Commodities*. London: Academic Press.

Griffith, Mary (1984 [1836]) 'Three Hundred Years Hence', pp. 29–48 in Kessler (1984), *q.v.*

Guenther, Irene V. (1997) 'Nazi "Chic"? German Politics and Women's Fashions, 1915–1945', *Fashion Theory*, 1 (1): 29–58.

Gullestad, Marianne (1984) *Kitchen-Table Society*. Oslo: Universitetsforlaget.

Gustav III (1778) *Réflexions*. La Haye: Detune. Exemplar B i Kongliga Biblioteket, Stockholm.

Haldane, Charlotte (1926) *Man's World*. London: Chatto and Windus.

Harberton, F. (1882) 'Rational Dress Reform', *Macmillan's Magazine*, 45 (April): 456–61.

Harley, Kirsten (2000) 'Polynymity and the Self: Testing the Limits of Foucault'. Unpublished BA Honours thesis, School of Social Science, University of New England, Armidale, Australia.

Harrington, James (1992 [1656]) *The Commonwealth of Oceana* and *A System of Politics*. Edited by J.G.A. Pocock. Cambridge: Cambridge University Press.

Harris, Rosemary (1972) *Prejudice and Tolerance in Ulster*. Manchester: Manchester University Press.

Harvey, David (1990) *The Condition of Postmodernity*. Cambridge, MA: Blackwell.

Hashemi, Fereshti (1982 [1980]) 'Discrimination and the Imposition of the Veil', pp. 193–4 in *In the Shadow of Islam. The Women's Movement in Iran*. Edited by Azar Tabari and Nahid Yeganeh. London: Zed Press.

Haweis, Mary Eliza (1879) *The Art of Dress*. London: Chatto and Windus.

Heringa, R. (1988) 'Textiles and Worldview in Tuban', pp. 55–61 in *Indonesia in Focus. Ancient Traditions – Modern Times*. Edited by R. Schefold, V. Dekker and N. de Jonge. Meppel: Edu'Actief. As quoted by Geirnaert (1992), *q.v.*

Herzfeld, Michael (1990) 'Pride and Perjury. Time and the Oath in the Mountain Villages of Crete', *Man* (n.s.), 25 (June): 305–22.

Higson, Rosalie (2000) 'Made to Measure', *The Australian Magazine*, 8–9 April: 30–3.

Hobbes, Thomas (1991 [1651]) *Leviathan*. Edited by Richard Tuck. Cambridge: Cambridge University Press.

Hollander, Anne (1978) *Seeing through Clothes*. New York: The Viking Press.

Homans, George Casper (1961) *Social Behaviour. Its Elementary Forms*. London: Routledge and Kegan Paul.

Howland, Marie Stevens Case (1984 [1874]) 'Papa's Own Girl' (1874), pp. 95–103 in Kessler (1984), *q.v.*

Huxley, Aldous (1994 [1932]) *Brave New World*. London: Flamingo.

Jackson, Margaret (1936) *What They Wore. A History of Children's Dress*. Woking: George Allen and Unwin.

Jandreau, Charles (2002) 'Social Rituals and Identity Creation in a Middle Class Workplace', *Emory Center for Myth and Ritual in American Life (MARIAL) Working Paper 14*, Spring.

Jordan, Tim (1999) *Cyberpower. The Culture and Politics of Cyberspace and the Internet*. London: Routledge.

Kauffmann, Sylvie (2000) 'Wall Street accepte les hommes sans cravate mais pas les femmes en caleçon', *Le Monde Sélection Hebdomadaire*, 6 May.

Kaufmann, Jean-Claude (1992) *La trame conjugale. Analyse du couple par son linge*. Paris: Nathan.

Kessler, Carol Farley (ed.) (1984) *Daring to Dream. Utopian Stories by United States Women: 1836–1919*. London: Pandora Press.

Khomeiny, Ayatollah Ruhollah (1985 [1943]) 'A Warning to the Nation', pp. 169–73 in his *Islam and Revolution. Writings and Declarations*. Translated and annotated by Hamid Algar. London: KPI.

King, E.M. (1882) *Rational Dress, or the Dress of Women and Savages*. London: Kegan Paul, Trench and Co.

Kintzler, Catherine, Taguieff, Pierre-André, Teper, Bernard and Tribalat, Michèle (2003) *L'école publique doit être soustraite à la pression des groupes politico-religieux.* www.ufal.org/spip/article.php3?id_article=28. Accessed 19 January 2005.

Kiser, Edgar and Drass, Kriss A. (1987) 'Changes in the Core of the World-System and the Production of Utopian Literature in Great Britain and the United States, 1883–1975', *American Sociological Review,* 52: 286–93.

Klietsch, Ronald G. (1965) 'Clothesline Patterns and Covert Behavior', *Journal of Marriage and the Family* February: 78–80.

König, René (1973) *The Restless Image. A Sociology of Fashion.* London: George Allan and Unwin Ltd.

Kopytoff, Igor (1986) 'The Cultural Biography of Things: Commoditization as Process', pp. 64–91 in Arjun Appadurai (ed.), *The Social Life of Things. Commodities in Cultural Perspective.* Cambridge: Cambridge University Press.

Kroeber, A.L. (1919) 'On the Principle of Order in Civilization as Exemplified by Changes of Fashion', *American Anthropologist,* 21 (3) July–September: 235–63.

Kumar, Krishan (1991) *Utopianism.* Milton Keynes: Open University Press.

Kunzle, David (1982) *Fashion and Fetishism.* Totowa, NJ: Rowman and Littlefield.

Lane, Mary E. Bradley (1984 [1880–81]) 'Mizora: A Prophecy', pp. 117–37 in Kessler (1984), *q.v.*

Lang, Carl (2003) 'Vous avez aimé l'immigration? Vous allez adorer l'islamisation'. *Français D'abord – Le Magazine de Jean-Marie Le Pen.* 15 December. www.francaisdabord.info/editoriallang_detail.php?id_inter=1. Accessed 19 January 2005.

Laqueur, Thomas (1990) *Making Sex. Body and Gender from the Greeks to Freud.* Cambridge, MA: Harvard University Press.

Lash, Scott and Urry, John (1994) *Economies of Signs and Space.* London: Sage.

Laver, James (1937) *Taste and Fashion. From the French Revolution until To-Day.* London: Harrap.

Laver, James (1951) *Children's Fashions in the Nineteenth Century.* London: Batsford.

Laver, James (1964) *Costume through the Ages.* London: Thames and Hudson.

Laver, James (1969) *Modesty in Dress.* London: Heinemann.

Lawrence, James (1981 [1811]) *The Empire of the Nairs; or, the Rights of Women. An Utopian Romance,* Four volumes. London: T. Hookham, Jun. and E.T. Hookham, quoted in Lyman Tower Sargent, 'An Ambiguous Legacy: The Role and Position of Women in the English Eutopia', pp. 88–99 in Marleen S. Barr (ed.), *Future Females: A Critical Anthology,* Bowling Green, OH: Bowling Green State University Popular Press.

Le Guin, Ursula K. (1975 [1974]) *The Dispossessed.* London: Grafton Books.

Lefferts, H. Leedom Jr (1992) 'Cut and Sewn. The Textiles of Social Organization in Thailand', pp. 44–55 in *Dress and Gender. Making and Meaning in Cultural Contexts.* Edited by Ruth Barnes and Joanne B. Eicher. New York and Oxford: Berg Publishers.

Levitas, Ruth (1990) *The Concept of Utopia.* Hemel Hempstead: Philip Allan.

Lhez, Pierrette (1995) *De la robe de bure à la tunique pantalon. Etude sur la place du vêtement dans la pratique infirmière.* Paris: InterEditions.

Lipovetsky, Gilles (1987) *L'empire de l'éphémère. La mode et son destin dans les sociétés modernes.* Paris: Gallimard.

Littlestar, Miss (2005) www.malesubmission.com/littlestar/who.htm. Accessed 1 February 2005.

Luck, Kate (1992) 'Trouble in Eden, Trouble with Eve. Women, Trousers & Utopian Socialism in Nineteenth-Century America', pp. 200–12 in Juliet Ash and Elizabeth Wilson (eds), *Chic Thrills. A Fashion Reader*. Berkeley and Los Angeles, CA: University of California Press.

Lurie, Alison (1981) *The Language of Clothes*. New York: Random House.

Lyotard, Jean-François (1991 [1988]) *The Inhuman. Reflections on Time*. Translated by Geoffrey Bennington and Rachel Bowlby. Oxford and Cambridge: Polity Press.

Lytton, Lord (1871) *The Coming Race*. London: George Routledge and Sons, no date [probably 1871].

MacKinnon, Richard C. (1997) 'Punishing the Persona: Correctional Strategies for the Virtual Offender', pp. 206–35 in Steven G. Jones (ed.), *Virtual Culture. Identity and Communication in Cybersociety*. London: Sage.

Maffesoli, Michel (1996 [1988]) *The Time of the Tribes. The Decline of Individualism in Mass Society*. Translated by Don Smith. London: Sage Publications.

Maines, David R. (1987) 'The Significance of Temporality for the Development of Sociological Theory', *Sociological Quarterly*, 28 (3): 303–11.

Makeupalley (2007) *Makeup Alley Swap FAQ*. Available online at: makeupalley.com/content/content.asp/s=1/c=Swap_FAQ/. Accessed 16 May 2007.

Malinowski, Bronislaw (1922) *Argonauts of the Western Pacific*. London: Routledge and Kegan Paul.

Marcuse, Herbert (1979 [1977]) *The Aesthetic Dimension. Towards a Critique of Marxist Aesthetics*. London: Macmillan.

Martin, Emily (1987) *The Woman in the Body. A Cultural Analysis of Reproduction*. Milton Keynes: Open University Press.

Martin-Fugier, Anne (1979) *La place des bonnes. La Domesticité féminine à Paris en 1900*. Paris: Grasset.

Marx, Karl (1974 [1867]) *Capital. A Critical Analysis of Capitalist Production*. Volume I. Translated from the third German edition by Samuel Moore and Edward Aveling and edited by Frederick Engels. London: Lawrence and Wishart.

Marx, Karl (1975 [1844]) *Economic and Philosophical Manuscripts*, pp. 279–400 in his *Early Writings*. Translated by Rodney Livingstone and Gregor Benton. Harmondsworth: Penguin, in association with *New Left Review*.

Marx, Karl and Engels, Frederick (1968 [1847]) *The Manifesto of the Communist Party*, pp. 31–63 in their *Selected Works in One Volume*. London: Lawrence and Wishart.

Marx, Karl and Engels, Frederick (1989 [1846]) *The German Ideology*. Part One, with selections from Parts Two and Three. Edited with an Introduction by C.J. Arthur. London: Lawrence and Wishart.

Maslova, Gali Semeonovna (1984) *Narodnaya odezhda v vostochnoslavyanskikh traditsionnikh obichayakh i obryadakh XIX-nachala XX v*. Moskva: Nauka.

Mason, Eveleen Laura Knaggs (1984 [1889]) 'Hiero-Salem: The Vision of Peace', pp. 138–47 in Kessler (1984), *q.v.*

Maududi, Syed Abul A'la (1988 [1939]) *Purdah and the Status of Woman in Islam*. Third Edition translated and edited by Al-Ash'Ari. Delhi: Markazi Maktaba Islami.

Mauss, Marcel (1969 [1925]) *The Gift*. Translated by Ian Cunnison. London: Routledge and Kegan Paul.

Mauss, Marcel (1978 [1905]) 'Essai sur les variations saisonnières des sociétés eskimos', pp. 389–477 in his *Sociologie et anthropologie*. Sixième édition. Paris: Presses Universitaires de France.

McLaren, Leah (2000) 'Halifax Hysteria. Non-scents in Nova Scotia'. *The Globe and Mail*, April 29. www.fumento.com/halifax2.html. Accessed 9 February 2005.

McVeigh, Brian (1997) 'Wearing Ideology: How Uniforms Discipline Minds and Bodies in Japan', *Fashion Theory*, 1 (2): 189–214.

Méan, J.B. (1774) 'Mémoire, sur la Question suivante, proposée par la Société Royale Patriotique de Stockholm. Scavoir, si afin d'éviter les variations multi-pliées des Modes et empêcher le Commerce des Marchandises prohibées, il seroit avantageux à la Suède, d'y introduire une façon d'Habillement National, proportionné au Climat et différent des vêtemens d'autres Nations &c'., pp. 115–28 in *Kongl. Svenska Sällskapets Handlingar*. III stycket. Stockholm: Joh. Georg Lange.

Mellor, Philip A. and Shilling, Chris (1997) *Re-forming the Body. Religion, Community and Modernity*. London: Sage.

Mercier, Louis-Sébastien (1974 [1771]) *Memoirs of the Year Two Thousand Five Hundred*. Translated by W. Hooper in two volumes. London: Printed for G. Robinson in Pater-noster-Row, 1772. Facsimile reprint, New York and London: Garland Publishing.

Merrifield, Mary Philadelphia (1854) *Dress as a Fine Art*. London: Arthur Hall, Virtue, and Co.

Michelman, Susan O. and Ereksima, Tonye V. (1992) 'Kalabari Dress in Nigeria. Visual Analysis and Gender Implications', pp. 164–82 in *Dress and Gender. Making and Meaning in Cultural Contexts*. Edited by Ruth Barnes and Joanne B. Eicher. New York and Oxford: Berg Publishers.

Minai, Naila (1981) *Women in Islam. Tradition and Transition in the Middle East*. London: John Murray.

Mintz, S.W. and Wolf, E.R. (1971 [1950]), 'Ritual Co-Parenthood (*compadrazgo*)', pp. 346–61 in Jack Goody (ed.), *Kinship*. Harmondsworth: Penguin.

Modéer, Adolph (1774) 'Svar på Samma Fråga', pp. 58–82 in *Kongl. Svenska Sällskapets Handlingar*. III stycket. Stockholm: Joh. Georg Lange.

Molloy, John T. (1980) *Women. Dress for Success*. London: Foulsham.

Monneyron, Frédéric (2001) *La frivolité essentielle. Du vêtement et de la mode*. Paris: Presses Universitaires de France.

Moore, Doris Langley (1929) *Pandora's Letter Box, being a Discourse on Fashionable Life*. London: Gerald Howe.

Moore, Doris Langley (1953) *The Child in Fashion*. London: Batsford.

More, Thomas (1965 [1516]) 'Utopia', in *The Complete Works of St. Thomas More*, Volume 4. Revised version of 1923 translation by G.C. Richards. Edited by Edward Surtz and J.H. Hexter. New Haven, CT and London: Yale University Press.

Morelly (1970 [1755]) *Code de la nature, ou le véritable esprit de ses lois, de tout temps négligé ou méconnu*. Paris: Editions Sociales.

Morris, William (1912 [1890]) *News from Nowhere*, pp. 1–211 in *The Collected Works of William Morris*, Vol. XVI. London: Longmans Green and Company.

Mouedden, Mohsin (2003a) 'La France, terre des libertés'. *Al-Muslimah*. www.al-muslimah.com/articles/2003_12_20_la_france_terre_des_libertes.html. Accessed 11 March 2005.

Mouedden, Mohsin (2003b) 'Ne tombons pas dans le piège du foulard'. *Al-Muslimah*. www.al-muslimah.com/articles/2003_11_18_ne_tombons_pas_dans_le_piege_du_foulard.html. Accessed 11 March 2005.

Mukerji, Chandra (1983) *From Graven Images. Patterns of Modern Materialism*. New York: Columbia University Press.

Mustafa, Naheed (2003) 'La peur du hijab'. *Al-Muslimah*. www.al-muslimah.com/ articles/2003_07_27_la_peur_du_hijab.html. Accessed 4 September 2005.

Newton, Stella Mary (1974) *Health, Art and Reason. Dress Reformers of the Nineteenth Century*. London: John Murray.

Nichols, Mary S.G. (1878) *The Clothes Question Considered in its Relation to Beauty, Comfort, and Health*. London: published by the author.

Oliphant, Margaret (1878) *Dress*. London: Macmillan.

Orwell, George (1984 [1949]) *Nineteen Eighty-Four*. Harmondsworth: Penguin.

Paget, Lady W. (1883) 'Common Sense in Dress and Fashion', *The Nineteenth Century*, 13 (March): 458–64.

Pahl, Jan (1980) 'Patterns of Money Management Within Marriage', *Journal of Social Policy*, 9 (3): 313–35.

Pahl, Jan (1983) 'The Allocation of Money and the Structuring of Inequality Within Marriage', *Sociological Review*, 31: 237–62.

Pahlavi, Mohammed Reza Shah (1961) *Mission for My Country*. London: Hutchinson.

Parmelee, Maurice (1929) *Nudity in Modern Life; the New Gymnosophy*. London: Noel Douglas.

Peacham, Henry (1942 [1638]) *The Truth of Our Times*. New York: The Facsimile Text Society, published by Columbia University Press.

Perrot, Philippe (1977) 'Aspects socio-culturels des débuts de la confection parisienne au XIXe siècle', *Revue de l'Institut de Sociologie*, 2: 185–202.

Petitfils, Jean-Christian (1982) *La vie quotidienne des communautés utopistes au XIXe siècle*. Paris: Hachette.

Piercy, Marge (1979 [1976]) *Woman on the Edge of Time*. London: The Women's Press.

Pitt-Rivers, Julian (1968) 'Pseudo-Kinship', pp. 408–13 in *International Encyclopaedia of the Social Sciences*. Volume 8. London: Macmillan and Co.

Planché, J.R. (1900) *History of British Costume from the Earliest Period to the Close of the Eighteenth Century*. Third edition. London: George Bell.

Prynne, William (1628) *The Vnlouelinesse, of Lovelockes*. London.

Quicherat, J. (1879) *Histoire du costume en France depuis les temps les plus reculés jusqu'à la fin du XVIIIᵉ siècle*. Paris: Hachette. Referenced by Roche (1991 [1989]), *q.v.*

Reid, Elizabeth (1999) 'Hierarchy and Power. Social Control in Cyberspace', pp. 107–33 in Marc A. Smith and Peter Kollock (eds) *Communities in Cyberspace*. London: Routledge.

Rheingold, Howard (1993) *The Virtual Community. Homesteading on the Electronic Frontier*. Reading, MA: Addison-Wesley. Available online at: www.rheingold.com/ vc/book/ 16 May 2007. Accessed 16 May 2007.

Ribeiro, Aileen (1992) 'Utopian Dress', pp. 225–37 in Juliet Ash and Elizabeth Wilson (eds), *Chic Thrills. A Fashion Reader*. Berkeley and Los Angeles, CA: University of California Press

Richardson, Jane and Kroeber, A.L. (1940) 'Three Centuries of Women's Dress Fashions: A Quantitative Analysis', *Anthropological Records*, 5 (Part 2): 111–53.

Roche, Daniel (1991 [1989]) *La culture des apparences. Une histoire du vêtement XVIIᵉ-XVIIIᵉ siècle*. Paris: Seuil, collection 'Points Histoire'.

Roth, Bernard (1880) *Dress: Its Sanitary Aspect*. London: J. and A. Churchill.

Russ, Joanna (1985 [1975]) *The Female Man*. London: The Women's Press.

Sahlins, Marshall (1974) *Stone Age Economics*. London: Tavistock.

Sahlins, Marshall (1976) *Culture and Practical Reason*. Chicago, UL: The University of Chicago Press.

Schiebinger, Londa (1987) 'Skeletons in the Closet: The First Illustrations of the Female Skeleton in Eighteenth-Century Anatomy', pp. 42–82 in Catherine Gallagher and Thomas Laqueur (eds), *The Making of the Modern Body. Sexuality and Society in the Nineteenth Century*. Berkeley, CA: University of California Press.

Schreiber, Mark (2001) 'What am I bid for My Boxers? Famous Fetish Turned Topsy-turvy'. *The Japan Times Online* June 24. www.japantimes.co.jp/cgi-bin/getarticle.pl5?fl20010624tc.htm. Accessed 7 February 2005.

Schwartz, Barry (1967) 'The Social Psychology of the Gift', *American Journal of Sociology*, 73: 1–11.

Sciama, Lidia D. (1992) 'Lacemaking in Venetian Culture', pp. 121–44 in Ruth Barnes and Joanne B. Eicher (eds), *Dress and Gender. Making and Meaning in Cultural Contexts*. New York and Oxford: Berg Publishers.

Sen, Amartya (1984) *Resources, Values and Development*. Oxford: Blackwell.

Sex Toys (2005) www.sex--toys.org/edible.php. Accessed 6 February 2005.

Shilling, Chris (1993) *The Body and Social Theory*. London: Sage.

Simmel, Georg (1957 [1904]) 'Fashion', *The American Journal of Sociology*, 62 (6): 541–58.

Simmel, Georg (1971 [1907]) 'Prostitution', pp. 121–6 in *On Individuality and Social Forms*. Selected writings edited by Donald N. Levine. Chicago, IL: University of Chicago Press.

Simmel, Georg (1997 [1908]) 'Sociology of the Senses', pp. 109–20 in David Frisby and Mike Featherstone (eds), *Simmel on Culture. Selected Writings*. London: Sage.

Skinner, B.F. (1976 [1948]) *Walden Two*. With a new Introduction by the author, New York: Macmillan.

Smith, Marc A. (1999) 'Invisible Crowds in Cyberspace. Mapping the Social Structure of the Usenet', pp. 195–219 in Marc A. Smith and Peter Kollock (eds), *Communities in Cyberspace*. London: Routledge.

Snow, C.P. (1974 [1964]) *The Two Cultures* and *a Second Look*. London: Cambridge University Press.

Sorokin, Pitirim A. and Merton, Robert K. (1937) 'Social Time. A Methodological and Functional Analysis', *American Journal of Sociology*, 42 (5) March: 615–29.

Sound Vision Staff Writer (2004) *The Question of Hijab and Choice*. www.soundvision.com/Info/news/hijab/hjb.choice.asp. Accessed 4 September 2005.

Squire, Geoffrey (1974) *Dress Art and Society 1560–1970*. London: Studio Vista.

Steele, Valerie (1999) 'The Corset: Fashion and Eroticism', *Fashion Theory*, 3 (4): 449–74.

Strizhenova, Tatyana (1989) 'Textiles and Soviet Fashion in the Twenties', pp. 3–14 in Strizhenova and Organizing Committee (1989), *q.v.*

Strizhenova, Tatyana Konstantinova (1972) *Iz istorii sovetskogo kostyuma*. Moskva: Sovetskii khudozhnik.

Strizhenova, Tatyana and Organizing Committee (1989) *Costume Revolution. Textiles, Clothing and Costume of the Soviet Union in the Twenties*. London: Trefoil Publications.

Stubbes, Philip (1836 [1585]) *The Anatomie of Abuses*. London: W. Pickering, Edinburgh: W. & D. Laing.

Swift, Jonathan (1967 [1726]) *Gulliver's Travels*. Edited by Peter Dixon and John Chalker, with an Introduction by Michael Foot. Harmondsworth: Penguin.

Tabari, Azar (1982) 'Islam and the Struggle for Emancipation of Iranian Women', pp. 5–25 in Azar Tabari and Nahid Yeganeh (eds), *In the Shadow of Islam. The Women's Movement in Iran*. London: Zed Press.

Taheri, Amir (1985) *The Spirit of Allah. Khomeini and the Islamic Revolution*. London: Hutchinson.

Tait, Gordon (1993) ' "Anorexia Nervosa": Asceticism, Differentiation, Government Resistance', *The Australian and New Zealand Journal of Sociology*, 29 (2): 194–208.

Taleghani, Ayatollah (1982 [1979]) 'On Hejab', pp. 103–7 in Azar Tabari and Nahid Yeganeh (eds), *In the Shadow of Islam. The Women's Movement in Iran*. London: Zed Press.

Tepper, Michele (1997) 'Usenet Communities and the Cultural Politics of Information', pp. 39–54 in David Porter (ed.), *Internet Culture*, New York: Routledge.

Thompson, E.P. (1967) 'Time, Work-Discipline, and Industrial Capitalism', *Past and Present*, 38: 56–97.

Thoreau, Henry David (1980 [1854]) *Walden*. London: The Folio Society

Treves, Frederick (1883) 'The Influence of Dress on Health', pp. 461–517 in Malcolm Morris (ed.), *The Book of Health*. London: Cassell & Co.

Turner, Bryan S. (1984) *The Body and Society. Explorations in Social Theory*. Oxford: Blackwell.

Turner, Bryan S. (1992) *Regulating Bodies. Essays in Medical Sociology*. London: Routledge.

Vahdat, Farzin (2003) 'Post-Revolutionary Islamic Discourses on Modernity in Iran: Expansion and Contraction of Human Subjectivity', *International Journal of Middle-Eastern Studies*, 35: 599–631.

Varst [Stepanova, Varvara Fedorovna] (1923) 'Kostyum sevodnyashnego dnya – prozodezhda', *LEF*, 2: 65–8.

Veblen, Thorstein (1975 [1899]) *The Theory of the Leisure Class*. New York: Augustus M. Kelly.

Vigerie, Anne and Zelensky, Anne (nd) '*Laïcardes', puisque féministes*. touscontrelevoile.free.fr/laicardes.html. Accessed 19 January 2005.

Vogue Australia (1993) January–April and June–December issues.

Waisbrooker, Lois Nichols (1984 [1894]) 'A Sex Revolution', pp. 176–91 in Kessler (1984), *q.v.*

Watts, G.F. (1883) 'On Taste in Dress', *The Nineteenth Century*, 13 (January): 45–57.

Webb, Wilfred Mark (1912) *The Heritage of Dress*. New and revised edition. London: The Times Book Club.

Wells, H.G. (1967 [1905]) *A Modern Utopia*. Lincoln, NE and London: University of Nebraska Press.

Wells, H.G. (1976 [1923]) *Men Like Gods*. London: Sphere Books.

Wilde, Oscar (1909 [1882]) 'House Decoration', pp. 159–71 in his *Essays and Lectures*. Second edition. London: Methuen.

Wilde, Oscar (1920a [1884]) 'Woman's Dress', pp. 60–5 in his *Art and Decoration. Being Extracts from Reviews and Miscellanies*. London: Methuen.

Wilde, Oscar (1920b [1884]) 'More Radical Ideas upon Dress Reform', pp. 66–79 in his *Art and Decoration. Being Extracts from Reviews and Miscellanies*. London: Methuen.

Wilson, Elizabeth (1992) 'Fashion and the Postmodern Body', pp. 3–16 in Juliet Ash and Elizabeth Wilson (eds), *Chic Thrills. A Fashion Reader*. Berkeley, CA and Los Angeles: University of California Press.

Wilson, Gail (1987) *Money in the Family. Financial Organisation and Women's Responsibility*. Aldershot: Avebury.

Woolf, Virginia (1938) *Three Guineas*. London: Hogarth Press.

Young, Agatha (Agnes) Brooks (1966 [1937]) *Recurring Cycles of Fashion 1760–1937*. New York: Cooper Square Publishers.

Zerubavel, Eviatar (1977) 'The French Republican Calendar. A Case Study in the Sociology of Time', *American Sociological Review*, 42 (December): 868–77.

Zerubavel, Eviatar (1979) *Patterns of Time in Hospital Life. A Sociological Perspective*. Chicago, IL and London: The University of Chicago Press.

Zerubavel, Eviatar (1989 [1985]) *The Seven Day Circle. The History and Meaning of the Week*. Chicago, IL and London: The University of Chicago Press.

Zickmund, Susan (1997) 'Approaching the Radical Other: The Discursive Culture of Cyberhate', pp. 185–205 in Steven G. Jones (ed.), *Virtual Culture. Identity and Communication in Cybersociety*. London: Sage.

Index